ISLAND SOCIETIES

T0370896

ISLAND SOCIETIES

ARCHAEOLOGICAL APPROACHES TO
EVOLUTION AND TRANSFORMATION

EDITED BY PATRICK VINTON KIRCH

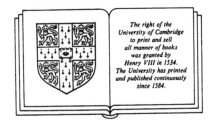

CAMBRIDGE UNIVERSITY PRESS

CAMBRIDGE
LONDON   NEW YORK   NEW ROCHELLE
MELBOURNE   SYDNEY

CAMBRIDGE UNIVERSITY PRESS
Cambridge, New York, Melbourne, Madrid, Cape Town, Singapore, São Paulo, Delhi

Cambridge University Press
The Edinburgh Building, Cambridge CB2 8RU, UK

Published in the United States of America by Cambridge University Press, New York

www.cambridge.org
Information on this title: www.cambridge.org/9780521105439

First published 1986
This digitally printed version 2009

A catalogue record for this publication is available from the British Library

Library of Congress Cataloguing in Publication data
Main entry under title:
Island societies.
Bibliography p.
Includes index.
1. Man, Prehistoric– –Oceania– –Addresses, essays,
lectures. 2. Oceania– –Social conditions– –Addresses,
essays, lectures. 3. Oceania– –Antiquities– –Addresses,
essays, lectures. I. Kirch, Patrick Vinton.
GN871.I85 1986   990   85-30907

ISBN 978-0-521-30189-3 hardback
ISBN 978-0-521-10543-9 paperback

CONTENTS

CONTRIBUTORS

R. C. Green, Department of Anthropology, University of Auckland
    New Zealand
George J. Gumerman, Center for Archaeological Investigations,
    Southern Illinois University, Carbondale
Robert J. Hommon, Archaeologist, Naval Facilities Engineering
    Command, Pearl Harbor, Hawai'i
Terry L. Hunt, Department of Anthropology, University of Washing
    ton, Seattle
Patrick V. Kirch, The Burke Museum, University of Washington,
    Seattle
Barry Rolett, Department of Anthropology, Yale University, New
    Haven
Matthew Spriggs, Department of Anthropology, University of Hawa
    at Manoa, Honolulu
Christopher M. Stevenson, Department of Anthropology, The
    Pennsylvania State University, Pennsylvania

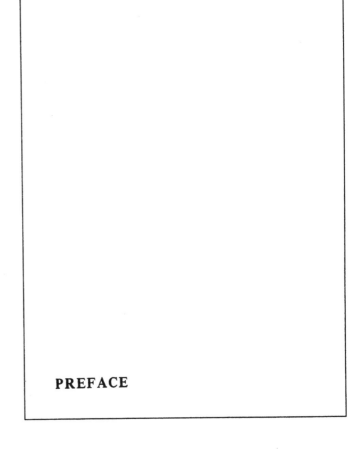

PREFACE

Despite a long and significant tradition in Oceanic anthropology, the islands of the Pacific are one of the last areas of the world to have received archaeological scrutiny. Barely three decades ago, a host of unwarranted assumptions that had thwarted the development of archaeology in Oceania were finally swept aside with the unanticipated results of excavations in Fiji, the Marianas, and Hawai'i. In the past few years, as major problems of cultural origins and island sequences have been resolved, island archaeologists have increasingly turned their attention to significant issues of social change. Such studies frequently attempt to integrate the vast new corpus of archaeological data with the older but rich ethnographic and ethnohistorical materials. Much of this recent work centers on the evolution of complex Oceanic chiefdoms, several of which (such as Hawai'i) were advanced enough in terms of the classic indices to be arguably termed 'archaic states'.

In order to bring together some of the more prominent investigators active in the archaeological study of island societies, I organized a symposium on 'The Evolution of Island Societies' for the XIth International Congress of Anthropological and Ethnological Sciences in Vancouver, British Columbia, in August 1983. A parallel symposium, 'Recent Advances in Pacific Prehistory', organized by Professor William Ayres of the University of Oregon, also included several papers with overlapping or relevant themes. Following the symposia and discussions among several participants, it was agreed that I would edit a selected group of revised papers drawn from these two symposia. Cambridge University Press expressed interest in the project, and offered to publish the work in the present series. Ten participants were originally invited to submit revised papers for consideration; in the end, two of these authors were unable to meet their commitments. While their contributions are missed, the eight papers compiled here present a fair sampling of current archaeological work on the evolution and transformation of island societies. It is to be hoped that the approaches developed here, and the unique characteristics which islands offer, will be of interest not only to Oceanic specialists, but to all archaeologists and prehistorians grappling with the complex problems of tracking and explaining prehistoric social change.

Professor Richard Pearson of the University of British Columbia and a member of the Organizing Committee of the XIth International Congress is owed a debt of thanks for first proposing that such a symposium be held, and for inviting me to organize it. The Bishop Museum in Honolulu provided organizational support and also underwrote my own travel costs to and from the Congress. I am particularly grateful to the contributors for responding so cheerfully, and for the most part promptly, to my varied editorial queries and suggestions.

Chapter 1

**Introduction: the archaeology of
island societies**

Patrick V. Kirch

Island societies have always provided fertile intellectual
terrain for the nurturance of anthropological theory. Well
before anthropology had been codified as an academic discipline, the accounts of Bougainville, Banks, Cook, and other
explorers to the 'South Seas' inspired philosophical debates in
the salons of Europe as to the nature of human society, and
of the 'social contract'. The real impact of islands on anthropology, however, came with the initiation of systematic
ethnography. It was in the Trobriand Islands of western
Melanesia that Bronislaw Malinowski worked out many of the
fundamental principles and methods of modern ethnographic
fieldwork. Not only did the isolation of island societies render
them enclaves for the documentation of 'primitive' cultures,
but their very boundedness seemed to make them almost the
perfect unit for the 'structural-functionalist' approach to
ethnographic description and analysis. Sir Raymond Firth's
classic monographs on the Tikopia exemplify the role of island
societies in the development of the structural-functionalist
paradigm of mid-century social anthropology. Then, too, the
developing psychological approaches of Margaret Mead and
Gregory Bateson found a ready arena of application in small
island communities such as Samoa and Manus, where differing
cultural ethos could be neatly contrasted.

The resurgence of an evolutionary paradigm within
anthropology in the 1950s and 60s also drew upon the island
theme. Synthesizing frameworks for political evolution, such
as those of Elman Service (1967) and Morton Fried (1967),
drew upon Polynesian examples as the virtual 'type' for a
major evolutionary stage, the 'chiefdom' or 'ranked' society.
Marshall Sahlins (1958) mined the Polynesian ethnographic
literature to produce an elegant argument for the diversification
of social structures through a process of 'adaptive radiation'
to varied ecological conditions. The *control* provided by
island societies was essential to this kind of theoretical structure
(Goodenough 1957). Goldman (1970) used the same ethnographic corpus to produce a contrastive theory of Polynesian
social change in which inherent status rivalry provided the
engine of change. The range of island political systems inspired
yet another theoretical paradigm of wide application, the 'big
man–chief' distinction proposed by Sahlins (1963). One may
also cite the role of island data in the development of ecological
perspectives (e.g., Rappaport 1968; Fosberg 1963), of theories
of exchange (dating as far back as the classic essay of Mauss
1923), and recently, in the movement toward an 'anthropology
of history' (Sahlins 1983).

This admittedly sketchy historic overview makes the
point clearly enough: island societies have long provided
inspirational material for the advance of anthropological
method and theory. But where, in all this, have archaeology
and prehistory figured? The answer – hardly at all, at least,

until quite recently. The history of archaeology amongst the Pacific islands is a curious one, and bears a brief synopsis as background to the papers which follow in this volume.

With the problem of cultural origins and 'migration routes' monopolizing early twentieth-century ethnography in the Pacific, one might have expected archaeology to have dominated the scene. Instead, it took on a distinctly secondary role, relegated to the descriptive cataloging of surface monuments and stone tools. As various scholars have noted (e.g. Danielsson 1967; Kirch 1982, 51–2), a set of unwarranted assumptions were responsible for the underdevelopment of archaeology in the study of island societies. Among these were assumptions of shallow time depth, lack of significant stratification, and most importantly, the absence of ceramics or other stylistically varied artifacts which could readily supply the basis for relative chronology and areal comparison.

This situation was dramatically reversed after World War II, when a small group of pioneer excavators (Gifford in Fiji, and later, Yap and New Caledonia; Spoehr in the Marianas; Emory in Hawai'i) quickly dispelled the prevailing, unwarranted assumptions that had held back the development of island archaeology. Libby's invention of radiocarbon dating played a part here, too, with the empirical demonstration of substantial time depth for island settlement. However, despite the suggestions of a few prehistorians that archaeology could now contribute directly to the study of island *societies* and their change over time, the early post-war era continued to be dominated by issues of cultural origins and migrations. Not until the mid-60s, and on into the 1970s, did island archaeologists begin to tackle issues beyond those of defining cultural origins and outlining local phase sequences (Kirch 1982, 70–3).

Over the past fifteen to twenty years, however, the conduct of island archaeology has changed dramatically. Perhaps because the nagging old questions of origins and 'migration routes' have now been met with at least a general model (even if arguments still rage over minutiae), and because the basic time–space sequences for a substantial number of Pacific islands have been established (Bellwood 1979; Jennings 1979; Kirch 1982), island archaeologists have broadened the scope of their inquiries to address such issues as variation in prehistoric subsistence economies, the adaptation of technology and settlement pattern to contrastive environments, the development and intensification of production systems, the modification of island landscapes and biota by human populations, the analysis of trade and exchange between island communities, and the reconstruction of former social structures through the use of settlement pattern, mortuary, and other data.

One area in which archaeology is making a significant impact is that of the description as well as explanation of long-term change in island societies. As noted earlier, the explanations offered for variation and differentiation in island societies have traditionally been promulgated by ethnographers (e.g. Burrows 1939; Sahlins 1958; Goldman 1970), who based their theories of diachronic process (warfare, adaptive radiation to local ecology, status rivalry, etc.) on the comparative analysis of synchronic ethnographic descriptions. To be sure, the analytical control inherent in the island world – where a variety of societies can be shown to have descended from a common historical ancestor – does permit such comparative ethnographic exercises, and these have indeed been a fruitful source of theories or models for the evolution and transformation of island societies. The problem with such theories, however, is precisely that they are not amenable to independent testing and verification on the same corpus of ethnographic materials, without succumbing to logical tautology. Only archaeology can offer the direct, material evidence for social change on which theories of evolutionary or historical process can be tested. Archaeology, of course, is not restricted to a secondary role of theory testing, for the material evidence of prehistoric change itself contributes directly to theory building.

This volume is a sampling of some current archaeological efforts to address problems of long-term change in island societies. The approaches range from the strongly evolutionary and ecological in basic orientation, to those which have been inspired by recent Marxist discussions of contradiction and dominance in social formations, or of the role of ideology in structuring material culture. Though eclectic in orientation, the papers are united by a common goal of bringing the material evidence of archaeology to the problems of understanding social change in island settings.

Aspects of island societies
The essence of islands is discreteness, that is, their bounded and circumscribed nature. This essential characteristic has prompted more than one anthropologist to speak of islands and island societies as 'laboratories' (Suggs 1961, 194; Sahlins 1963; Clark and Terrell 1978; Kirch 1980; Friedman 1981, 275). Historian O. H. K. Spate echoed this theme in describing the insular Pacific as 'so splendidly splittable into Ph.D. topics' (1978, 42). Certainly the boundedness of island ecosystems and insular societies is one of the great advantages offered by the Oceanic region for controlled studies of prehistoric change. Yet the laboratory analogy can easily be pushed too far, especially if boundedness is confused with *closure*. Too often it has been assumed that because islands are discrete and isolated, their societies have developed as closed systems, a facile but frequently unwarranted assumption. More will be said on this matter of closed and open systems shortly.

A corollary of boundedness, particularly on smaller islands, is *limitation* of resources. Space (especially arable land) is the most fundamental of these limited resources, but water, isotropic stone, clay or other materials for ceramics, edible flora and fauna, and a host of other necessities may be in scarce supply or totally absent on any island. Competition for limited resources is not surprisingly a dominant theme in explanations for the evolution of island societies (e.g. Burrows 1939), and is considered by several of the papers to follow.

Gumerman, in particular, considers the alternate strategies of competition and cooperation in situations of limited resources.

Another property of oceanic ecosystems makes them especially intriguing for tracing the long-term interactions between human societies and their environmental settings. This is the 'extreme vulnerability, or tendency toward great instability when isolation is broken down' (Fosberg 1963, 5), particularly following upon human colonization. Thus, the evolution of any island society must be tracked not only in terms of changing demographic and social structures, but in the context of a frequently dynamic ecosystem and varying resource base. The evidence for human-induced environmental change on Pacific islands has rapidly accumulated over the past decade (Kirch 1984, 135–50). This theme is echoed by several papers in this volume, most strongly by Spriggs, who demonstrates the massive deforestation and erosion of Aneityum Island by early Austronesian colonizers. The late prehistoric transformation of both Easter Island and Hawai'ian societies, however, are also linked with human-induced environmental change, as Stevenson and Hommon note.

Along with isolation, one aspect of islands that has contributed to the 'laboratory' analogy is the seemingly endless recombination of environmental attributes. Amongst the approximately 7500 islands in the inner Pacific (excluding island Southeast Asia) is represented virtually every imaginable combination of climatic, geologic, hydrologic, edaphic, and biotic variables. High islands range in size from near-continental New Zealand to diminutive Nihoa or Anuta; the sub-Antarctic Chathams contrast with tropical Samoa; atolls can be found with every possible lagoon configuration; and so forth. It was precisely this environmental variation that Sahlins (1958) found so enticing in developing his theory of social stratification in relation to the distribution of resources.

So far, we have mainly considered those aspects of island *environments* that render them attractive theatres for the study of long-term social change. But the great advantage of the inner Pacific for such pursuits lies in the demonstrable common cultural origins of its myriad bounded societies. Excepting parts of New Guinea and certain adjacent islands, all of the indigenous populations of the Pacific islands are or were members of the widespread Austronesian language family, which itself attests to their cultural affinity. The societies of certain regions, of course, are more closely related than others. The Polynesian societies, for example, can be demonstrated (linguistically, archaeologically, and genetically) to have diverged from a common ancestral society beginning about 1000–500 BC (Kirch 1984). Likewise, the societies of Eastern Micronesia probably have a common origin in the southeast Solomons–north Vanuatu region, of about the same time depth. The important point is that Oceania offers sets of *phylogenetically related societies*, distributed over a widely varied range of discretely bounded ecosystems. Thus, for example, closely related Eastern Polynesian societies which diverged from a common ancestral group no more than 1600 years bp successfully occupied a spectrum of islands including

atolls, high islands, and upraised coral islands in tropical, subtropical, and temperate climates. Such groups of genetically related societies offer marvellous opportunities for controlled comparisons, a situation exploited by Green in his reconstruction of the Ancestral Polynesian settlement system, and also by Rolett in his interpretation of turtle petroglyphs.

Recent approaches to social archaeology in Oceania

The papers which follow in this volume are a fair representation of the environmental and ethnographic diversity of Oceania, with a geographic range including Melanesia, Micronesia, and Polynesia (Fig. 1.1). As well, they offer a sampling of the variety of approaches currently being applied in the archaeological investigation of island societies. To close this brief introduction to the volume, I offer a few comments on these diverse approaches.

Spriggs has tackled the southern half of an extensive east Melanesian archipelago – Vanuatu (formerly the New Hebrides) – the archaeological record of which is known only in the barest outlines (so spotty had been the previous survey work in this region that southern Vanuatu was regarded as 'aceramic' until Spriggs' most recent expedition rapidly demonstrated the absurdity of that claim). The long-term goal in his work is to understand the social dynamics of a region with several ethnographically known societies all of which are presumed to have descended from a common founding culture. As a basis for formulating research strategy, Spriggs has made use of controlled comparisons of the 'endpoint societies' to generate a series of working hypotheses on social dynamics. As noted earlier, this exploitation of the advantages offered by a set of phylogenetically related societies is common to many current Oceanic studies, and is utilized also by Green and Rolett (this volume). Drawing the results of initial archaeological work on Aneityum and Tanna together with his ethnohistorical materials, Spriggs offers a preliminary model for the divergent development of social systems in the Tafea region. He argues that social dynamics will be explained not in simple causal terms (such as those of population pressure or ecological constraint), but rather as a complex dialectic between social and ecological relations. For example, while Spriggs' archaeological work on Aneityum clearly shows the role of environmental change in the development of large-scale irrigation systems, it is also evident that the limiting factor in agricultural intensification was the availability of labor, itself a socially defined relation of production.

The large Fijian archipelago to the east of Vanuatu (Fig. 1.1) attracted some of the earliest archaeological excavation in Oceania (by E. W. Gifford in 1947). Perhaps because these islands lie at the interface between the classic ethnographically defined regions of 'Melanesia' and 'Polynesia', discussions of Fijian prehistory have always been couched in episodic terms of 'migrations' and cultural 'replacements'. Hunt has found such conventional culture-historical explanations for prehistoric change in Fiji wanting. In particular, he points to the emphasis on a single body of material – ceramics – and

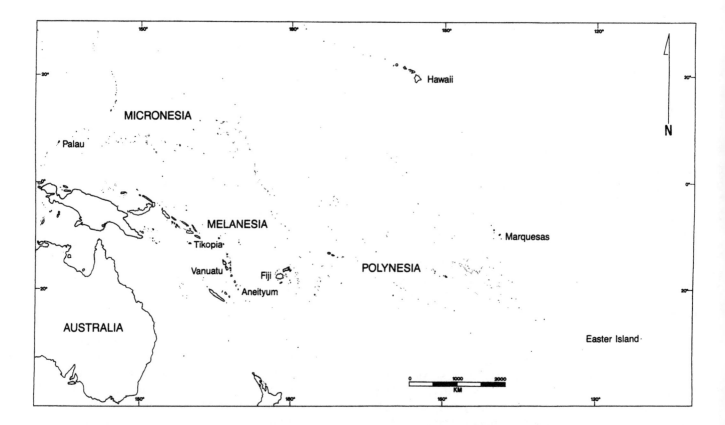

Fig. 1.1. The Pacific Region, indicating the locations of island societies considered in this volume.

on the tendency to extend patterns of stylistic change in ceramics as 'explanations' for large-scale culture change. A careful analysis of the ceramic evidence from the Yanuca rockshelter demonstrates that quite different patterns of quantitative change can be obtained depending upon the selection of stylistic or 'functional' attributes. Without denying the reality of population movements or diffusion in the southwestern Pacific, Hunt suggests how a processual model of prehistoric change in Fiji might be constructed.

In the third contribution, I turn to one of the most anthropologically famous Oceanic communities, Tikopia, for an assessment of the notion of island societies as closed systems. This idea that the evolution of island societies can be accounted for largely if not wholly in terms of internal processes of change has been implicit in much ethnographic as well as archaeological work on island societies, and has often been explicitly advanced under the rubric of island 'laboratories'. Tikopia offers an instructive case, for on the strength of Firth's structural-functionalist analyses, its people are as self-contained as one could imagine. Yet both the ethnohistoric and archaeological data leave no doubt as to the frequency of external contacts in Tikopia prehistory, including both incorporation into now-defunct regional exchange networks and the repeated arrival of drift-voyage immigrants. Rather than being extraneous to the analysis of social change, the elucidation of such external relations proves

to be a vital key in an historical understanding of the structure of modern Tikopia society.

Gumerman focusses on the Palau Islands of western Micronesia, notable for their hierarchical social system as well as for their archaeological vestiges of intensive agriculture. He has made one of the characteristic aspects of islands, resource limitation, a central element of scrutiny in a model that focusses on the role of competition and cooperation. In particular, a simple game theory model of iterated 'Prisoner's Dilemma' is used to suggest that the most appropriate strategy in an island environment with limited resources may be one of competition. It can be further argued that a hierarchical social order offers certain advantages in such a competitive situation.

As noted earlier, the island societies of Polynesia have long been known to form a discrete phylogenetically-related group, descended from a common ancestral community. The last four papers in this volume are concerned with this region, and demonstrate some of the possibilities for analytical control which Polynesia offers. Green is not concerned with any particular island group, but rather with an attempt to reconstruct certain aspects of the 'Ancestral Polynesian' society itself, namely the components of its settlement system. The importance of such a task clearly lies in delineating the baseline against which subsequent change in the variety of Polynesian islands can be assessed. To accomplish this goal,

Green outlines a tripartite approach using lexical reconstruction, controlled ethnographic comparison, and archaeological evidence. Although Green's paper focusses on a narrow domain of Ancestral Polynesian culture, the approach is expandable to virtually any other aspect of culture and society, and provides a powerful tool for establishing the baseline from which subsequent social systems derived.

It has often been suggested that Hawai'ian society represented an apogee of socio-political evolution within Polynesia, and the late prehistoric Hawai'ian system has even been described as an 'archaic state'. A wealth of archaeological data accumulated from a variety of sites over the past thirty years now permit a diachronic analysis of Hawai'ian social evolution, as Hommon attempts. Hommon pays particular attention to the chronometric assessment of evidence for 'inland expansion' and for the formation of the pattern of territorial units which typified the contact-period socio-political system. His model suggests that population growth combined with the establishment of extensive inland agricultural complexes after about AD 1400 led to the formation of these self-sufficient territorial units, and to the disintegration of an ancestral pattern of corporate kinship units. By AD 1600 attainment of high political office and the establishment and defense of boundaries were no longer solely expressions of the kinship structure, but were increasingly manifestations of the power monopoly of the newly established chiefly *class*. This sundering of the Ancestral Polynesian kinship structure and its replacement with a fundamentally different kind of political system based on (among other things) a power monopoly and class endogamy demonstrate the degree of social transformation possible in isolated island settings over even relatively short time spans (e.g., less than two millennia).

The Easter Island case considered by Stevenson provides a fruitful comparison with Hawai'i, since both societies diverged from a common East Polynesian ancestral community probably no more than 1500–2000 years ago. Stevenson approaches the problem of socio-political change by focussing on the ritual structures termed *ahu*, renowned for the large stone statues they were constructed to support. As in many societies with corporate lineage organizations, the Easter Island *ahu*

were constructed by corporate descent groups, each occupying a radial territorial unit analogous to the Hawai'ian *ahupua'a* examined by Hommon. Using the method of obsidian hydration dating, Stevenson has established a chronological sequence for *ahu* construction along a 9 km long section of the southern coast of Easter Island, during the period from AD 1300 to 1864. An early phase of rapid construction of single-lineage *ahu* was followed by a period of increased socio-political integration reflected in the construction of multiple-lineage centers at more or less regular intervals along the coast. The presence of four major socio-political groups within the study area is suggested by the spatial arrangement of *ahu*. The subsequent replacement of image *ahu* with 'semi-pyramidal' interment structures reflects yet another phase of significant socio-political change, possibly associated with demographic stresses and environmental deterioration.

This volume's final essay takes up a theme of considerable debate in contemporary archaeology – namely, whether the 'recovery of mind', or the reconstruction of prehistoric cognitive patterns is an attainable archaeological goal. Rolett addresses this issue through the application of controlled iconographic analysis of a set of Marquesan turtle petroglyphs. His study is noteworthy not only because it is a first attempt to apply iconographic methods in Polynesian archaeology, but because it infuses new life into the study of petroglyphs. These rock carvings have long attracted archaeological attention in Oceania, but attempts to deal with them have usually been either purely descriptive, or have uncritically used petroglyphs as a basis for linking island cultures in grand migrationist reconstructions. Rolett is concerned not only with the iconographic analysis of the Marquesan turtle glyphs, but with their archaeological context, which proves critical to their structural interpretation. Furthermore, he makes use of the model of phylogenetically related cultures within Polynesia in order to set his pan-Polynesian turtle petroglyph comparisons in a systematic framework. His tentative interpretation of the symbolic content of the Marquesan turtle petroglyphs is a highly plausible one, meshing neatly with the ethnohistoric evidence. While Rolett's analysis is a trial foray into an area of much theoretical contention, in my view it augurs well for continued efforts in this direction.

Chapter 2

Landscape, land use, and political transformation in southern Melanesia

Matthew Spriggs

The southern islands of Vanuatu (formerly the New Hebrides) form the administrative district of Tafea, an acronym referring to the five inhabited islands of the area – Tanna, Aneityum, Futuna, Erromango and Aniwa (fig. 2.1). They are currently under investigation by *The Southern Vanuatu Culture History Project* which follows on from research conducted by the author on the island of Aneityum in 1978 and 1979. Prior to that research little archaeological work had been conducted in southern Vanuatu.[1]

The languages of the three main islands of Tafea (Aneityum, Tanna and Erromango) form a distinct Southern Vanuatu subgroup of Oceanic Austronesian (Lynch 1978), while the inhabitants of the two small islands of Futuna and Aniwa speak a Samoic Outlier language of the Polynesian subgroup (Clark 1978). Prior to the adoption of this intrusive language within the last millennium it can be presumed that the languages of these two islands were related to the Southern Vanuatu subgroup. At European contact in the late eighteenth and early nineteenth centuries the islands of Tafea were linked by a regional exchange system with considerably more contact between them than any one island had with places outside the group.

Settlement of Tafea (indeed of all of Vanuatu) probably first took place about 3500 bp during the 'Lapita expansion' of population from the Bismarck Archipelago area and out across the southwestern Pacific as far as Tonga and Samoa

(Spriggs 1984). Since Lapita colonization the cultures of the region have changed and diverged and it is the explanation of these transformations which the current project seeks to investigate. The environments of the several islands of Tafea offered different challenges and opportunities to their human settlers because of contrasts in geology, soils, and water resources. After discussing these, I shall focus on Aneityum as a detailed case study. This island is the only part of Tafea where a rudimentary prehistoric sequence has yet been established, based mainly on evidence of geomorphological and land use changes. In order to assess these changes, a reconstruction is given of Aneityumese society at European contact (circa 1830). This is followed by a discussion of the interplay of land use changes and suggested changes in socio-political structure.

The wider project will consider the Tafea 'regional system' as a whole. Similarities and differences between the several islands can be brought out by a study of the 'endpoints' provided by European contact history. These endpoints are the result of differential socio-political transformation from a presumed single founding culture, processes whose archaeological investigation has only just begun. As a first step in this direction a tentative reconstruction of Tannese social structure is offered for comparison with Aneityum. Historical and archaeological investigation of the other islands of Tafea are too little advanced for further comparison at this stage,

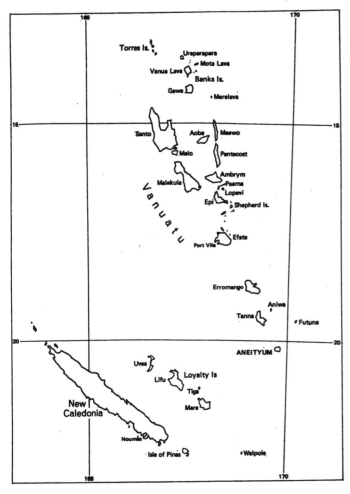

Fig. 2.1. Map of Vanuatu and New Caledonia.

being close to saturation most of the time. The ridge crests are high enough to induce orographic rainfall and Quantin (1979) suggests that rainfall in this zone is probably above 4000 mm annually and the temperature cooler by 2–3°C. As the highest point of Aniwa is only 42 m this zone is not present on that island. The western slopes and particularly the northwest of the islands have a leeward climate with mean annual rainfall of 1600–1800 mm (1643 mm for Lenakel on Tanna, 1740 mm for Noumpon on Erromango) and a more marked seasonality. Tafea is in a belt of frequent tropical storms and hurricanes, generally between December and March. Hurricanes tend to affect the north coasts of islands more severely.

Many of the watercourses of Aneityum and the southern mountainous areas of Tanna are deeply dissected and perennial, although only those of Aneityum appear to have produced significant alluvial plains. On leeward Aneityum, however, between Uche on the south coast and the Aname river on the north coast only two rivers are perennial. In the limestone areas of Tanna surface water quickly drains and many of the rivers cease running during prolonged spells of dry weather. On Erromango there is a predominantly radial pattern of drainage but when rivers reach the limestone fringe they are often diverted and as a result they become bottle-necked with only one coastal outlet serving large networks of tributaries. This limestone fringe constricts the buildup of alluvium at river mouths and creates a 'flushing' effect in periods of high rainfall when areas of coastal alluvium are often eroded in floods. Futuna has near vertical slopes and run-off is rapid. On this island perennial water occurs only as seepages at the contact between the limestones and the underlying volcanics. Aniwa has running water only after heavy rain (Carney and McFarlane 1979, 1; Colley and Ash 1971, 12).

Climate and geology together influence the soils and vegetation of the islands. Aneityum is a high island formed from two coalesced Pleistocene volcanoes. It is 160 km² in area and its highest peak is at 852 m. There is one small area of late Pleistocene or Holocene raised reef and quite extensive areas of recent alluvium in part overlying reefal materials laid down at or near present sea level. The soils reflect this simple geology, but climatic zonation and human influence have complicated the picture. Eighty-eight per cent of the soils are strongly leached ferrallitic soils (ferralsols and cambisols) of poor to moderate fertility while the other main soil type (about 9% of the area) is that of the alluvial soils, the most fertile on the island.

Tanna is considerably larger, 572 km² with its highest point at 1084 m. Again it is basically volcanic in origin, although the vulcanism of the southeast is considerably more recent, continuing today with the continuously active cone of Yasur volcano. Ash enrichment of soils on the island is important in maintaining their fertility. Along the west coast is a strip of recent raised reef, backed by older Pleistocene reef which is also found in many river valleys. In the northern part of the island are found extensive older raised limestones and Pliocene volcanics. From near the northernmost point of

but analysis will be extended to them in the future. The present study should thus be seen as a preliminary statement of Southern Melanesian social dynamics, certainly not as the last word.

Island environments of Tafea

The islands stretch from 18°37′ S to 20°16′ S with a mean difference in temperature between Aneityum and Erromango of only 1°C. This far south of the equator there is some seasonality of climate, with a wetter, hotter period from January to March and a drier, cooler period from July to October. Three climatic zones can be recognized on all islands except the low island of Aniwa: windward, perihumid and leeward (Quantin 1979, 2–3).

Below 500 m on the windward slopes exposed to the south and east, mean annual rainfall is between 2000 and 3000 mm (2290 mm for Anelcauhat on Aneityum, 2822 mm for Potnarevin on Erromanga). The second zone, the perihumid, is found generally above 500 m. It is more constantly humid, the island along the east coast to just north of Waesisi is a coastal fringe of raised beach deposits, with alluvium in the larger river valleys. The interior of the northern two-thirds of Tanna presents a relatively flat plateau while the southern third gives a much more dissected appearance. The soils of Tanna are predominantly andosols (65% of land area) of variable fertility. Most important of these is a type of mollic andosol found on the central plateau and lower windward slopes which is very fertile and covers nearly 26% of the land area. Eutric lithosols cover a further 25% of land area and are very infertile (Quantin 1979, 51–2).

Erromango (902 km²) has a Plio-Pleistocene volcanic core with peaks up to 886 m. Much of the island is fringed by a series of raised limestone terraces up to 300 m in altitude and representing a third of the total area of the island. Along the east coast of the island some of this raised reef was uplifted in the later Holocene period. Areas of alluvium occur at the mouths of some of the major rivers, particularly in the Cook Bay area. As on Aneityum the majority of the soils are ferrallitic (78%), with eutric lithosols covering a further 12% of the area and alluvial soils only 3% (Quantin 1979).

Although Futuna is only 11 km², its high central plateau has an average altitude of 500–600 m. Seventy per cent of its surface area is limestone, overlying Pliocene volcanics. There is a coastal fringe of recent raised reef. Nearly 45% of its soils are useless eutric lithosols, with a further 39% of ferrallitic soils varying in fertility, and other, minor limestone-derived soil types making up the rest of the island. Aniwa is even smaller (8 km²) and in contrast is a low island, 42 m maximum altitude. Apart from the tuff deposits on its central plateau it is a raised reef island. Ferrallitic soils (cambisols) have developed on the tuffs (nearly 53% of the area) while the other soil types all derive from reefal deposits.

Quantin (1979, 53–4) has rated the soils of these islands for agricultural potential from most fertile (type 1) to little or no potential (type 5). Although he is rating for modern potential rather than taking account of traditional agricultural methods his work serves as a useful guide in comparing traditional agricultural production of the islands (table 2.1). There has been considerable human influence on the vegetation

and soils of these islands. This will be examined in detail below in relation to the Aneityum case study where human impact affected not only vegetation but also led to an increase in land area through erosion and deposition.

The Aneityum case study — a transformed environment: humans and hurricanes

The vegetation over nearly the whole of Aneityum (fig. 2.2) immediately before human colonization was probably dense forest except in some swampy areas (Schmid, 1975, 335; Hope and Spriggs 1982). By the time of European contact, however, the island presented a very different appearance:

> As you coast along in a boat you observe three belts or zones, in many places pretty well defined, which we may name the alluvial or arable, the sterile, and the woody. The first lies along the shore, is flat, and consists of a dark, rich soil. As it furnishes a great proportion of the food, most of the natives are found on it. Here flourish luxuriantly the Cocoa-nut and bread-fruit trees, with taro, bananas, sugarcane etc. The second or sterile is of larger extent, and can be best seen. In some places there is no vegetation, nothing but red earth. On the most of it, you find grass, ferns, and a few stunted trees . . . . The woody belt occupies the summit and centre of the island. (Copeland 1860, 346)

The 'red earth' refers to the eroded ferrallitic soils of the slopes. Clearance of the original forest for gardening or other purposes would have had different results in the wetter south and east than it would in the drier north and west. In the windward zone a more woody regrowth is usual after burning, and forest regeneration takes place quite rapidly (Quantin 1979, 9). The leeward zone constitutes a more stressful environment and burning of the forest here would have tended to give rise to a succession of more open vegetation types. Forest regeneration in this zone would have been much slower and could have been easily interrupted by further burning.

The burning off of forest for cultivation would have resulted in the formation of savanna vegetation. When not

Table 2.1. *Quality of soils in Tafea (After Quantin 1979)*

Quality	Erromango		Tanna		Aneityum		Futuna		Aniwa	
	Area (km²)	%	Area (km²)	%	Area (km²)	%	Area (km²)	%	Area (km²)	%
1	104	11.5	219	38.3	7.5	4.7	1.5	13.6	4.2	52.5
2	102	11.3	94	16.4	6.4	4.0	0.9	8.2	1.8	22.5
3	297	33.0	44	7.7	28.0	17.5	3.7	33.6	–	–
4	247	27.4	69	12.1	91.6	57.2	–	–	–	–
5	152	16.8	146	25.5	26.5	16.6	4.9	44.6	2.0	25.0
Total	902		572		160		11		8	

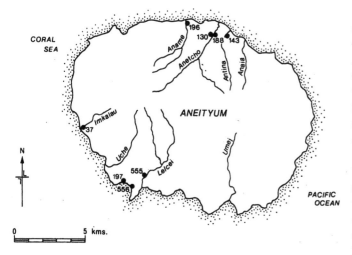

Fig. 2.2. Map of Aneityum, with sites mentioned in the text.

regularly burned this would tend to be replaced by forest once again. Under repeated burning, however, *maquis* scrub would develop, with open, unvegetated areas subject to erosion. Extensive degraded pyrophytic savanna areas are found as well in the north and west of Tanna and Erromango, and even on the northern side of Futuna. Vegetation consists of *Miscanthus*, *Chrysopogon*, and *Imperata* grasses.

Once serious degradation of the vegetation and soils had begun, the economic value of such areas to the inhabitants would have decreased. Fire control may have become less strict when burning off garden areas in the valley bottoms, thus allowing fires to burn freely upslope to the ridges. A further major factor inhibiting forest regeneration after initial burning would have been the devastating hurricanes which affect the region. The northern and western sides of the island bear the brunt of the wind and rain, as attested by historical reports. It is precisely in these areas that the most eroded landscapes are found.

The extremely high runoff associated with hurricanes and other periods of exceptional rainfall would have led to greatly accelerated erosional processes and the strong winds would have damaged regenerating vegetation. On land recently cleared by fire for agricultural or other purposes, or in areas of open anthropogenic vegetation created by regular burning, rates of erosion would have been much higher during hurricanes than in forested areas. The interplay between human interference with the vegetation and natural catastrophic events can be clearly seen at work in this situation. Once serious erosion had begun, the process would have been cumulative and with removal of soil occurring at much faster rates than that at which weathering of the substrata could renew it, the soils could never recover. Erosion certainly occurred in the wetter windward side of Aneityum but to a lesser extent. Between 1848 and 1918 at least thirty-three hurricanes affected Aneityum. The occasional strong earthquake could also cause slope instability.

Deposition of the products of erosion has created the extensive alluvial plains at the mouths and along the valleys of the three main rivers on the island (the Lelcei, Umej and Anetcho rivers) and also at the mouths of many of the smaller streams. These plains are at their most extensive in the north where the Anetcho and several smaller rivers empty into a lagoon protected by an extensive fringing reef. The largest alluvial plains occur below the most eroded slopes, on the coast most affected by hurricanes.

The rivers cutting through these plains reveal in their bank sections traces of past agricultural systems in the form of stone walls and plot boundaries and stone-lined drains, up to 2 m beneath the present ground surface. Deep soil profiles are often revealed in the river banks and former topsoil layers can be traced extending along the river sections sometimes for hundreds of metres – up to four such horizons can often be distinguished, each buried by alluvial material deposited in flash floods associated with major storms in the past. In some places up to 300 m from the current coastline, coral reef platforms are revealed in the river bed at or very close to present sea levels and are considered to be mid–late Holocene in age.

Analysis of these sections and other geomorphological evidence allow us to establish a three phase model for human–environmental interaction on the island (see also Spriggs 1981, chapter 5). A brief summary is given below (see fig. 2.2 for locations of sites discussed in the text):

1. *Human arrival and initial sedimentation*
When the sea reached its present level at about 6000 bp, stream downcutting would have been halted and the valley floors would have begun to silt up, leading to marshy valley bottoms with the streams meandering through them subject to frequent changes of course in response to heavy rainfall. A natural succession in the valley bottoms over time, caused by siltation of the valleys and some attendant progradation of the coastline, would be from marsh to meadow and eventually to forest. Thus when people arrived on the island, at about 2890 ± 60 bp (ANU-2421B), many of the valley floors may have been too swampy to be cultivated easily, as well as being prone to flooding. In addition, the coastlines at the valley mouths may have been in some cases a kilometre or more inland of their present location. The early inhabitants may have concentrated agricultural activities on the hillsides near the coast in order to utilize both marine and terrestrial resources with the minimum of effort. The sequence from the coastal Anauwau swamp (Site AT556) suggests clearance of the adjacent hillsides and accelerated erosion beginning at initial settlement (fig. 2.3; cf. Hope and Spriggs 1982).

It seems plausible that some areas of swamp were used for growing taro, perhaps with small canal-fed irrigation systems in upstream valley floor areas. Many of the largest areas of swamp, however, those on the coastal flatlands against the hillside or immediately adjacent to the beach, have developed above Holocene reef deposits and may have come

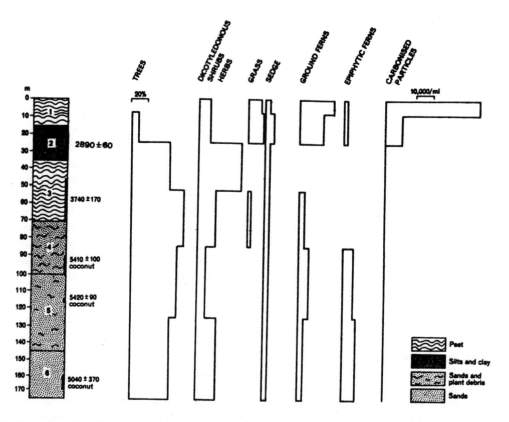

Fig. 2.3. Summary pollen diagram from Anauwau Swamp, Trench 1.

into existence only in the last few hundred years as coastal progradation was accelerated. Previous to this, many of them would have only been small seepages at the base of coastal cliffs or small springs on the beach.

At Imkalau (AT37) there is evidence of initial sedimentation on the valley floor during the period 2180 ± 80 bp (ANU-2188), and then a break in alluvial deposition of nearly 1000 years. This may reflect serious degradation of the hillslope garden areas soon after initial occupation and subsequent abandonment of the area because of its now marginal agricultural value. Changed circumstances a thousand years later, possibly representing population expansion or other forms of pressure on resources, led to the re-occupation of the area perhaps initially with a focus on offshore reef resources. In the Lelcei valley (AT555) in-filling was underway by about 1720 ± 150 bp (ANU-2367) with gardening on the slopes of a volcanic promontory on the east side of Anelcauhat bay leading to erosion and the creation of a colluvial apron at the base of the promontory some time before 1830 ± 70 bp (Beta-7676).

2. *The move on to the valley flats*

Erosion caused by the combined effects of people and the elements was not totally deleterious in effect. It is true that it stripped the hillsides near the coast of much of their soil and vegetation and rendered them useless for gardening, but these hillside soils would have been of low fertility and needed extensive terracing to fit them for any sustained form of cultivation. On the other hand, the alluvial soils created in the valley bottoms and coastal plains are the most fertile on the island. They are deep and well-drained and, unlike the case of some of the extremely narrow valleys elsewhere on the island, sunlight hours at the wide valley mouths and on the coastal plains are optimal for crop growth, with a cropping time shorter than further up the valleys. Similar processes of alluviation also occurred in all the other smaller valleys of the island.

On the north coast, where much more massive erosion has occurred, the evidence for human interference with the landscape is generally more deeply buried, and basal dates from river sections at best relate only to the last 1000 years or so. At Aname (AT196) there is evidence for substantial valley in-filling and progradation of the shoreline since about 570 ± 90 bp (ANU-2360) and 2.5 m of alluvium has been deposited over large areas of the Aname floodplain since that time. In the Anetcho valley such in-filling had already begun to occur by 1000 BP. In the Antina valley the datable sequences do not go back so far, but the major phases of valley in-filling there have certainly occurred within the same time scale. At Aname (AT196, RS2) there is evidence for burning in the catchment by about 1650 ± 290 bp (ANU-2361) but no evidence for accumulation of alluvium on the valley floor at that time, when the shore at this point was some 300 m inland of its present location.

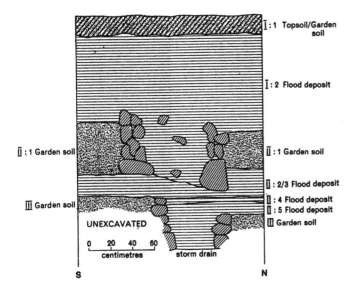

Fig. 2.4. Section of Site AT 130, Anetcho River floodplain, with buried agricultural drainage channels.

The first direct evidence for the use of the valley mouths and plains for agriculture and habitation, as opposed to the indirect evidence their sediments contain of burning activities in the catchment, comes from within the last 1000 years. On the Lelcei floodplain (AT555) an earth oven was revealed in the river bank dating to 540 ± 75 bp (ANU-2368) and slightly downstream stone walls associated with agriculture have been found in the same horizon. At Imkalau (AT37) a settlement on the valley bottom with probable agricultural associations was occupied at about 1000–700 bp (ANU-1064, 1069, 2242) and dry land gardening was certainly underway by about 440 ± 80 bp (ANU-2241). In the north there is no direct evidence of use of the Aname valley floor until after about 300 ± 170 bp (ANU-2363)(Site AT196), whereas in the Anetcho valley an earth oven dates occupation at AT188 to 1020 ± 120 bp (ANU-2356). This occurred during rapid accumulation of alluvium on the valley floor, and structural evidence associated with agriculture does not appear until some metres higher in the section. No direct dates have been obtained from the garden soils associated with the parallel storm drains found both on the Anetcho (AT130; see fig. 2.4) and Antina (AT143) Rivers, but a date in the order of 1000 bp seems likely on stratigraphic grounds. Fluvial deposits covering these storm drains could have been laid down several hundred years later.

3. Agricultural intensification on the valley floors

In all cases where clear evidence is available, with the exception of the Aname floodplain, the initial use of the valley floors appears to have been for habitation and dry land gardening. At Anetcho and Antina, the initial labor investment in storm drains to prevent flooding and perhaps lower the water table may have been considerable. The process, however, was generally one of *extensification*, the use for the first time as gardens of the previously swampy and flood-prone valley flats. This may have been forced by over-exploitation of hillside swiddens near the coast. As alluvium accumulated, the valley floors would have become raised further above the base water table and flooding would have been less frequent.

On the same Aname floodplain, where massive alluviation has occurred since 500–600 bp, the initial form of gardening for which we have evidence is irrigation. There is evidence from the dating of the underlying alluvium to suggest that the irrigation system can only have been constructed since 300–400 bp. The AT196 system occurs at the end of the longest canal on the island (AT177), so this particular inter-district canal may be no more than a few hundred years old. The floodplains of the Anetcho and Antina rivers also present surface remains of large-scale irrigation systems, again often at the end of long inter-district canals. The evidence of the river sections, assumed to reflect deposition patterns over wide areas of the valley floors, would suggest that the large-scale systems represent a late intensification of agricultural production within the last few hundred years. Being surface features, such systems are hard to date, but the very fact that they are surface features would suggest a comparatively recent time period.

They were already of some antiquity, however, when the missionaries arrived. Copeland (1860, 346) wrote that the canals, 'according to the old opinions of natives, are the work of superhuman agents'. In his 1882 Dictionary, Inglis noted that:

> if you ask the natives who made these old canals for irrigation, they tell you they do not know; they suppose that they were made by the *natmasses*, that is, the gods, or, in other words, the spirits of their forefathers, which, of course means their forefathers themselves. (1882, xxiii)

Some of the larger canals are named after birds or freshwater crayfish which are supposed either to have built them or shown the people how to do so. A date of construction at least a few generations before the arrival of the missionaries would seem to be necessary for their origin to have become enshrined in myth and their human architects forgotten. However, the ultimate extension of irrigation on to the flattest areas of the plains may have occurred only immediately before European contact. The difficulties of maintaining a sufficient head of water on the flat plains were solved by leading the canals along the top of earthen embankments (*natawai*), some of which were over three metres high and hundreds of metres long, before letting the water down on to the flattest areas which could not otherwise be irrigated.

Before considering the effects of 3000 years of landscape change on economic and social structure we need to establish an ethnohistoric baseline, the socio-political organization of Aneityum at European contact.

The ethnohistoric baseline: Aneityum in 1830

Our sources for this period are written and oral history and archaeology. Many of the written sources date from the

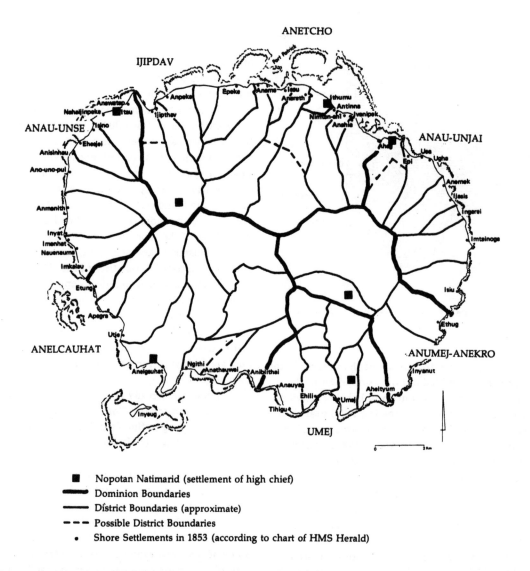

■   Nopotan Natimarid (settlement of high chief)

▬   Dominion Boundaries

─   District Boundaries (approximate)

- - -   Possible District Boundaries

•   Shore Settlements in 1853 (according to chart of HMS Herald)

Fig. 2.5. Dominion and district boundaries on Aneityum in the early contact period.

missionization period from 1848 onwards and so care in interpretation is warranted. This problem is addressed elsewhere and a detailed list of sources given in Spriggs (1981, chapters 3 and 4; 1985).

At contact the island was divided into seven dominions (or 'chiefdoms'), each further divided into a number of districts between fifty and sixty in number (fig. 2.5). Each dominion, called in Aneityumese *nelcau* or 'canoe', had at its head a high chief (*natimarid*) with a number of petty or district chiefs (*natimi alupas*) subservient to him. All early accounts agree as to the presence on the island of patrilineal hereditary chieftainship. It is often stressed in the missionary accounts that the 'civil' role of chiefs was inextricably bound up with their 'sacred' role. Chiefly power was based, as in many small-scale chiefdoms (cf. Godelier 1977, 201–2; 1978, 767), on ritual rather than physically coercive powers — power of sorcery against enemies, power over the elements to control success in agriculture and fishing, and so on.

There are various ways in which chiefs were distinguished from commoners. Only chiefs could regularly participate in *kava* drinking, and cannibalism was also their special prerogative. Polygamy was practiced principally among the chiefs, with three wives being the maximum number noted by the missionaries. Chiefs had some say (with family heads) in arranging marriages, and they themselves tended to intermarry with other chiefly families to extend alliances. Only *natimarid* had the right to be carried on men's shoulders in 'baskets' on ceremonial occasions and their person was considered sacred. There were various ceremonies on the accession of a chief and each chief had an area of sacred ground where rituals were performed. *Natimarid* were most clearly differentiated from all others at their death. The usual method of disposal of the dead was burial at sea, but the *natimarid* were buried in their houses with their heads exposed. Food offerings were placed before the corpse until the head could be separated from the body and then the skull was placed on a pole as an object of worship.

The basic settlement unit was the district under a *natimi alupas*, with households dispersed among the gardens. These districts usually consisted of a single catchment from the central chain of mountain ridges to the shore, forming wedge-shaped territories incorporating a range of environments from reef flat to cloud forest at several hundred metres above sea level. These districts, between 51 and 55 in number, have clear parallels with Hawai'ian *ahupua'a* as described by Earle (1978), which covered a similar range of environments (see also Hommon, this volume). However, not all *ahupua'a* correspond to Earle's 'ideal type' wedge segments, and nor do all Aneityumese districts. Radiating ridges from the central mountains of the island account for the boundaries in most cases (23–5 cases) but streams or rivers sometimes form boundaries (though rarely at points where irrigation supply canal take-offs are situated), while in other cases a coast–inland dichotomy in deeper valleys has been created by dividing up tributary catchments as districts (8 cases) or so designating valley segments away from the shoreline. Some shore districts with a wide expanse of coastal plain appear to have been created following no clear natural boundaries at all. Possibly they simply represent divisions of land into areas of equal population and/or equal resources in a uniform environment (4–6 cases).

Dominion boundaries are recorded on a map (fig. 2.6) prepared by missionary Geddie (probably in 1849) and in written and oral sources, although current land and political disputes make exact locations problematic. 'Border' districts may have shifted allegiance from time to time but the basic pattern recorded in 1849 was almost certainly a precontact one.

The agricultural system consisted then (as it does today) of both dryland and irrigated gardens, with taro (*Colocasia esculenta*) as the main staple grown in taro swamps (*inhenou*), and in canal-fed furrow irrigated gardens (*incauwai*), as well as by a range of dryland swidden techniques (Spriggs 1981, chapter 3).

The district inhabitants of non-chiefly status should not be considered homogeneous. The drudgery of women's lives is recorded in detail in oral and written sources. Much of the garden work, collecting of marine foods and cooking was done by them. When Geddie and Inglis took the first census in 1854 they noted a marked imbalance in numbers between the sexes which was attributed to greater infanticide of female children and the strangling of women upon the death of their husband or sometimes other close relatives.

A rule of endogamy restricted marriage usually to within the dominion, and perhaps more ideally within the district or contiguous districts. Chiefly marriage links were wider, however. Sister exchange was the preferred form according to informants, and there was no operation of bridewealth. If marriage was contracted outside the district a woman had to be obtained in return sooner or later. Sexual antagonism and violence against women leading to their death or subsequent suicide were frequently recorded by the missionaries. Such socially sanctioned violence against women elsewhere in Melanesia has been interpreted as coercion to extract obedience and in particular increased labor inputs into agricultural tasks (cf. Modjeska 1977, 252–8 for a discussion of sexual antagonism among the Duna of the Southern Highlands, PNG).

Agricultural production limits were effectively set by the amount of work women could be pressured into doing, but their numbers were limited by infanticide and strangulation of widows, monopolized by the polygamy of chiefs and elders, and rationed by these same men who allocated them as wives. At one level such limiting practices can be seen as operating as a social control over the behaviour of younger men, with obedience being demanded in return for a wife (cf. Terray 1972). As Geddie noted, the imbalance of the sexes meant that 'no less than 600 men are doomed to a life of hopeless celibacy' (1855, 125). Women were thus (to men) a scarce and extremely valuable exchange object controlled by chiefs and family heads. I do not pretend that this is a full explanation for the sexual oppression of women on the island: women were of course the producers of the producers, and selective infanticide, although probably not strangling of widows, may have served as a population limiting or stabilising mechanism (McArthur 1974, 65–8, chapter 5).

Continuously fluid and shifting alliances seem to have been the pattern of relations between dominions. Pressure on resources does not appear to have been the reason for warfare, territorial conquest was not the aim, and few men appear to have been killed in these engagements. The idea that traditional warfare was in some sense a ritualized form of competitive exchange, as put forward by Adams (1984, 12) to explain warfare on Tanna, may well be valid for Aneityum.

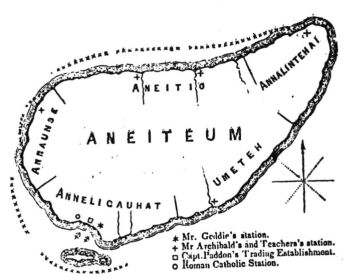

Fig. 2.6. Geddie's 1849 map of Aneityum showing chiefdom boundaries and mission outstations.

It is in the practice of feasting (so strongly condemned by the missionaries) that Aneityumese social structure and the position of chiefs is most clear. The central role of chiefs was in the giving and receiving of feasts (*nakaro*) involving the appropriation of surplus food production in their own dominions or districts and redistribution across dominion or district boundaries. In this way no one ate their own surplus. There were elements both of reciprocity, maintaining relations with potentially hostile groups, and of social competition. A chief's relative status was shown by the quantity of food collected and this was limited by the quantity he could appropriate from his own subjects. One way of concentrating food supplies for the feasts was the imposition of a taboo of up to six months on certain foods leading up to it, backed up by fear of angering the chief as possessor of malevolent powers, and of angering the spirits (*natmas*) in general. On occasion more directly coercive sanctions were employed to enforce taboos.

This fear was tempered by an ideology of giving. Within the district status would be achieved by the individual who produced the greatest quantity of food, successfully propitiating both chief and *natmas*. The chief carried this desire for status to the inter-district arena, where an impressive display of food showed that his garden magic was more powerful, therefore his propitiation of the *natmas* more successful, and his control over agricultural production more effective than that of his rivals.

That the social rather than nutritive aspects of feasting need to be stressed is clear from the fact that much of the collected and already cooked food that was exchanged was allowed to rot, the *quantity* of food collected rather than the food itself being important. Many foods were presented at feasts but taro was always the essential ingredient, a crop which once harvested lasts only a matter of days. The competitive element in these feasts would have led to a cycle of escalation of gifts and ever more lavish countergifts. This spiral was controlled only by the limits of agricultural productivity. One of the limits to this was the area of productive land, depending on available technology, another was climate, and the third was the labor available for agricultural production.

The third factor is perhaps the most crucial. Given the major role played by women in agricultural production it is clear that the appropriation of surplus depended on the labor inputs of women, and so increased demands on production represented increased demands on women's labor. Thus Mrs Geddie complained that when feasts were imminent the women had to fatten the pigs in addition to their usual tasks and her women's school had to be broken up. The crucial factor in limiting the 'inflationary' tendencies of competitive feasting was the extent to which women could be pressured to work harder. Modjeska (1977) has discussed a similar situation in Highland New Guinea where in many cases the limits to agricultural intensification (for instance in Kapauku) are set by the extent to which women's labor hours can be

increased. Thus as Modjeska notes (1977, 226) the social relations of production governing the division of labor rather than any factor of population, technology or environment set the limits to intensification in many Melanesian societies.

Links between dominions were extended to other islands. Certain dominions had links to the nearby islands of Futuna and Aniwa and to particular parts of Tanna. These links involved intermarriage, exchange and reciprocal feasting. Thus Anelcauhat had links with Port Resolution on Tanna, Anau-unse with Anuikaraka twelve miles south from Port Resolution, while Anetcho was linked to both Futuna (or at least a part of that island) and Aniwa. If a visiting canoe missed anchorage and landed in a different dominion its crew would be killed and eaten, a fate which befell a company of Aniwans who were shipwrecked at Anau-unjai in about 1820 en route for Anetcho, and a mixed party of Aneityumese and Tannese who were forced to put ashore in a hostile area of Tanna in 1852.

Archaeological settlement pattern

An archaeological reconnaissance of the whole island, and a detailed settlement pattern study of four of the seven dominions (Anau-unse, Ijipdav, Anetcho and Anau-unjai) were undertaken to examine the archaeological manifestations of this later prehistoric/early historic pattern.

Archaeologically the dominion or chiefdom level of political organization is shown most clearly by the long canal irrigation systems, some crossing major watersheds and over four kilometres in length. The significance of such substantial engineering works does not lie, however, in the required labor input for these necessitating a chief or equivalent as manager of such enterprises. It lies in there being that area of land under the political control of one unit, of there being in this case a supra-district polity. Initial labor input and labor organization would not have required the mobilization of large work teams above the level available in a single district or contiguous districts served by these canals. There are many examples in the ethnographic literature of social groups without 'chiefly' managers building and maintaining irrigation systems equivalent to or larger than those on Aneityum. In fact none of the irrigation systems in the Pacific is of such scale as to demand centralized direction in construction or maintenance, so the more extreme versions of the 'hydraulic hypothesis' of Karl Wittfogel (1957) and others must be rejected (cf. Earle 1978 for a detailed examination of Wittfogel's ideas in the light of research in the Hawai'ian Islands). The chief as overseer or manager is clearly *not* a necessary precondition for the existence of such systems.

Long canals are, however, vulnerable to any interference, and so political control above the district level was necessary to ensure the continuation of water supply. In the period for which we first have documentary evidence on Aneityum, such supra-district organization was provided by the dominions.

These canals never cross dominion boundaries as we know them from this period. Such supra-district organization might have been possible on a purely reciprocal basis between politically independent districts, but would have been a more tenuous arrangement. On the north coast of Aneityum between the Aname and Anaia rivers flood plain irrigation systems cover some 69 ha fed by eleven canals. Four of these canals, feeding approximately 58 ha or 85% of the total area, cross district boundaries. If water supply had been cut off to some of these lowland districts or to valleys (such as Uea and Igarei) which relied heavily on extra irrigation water from adjacent districts, their economies would have collapsed.

It is thus not surprising that the core of every dominion was a large permanent river or series of rivers. If we calculate the percentage of wetland (as opposed to rain-fed) garden area in use per year for the four northern dominions (combining Ijipdav and Anetcho, whose boundary is unclear) at about 1830 we find 5% for Anau-unse (the driest dominion, on the leeward end of the island), 20% for Ijipdav-Anetcho, and 31% for Anau-unjai. The higher yields from the irrigated gardens meant that somewhere in the order of 10% of total root crop production was supplied by irrigated gardens in Anau-unse, 27% in Ijipdav-Anetcho and 40% in Anau-unjai (details of the calculations are given in Spriggs 1981, chapter 4). It must be noted that these figures assume a year in which rainfall was adequate for good crop growth in the rain-fed sector. In drier years a higher percentage of total production would have come from the more reliable irrigated gardens. The irrigation systems form a permanent infrastructure of canals and sloped stone-faced terraces which could be brought back into use at any time. Such a permanent infrastructure leads to a greater tie to land, giving reason to remain in a particular locale. There is a potential for privatization of land ownership where such infrastructures exist, and a tendency towards this may have been occurring on Aneityum at European contact.

Sites recorded in the archaeological survey usually form discrete clusters in the valley bottoms and lower slopes of major catchments, extending inland but very rarely to above the 300 m contour. Above this were found occasional taro swamps, some dry gardens on flat areas but only very exceptionally any house sites. Only one canal take-off (AT177) occurred above 300 m altitude and this is the longest supply canal on the island. Connecting some of these settlement/ agricultural clusters are long canals such as AT177 which cross major watersheds between valleys. Apart from such canals the ridges between valleys are usually devoid of sites, thus clearly delimiting the areas of many of the districts. House sites represented by low stone-faced platforms are found dispersed among the gardens of the districts. On occasion up to four or five house platforms occur in clusters, and one or two clusters appear to have low banks and ditches around them. Although Geddie refers to 'villages', the pattern is best described as dispersed settlement. Associated with each district were one or more *intiptag*. These were (and are) usually

open spaces adjacent to large (particularly banyan) trees where the men drank *kava* at night. Although former *intiptag* sites are often known to informants, archaeologically they have no clear traces. In cases where a building was associated with them, it is indistinguishable from an ordinary house site.

The settlement and burial places of high chiefs (*nopotan natimarid*) are generally remembered. At Idumu the *nopotan natimarid* of Anetcho is surrounded by a bank and ditch. At Anelcauhat one such site (Unumej, AT197) adjacent to the present *natimarid*'s compound has been affected by recent gardening operations and at least two burial sites disturbed. One was recovered by the villagers in the mid-1970s, and the other partially disturbed burial was excavated by the author in 1983. Both burials contained a male and female with quantities of red ochre, necklaces of drilled pig teeth, large *Tridacna* and whale tooth (?) beads and *Conus* rings, all said to be part of a *natimarid*'s insignia. The burial excavated in 1983 contained parts of other individuals whose association with the primary inhumation is unclear.

A basic assumption has been made in assessing the significance of the site survey that all agricultural systems which are not known to informants to have been built in the period after missionization were in use (either as planted areas or in short-term fallow) at European contact. Using a 'welfare' approach to carrying capacity developed by the geographer Bayliss-Smith (1978, 1980), estimates of the 1830 population can be made (see Spriggs 1981, chapter 4, for detailed methodology). In 1854 the missionaries conducted a census and found that there were about 3800 people on the island. It is known however that in the 1830s and 1840s there were two epidemics which occasioned considerable mortality. Some early writers estimated the precontact population at somewhere between 9000 and 20,000. The settlement pattern study indicated an 1830 population of between 4600 and 5800 people, a density of 29–36 persons per square kilometre.

Agricultural intensification and political transformation on Aneityum

Convincing linguistic reconstructions allow us to suggest that the original settlers of this area were agriculturalists with a chiefly system of social organization (Pawley 1982; Pawley and Green 1973). Indeed one of the Proto-Oceanic reconstructions of a term for chief *qalapa(s)* is apparently cognate with Aneityumese *natimi alupas* (Pawley 1982, 42). At European contact in 1830 Aneityum had two ranks of chiefs, whose prestige was based on their ability to mobilize surplus production for competitive feasts.

The potential for agricultural intensification is the potential to increase surplus production to meet the demands of the socio-political system. As Godelier (1977, 110–11) has pointed out:

> If modern anthropology has confirmed the argument
> that the relationship between the development of
> productive forces and the development of social

inequalities is not mechanical, it has on the whole shown that social competition in class societies provides the major incentive to surplus production and, in the long term, leads indirectly to progress in productive forces. It is this competition and this progress which are detailed in the sequence from Aneityum. Thus we see a change in land use over time from dryland to more productive irrigated agriculture (cf. Spriggs 1985), and further intensification of particular irrigation techniques. Cropping of swampland gardens can be indefinitely extended by continually renewing the leaf mulch and turning over the soil, and yields can be increased in furrow irrigation by tillage. Tillage and deep mulching appear to have been used in dryland gardening as well. A presumably unintentional consequence of gardening on the steep hillsides was the massive erosion which appears to have begun almost immediately after initial settlement. This led to the creation of the extensive alluvial plains generally used first for dryland gardening and then for irrigation within the last few hundred years prior to European contact.

Much of the irrigated land fed by the long inter-district canals of the north coast was not in existence at settlement. It is within Anetcho dominion that the expansion of agriculture allowed by landscape change is most evident. Whole shore districts such as Itad, Anared and Anetcho Ecsina may have only become habitable at all within the last few hundred years, previously being swampy and flood-prone or even under the sea. As noted earlier, the boundaries of these districts do not follow clear natural features and give the appearance of having been purposefully divided up as equal areas of new productive land. It is in these districts that much of the irrigated land of Anetcho dominion is found, and it is perhaps significant that the *nopotan natimarid*, the headquarters of the Anetcho *natimarid*, occurs in one of these 'new' districts. Smaller areas of recent alluvium are found in all dominions and are everywhere highly significant within the agricultural system.

The growth of chiefly power and the expansion of irrigation on the island went hand in hand. As a chief's prestige grew he would become more able to command labor to expand the conditions of agricultural production by the building of new canals and the extension of irrigation systems to the flatter areas of the coastal plains. It was the chief's power to appropriate surplus production for feasts in order to maintain his prestige which required the expansion of the irrigation systems. An expansion in one district or dominion would necessitate expansion in the others to match food presentations, taro for taro, up to the limits of the productive capacity of the island. Irrigation is clearly an attractive path to intensify production in such expanding chiefdoms (cf. Spriggs 1985).

It is hard to imagine that the social system at European contact, based as it was on the sustained production of large agricultural surpluses, could have existed on anything like the same scale even five hundred years previously. Human interference with natural environmental processes had led, not to ecological disaster, but to a greatly expanded potential for agricultural intensification and social stratification.

First thoughts on Tanna

As already noted, there were exchange relations between particular districts on Tanna and on Aneityum and some intermarriage took place. Two Aneityumese products were much in demand on Tanna — red ochre and hawks' feathers. Red ochre was used as decorative body paint on Tanna and the feathers of the Australian goshawk (*Accipiter fasciatus*) were used 'for making plumes with which to adorn the heads of the Tannese chiefs' (Inglis 1890, 136). As Inglis noted, this hawk was not present on Tanna (cf. Medway and Marshall 1975, 455). *Kava* and pigs, both important in ritual life, were given in return. Tannese (and Aniwans and Futunese) also sailed to certain of the dominions on Aneityum to take part in feasts and dances which presumably were reciprocated on Tanna. Many early accounts noted the similarity in dress, hair styles, decoration and house and canoe types between the two islands, and the 'roads' (*swatu*) between *nakamal* (An: *intiptag*), the men's meeting places, which mediated relations between districts on Tanna (Bonnemaison 1979, 309–14; Brunton 1979, 99–101), certainly extended to Aneityum. I suspect they operated *within* Aneityum as well but there is no clear statement of this in the sources.

On Tanna there is no equivalent to the *natimarid* (high chief) or his dominion and 'chiefs' are usually *yeremwanu* (*yremera, yerumanu, yeremere*), equivalent in some ways to the *natimi alupas* (district chief) of Aneityum. The traditional power of *yeremwanu* on Tanna is now difficult to establish. The right to wear a large feather headdress (*kweriya*) is the most distinctive feature of the rank. Secondary roles such as that of crop magician, or the right to cannibalism appear to have contributed more to a person's power than the *yeremwanu* title (Adams 1984, 14–15), a point also made for Aneityum in relation to high chiefs and district chiefs. The feather headdress (to which the hawk feathers of Aneityum were presumably attached) was worn at the *nakwiari* or *nekoviaar*, 'the most prestigious and spectacular ceremonial exchange' (Brunton 1979, 100). Just as on Aneityum the *nakaro* (presumably a cognate term) was intimately connected with and initiated by the chiefs, so the *nakwiari*, its equivalent on Tanna, and other feasts and exchanges there, took place at the instigation of 'a local aristocracy whose highest ranked members, called *Yremera*, formed a network of alliances round the whole island' (Bonnemaison 1979, 309; translation by Spriggs).

Brunton's informants (1979, 100) claimed that *yeremwanu* had certain privileges such as not being required to work in the fields and access to a greater number of wives than other men. Another hereditary title on Tanna was the *yeniniko* (*yani niko, ieni entete, yani en dete*), the 'war chief' or 'talking chief' (Adams 1984, 15–18; Bonnemaison 1979, 311; Brunton 1979, 100). In warfare he was the local leader while the role of the *yeremwanu* was very limited, but generally the *yeniniko* was his subordinate and to some extent his assistant (Brunton 1979). While pointing out that it is probably an idealised view, Brunton (1979, 101) notes that:

Some informants claim that traditionally, sorcery (*netik*) was under the complete control of *yeremere* and *yeniniko* and was used to ensure compliance with their will.

This again is reminiscent of Aneityum, but many *natimarid* and *natimi alupas* privileges were not noted on Tanna. Thus *kava* drinking was a regular habit of all adult men on Tanna and while the right to cannibalism was restricted and inheritable, it was not a right many *yeremwanu* or *yeniniko* possessed. The degree of veneration of a *natimarid* during life as well as after death is not found associated with any rank on Tanna. As on Aneityum, however:

> Soon after birth girls would be set aside for a definite [marriage] alliance, often between lineages of the same tribe but sometimes between different tribes. The match was not related to land distribution so much as to the establishment and maintenance of political alliances . . . the acceptance of a bride entailed the obligation on the receiving line to provide a bride, and on the donor line to receive one, in the future. (Adams 1984, 10)

Brunton describes the marriage pattern as sister exchange between cross-cousins (1979, 97). A 'tribe' in the sense used above was a collection of hamlets sharing a common territorial name (Adams 1984, 7), corresponding to the district level of organisation on Aneityum. Interestingly enough these districts, about 115 in number, are called 'canoes' (*niko*) as are the largest independent territorial units on Aneityum, the dominions (*nelcau*). Bonnemaison (1983, 4–5) states that each *niko* consists of one or several clans and is organised around a network of strongholds and magic places according to natural topographic features such as catchments or clearly marked-off sections of plateau. Boundaries, as on Aneityum, are generally ridge crests or deeply embanked creeks. Bonnemaison sees the canoe terminology as being a folk memory of the original voyage of colonization and the *yeni niko* (literally 'spokesman of the canoe') as being the closest to what is understood elsewhere as 'chief' (1983, 11).

Exchange feasts between *niko* such as the *nakwiari* were as important on Tanna as on Aneityum, featuring the familiar elements of reciprocity and competition. Adams has stressed the principle of reciprocal exchange as essential to an understanding of Tannese social structure (1984, 8–10).

Comparisons between *yeremwanu* and *natimi alupas*, 'tribe' and 'district', can only get us so far, however. The *natimi alupas* operated within a hierarchical framework of which they were the second level, and no equivalent higher level of political integration operated on Tanna.

Brunton among others has characterised Tannese society as atomistic, creating a precarious balance between individual autonomy and interdependence (1979, 102). This balance is maintained by an almost inflexible, all-embracing network of relations between individuals and groups preventing them from forging new links or abandoning old ones. The possibilities for change lie in the hierarchical system of titles but, as Brunton points out, this system 'is unable to mobilise sufficient

power to constrain the autonomy of adult males' (1979, 102). He reflects that:

> Had there been effective foci of social power on Tanna sufficient to curb individual autonomy and provide some guaranteed range of internal peace, interaction and exchange may have been able to operate more smoothly. But there are few, if any, resources which could be monopolized to the extent necessary to provide the basis for such foci. (1979, 101)

The problem may well have been the limited possibilities for agricultural intensification on the island, in terms of both technology and labor. Given the topography and water resources of Tanna, irrigation systems for year-round production of taro could not have developed. Where rivers of permanent flow do occur on Tanna they are generally in deep gorges and unsuitable as irrigation sources. In addition, relative to its size, Tanna has a very limited area of alluvial plains, the prime locations where irrigation might be expected. The poorly developed fringing reef does not form the barrier against coastal erosion which allows the development of such plains.

On Tanna, however, there is fertile land for dry land agriculture, particularly in more leeward areas. Thus instead of taro it was the seasonal dry land yam crop on which attention was focussed. As a dry land crop, yam needed no appeal to resources beyond the immediate planting area and so no supra-district polity was necessary to allow the intensification of its production. The irrigation systems of Aneityum represented capital works which could be continually re-used and added to piecemeal. The yam mounds of Tanna, on the other hand, had to be remade before each planting and similar advantages did not accrue. While on Aneityum land use in many areas could be intensified from dry land untilled cropping, to tilled cropping, to canal-fed irrigation, with increasing yields obtainable per hectare, the productive limits of Tannese gardening systems were narrower. In a published review of my Ph.D. thesis, Bonnemaison (1981, 128) points out that intensification on Tanna was not a question of quantity but of quality and in particular of length of yam. Long, specially grown yams were an important part of ritual exchange. This is certainly true but 'ordinary' yams still had to be produced for feasts as well as the ritually exchanged yams and so quantity was also important.

A final limit to productivity could have been hours of labor. Following a typical southern Melanesian ideology and division of labor, yam gardening on Tanna was traditionally largely a male task (cf. Barrau 1965, 336–9). Women help remove weeds and clear the plot prior to making the yam mounds and also weed and harvest the crop. Men do the heavy clearing, construct the yam mounds and trellises on which they train the yam vines, plant the yam tops and also harvest the crop (L. Lindstrom, personal communication). Thus male labor may have set the limits to intensification rather than female labor. Given the autonomy of adult males as noted above, there were clear limits to the accumulation of surplus. An effective focus of social power on Tanna could therefore not be established with the social relations of production which existed and yam as the main crop.

Very little archaeological research has been conducted on Tanna and we have neither a good idea of the cultural sequence nor yet of traditional settlement pattern. The kind of massive humanly induced landscape change recorded for Aneityum has not occurred on Tanna, although the degraded 'white grass' vegetation of parts of the north and west of the island testifies to considerable alteration of at least the vegetation. The island is densely settled and appears not to have suffered as much from the massive depopulation which occurred on the other southern islands with European contact. The current population (1979 census) is 15,593, a density of just over 27 persons per square kilometre. Early 'guesstimates' gave figures of 15–20,000 people (26–35 per square kilometre) which may in fact not have been too wide of the mark.

Conclusions

Aneityumese social structure could be viewed as a transformation of the Tannese pattern with power and authority increasingly concentrated in the hands of a few and a stress on vertical social relationships. Influence on social structure of both islands from the nearby Polynesian outliers needs to be considered here. Lindstrom (1981b, 134, 140–1) has suggested for Tanna that the notion of talking and sacred chiefs may have diffused from Aniwa and/or Futuna in the last few hundred years with Polynesian settlement of those islands. Certainly Polynesian spiritual figures such as Mauitikitiki and Tangaroa feature in traditional stories all over Tafea, and Polynesian loan words occur in the languages. Lindstrom suggests that 'this new knowledge was used as is knowledge today – the men closest to the source became brokers and teachers and thus increase their political status'. But only initially. If chiefship were established this way in the area, the pre-existing social relations and economic structures of Aneityum and Tanna would explain why the idea 'stuck' in Aneityum but failed to take hold effectively on Tanna. Seeing chiefs in action on neighboring islands was not sufficient where permanent means of monopolizing power were not available.

While the outward trappings of chiefly rank on Aneityum and Tanna may owe a lot to Polynesian models, the basis for political power was indigenous. Indeed, instead of seeing Aneityum as an evolutionary transformation of a Tannese-style system it is possible to view Tanna as a 'devolution' in political power from a formerly more hierarchical system. Friedman's (1981, 1982) model for explaining the apparent diversity of Oceanic socio-political systems is pertinent here. The linguistic reconstruction of early Oceanic Austronesian social organization as hierarchical has already been alluded to. Friedman uses the linguistic reconstructions to suggest a 'prestige-good economy' as the basic building block of ancestral Oceanic society. Chiefly power was based on the monopolization

of wealth items necessary for social transactions (marriage, etc.) which were obtained by long-distance exchange, a monopoly which could be maintained only under conditions of trade scarcity. New Caledonian chiefly systems may well be of this kind and an exchange cycle between the main island of New Caledonia, the Isle of Pines, and the Loyalty Islands where shell valuables were exchanged against greenstone objects appears to have been important in stabilizing the system (Guiart 1963). This exchange system appears to have previously included Tafea. Tanna and Aneityum are visible from the Loyalty Islands and greenstone pendants clearly of New Caledonian origin were valuable personal wealth in Tafea at European contact (Cook [Beaglehole] 1969, 505; Golovnin n.d.; cf. Aubert de la Rue 1938). The supply appears to have already dried up by contact, however, representing a contraction of the exchange system. Trade density in general within Aneityum and between Aneityum and the neighboring islands appears to have been quite low at contact. If we follow Friedman's scenario, collapse of trade and loss of access to imported valuables would have meant no clear monopoly basis for power. Competition would have led to a stress on feasting with attendant intensification of production, intensified warfare and a stress on the religious sanctity of chiefs. This system Friedman calls 'theocratic feudalism' and it does bear a striking resemblance to the situation on Aneityum at contact.

Tanna is certainly more centrally placed with respect to external exchange than Aneityum and may have experienced an *increase* in trade density, probably pre-contact but certainly accelerated with the coming of the Europeans when Tanna became the major provisioning centre in the area for European vessels (as Aneityum did not produce many storable yams for sale to ships, it was largely ignored in the early contact period). Increasing trade density led to a breakdown of the monopoly hierarchy into competition between smaller groups as access to external goods became easier for all. A variant of the 'big man system' thus came to operate either shortly before or shortly after European contact.[2] Chiefly titles therefore may have been declining in importance on Tanna rather than being recent 'diffusions' from Polynesia which failed to take hold, whereas on Aneityum the basis for chiefship had shifted but chiefly status was maintained. In this model, both systems were transformations of an earlier ancestral 'prestige-good system' rather than being an evolutionary continuum with Tanna as a 'less-developed' version of Aneityum.

Future archaeological work in Tafea will seek to test these different models of political transformation while integrating the histories of the other Tafea islands to give a truly regional picture. What is already clear, however, is that the explanation of social dynamics in southern Melanesia will not come from invoking simple causes such as population pressure, adaptation, or environmental determinism. As the comparison of Aneityum and Tanna shows, the answers surely lie in the dialectic between social relations and ecological ones and the way in which this was worked out over three millennia of Tafea prehistory.[3]

Notes

1 In 1963–4 Mary and Richard Shutler conducted site survey and test excavations on Aneityum, Futuna, Aniwa, Tanna and Erromango, for which only a summary is published (Shutler and Shutler 1966; see also Shutler 1970, Shutler and Shutler 1975). Les Groube did further survey and excavation on Aneityum and Erromango in 1972 (Groube 1975, n.d.), and his work on Aneityum was expanded by Norma McArthur (1974, 1978).

Detailed ethnographic fieldwork has been undertaken on Tanna by several foreign researchers (Bastin 1981; Brunton 1979, 1981, Guiart 1956; Lindstrom 1981a, 1981b) while at present further research and recording of oral traditions in Tafea District are being carried out by local anthropologists, the fieldworkers of the Vanuatu Cultural Centre. The languages of the area and their history are being investigated by Professor John Lynch of the University of Papua New Guinea and there has been other research on languages by earlier linguists and missionaries (see in particular Lynch 1978; also Capell 1960; Tryon 1976).

2 This sequence may explain certain historic period and contemporary features of Tannese society as discussed by Lindstrom (1984). He sees control of esoteric and political knowledge as being more important on Tanna than control of material wealth, a situation which in part at least could be linked to high trade density where wealth is not easily monopolized.

3 I would like to acknowledge the help, interest and participation of the government and people of Vanuatu. 1978 and 1979 research was funded by the Department of Prehistory, Research School of Pacific Studies, Australian National University. 1983 research was funded by the University of Hawai'i. The manuscript was typed in the Department of Anthropology, University of Hawai'i at Manoa. Helpful comments on an earlier draft were given by Lamont Lindstrom. Special thanks go to Kirk Huffman, Jack Keitadi, *natimarid* Naulita, *natimarid* Yautaea, Philip Tepahae, Jack Yauotau and last but not least Ruth Saovana-Spriggs.

Chapter 3

Conceptual and substantive issues in Fijian prehistory

Terry L. Hunt

Many archaeologists agree that the discipline's strength lies in the explanation of prehistoric change, in particular long-term change accessible only in study of the archaeological record. This goal of contemporary archaeology is reflected in the Oceanic literature when islands are extolled as ideal laboratories for the investigation of change and diversification (e.g. Mead 1957; Sahlins 1957; 1958; Clark and Terrell 1978; Kirch 1980). For many Oceanic scholars the utility of islands as laboratories is realized in scientific applications of ecological and evolutionary approaches to prehistory. In spite of repeated and enthusiastic calls for exploiting islands as laboratories, much of our understanding of Oceanic prehistory remains limited in *explanatory* content (Clark and Terrell 1978; Kirch 1980).

Increasingly, it is obvious that understanding the course of Fijian prehistory will be an integral part of understanding the historical events or processes of diversification that led to the origins of Polynesians and to the ethnic boundary which Fiji represents today (Davidson 1977; Green 1967, 1981; Groube 1971). Davidson (1977, 91) understates the case: 'the proximity of Fiji and its differences from Polynesia pose numerous intriguing problems'. In this paper I explore the conventional cultural historical explanations offered for prehistoric change in the Fiji Islands, in particular, explanations that have focussed on ceramic change and its relation to other changes through time and over space. Culture historical research comprises an undeniably valuable and necessary step

in identifying patterns in the archaeological record. As a necessary link to understanding complex problems of the past, however, culture historical accounts must be accurate, empirically based and sufficiently textured to reflect the complexity and variability of the real world. Overly simplified explanations for change in the archaeological record offer an inadequate foundation for dealing with the issues of patterns and processes of prehistoric cultural change. If the varied islands and human histories of Oceania are to serve as laboratories of cultural change and diversification, then good culture history is an important, primary enterprise. But even a substantive foundation in culture history will provide only part of a scientific understanding of the past in Fiji and beyond.

Fijian culture history: the orthodox view

Western speculations concerning Fijian origins and prehistory began with some of the earliest continuous European contacts with islanders (e.g. Hale 1846). Later ethnographic studies and oral histories led to early culture historical syntheses (e.g. Hocart 1915; Thompson 1938). Archaeological excavations commenced in Fiji in 1947 with the pioneering efforts of E. W. Gifford (1949; 1951). Gifford, who sought to find 'traces of early Polynesians, if they had come via Fiji' (1951, 189) worked within a paradigm in which Oceanic scholars were preoccupied with defining cultural or racial

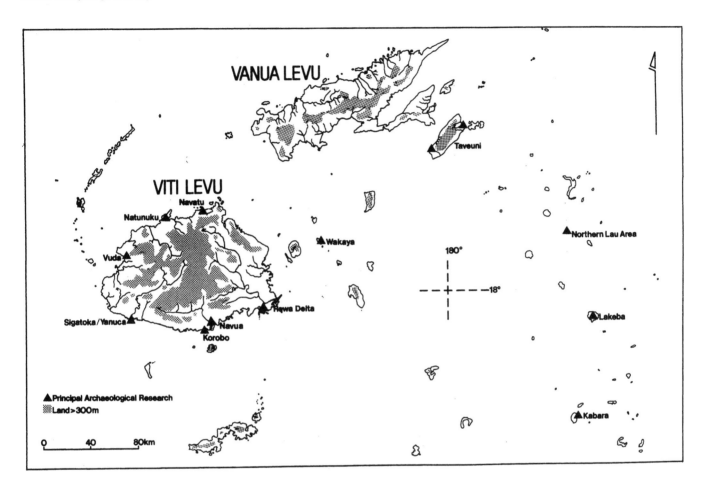

Fig. 3.1. The Fiji Islands, showing locations of principal archaeological research.

origins, particularly those of Polynesians. Gifford excavated two sites, Site 17 at Navatu and Site 26 at Vuda, both on Viti Levu (fig. 3.1). On the basis of this work, Gifford divided Fijian prehistory into a late horizon, characterized by midden dumping and ceramics with incised decoration, and an early horizon distinguished by 'relief wares' or ceramics decorated with carved paddle-impressions. Gifford speculated that a possible middle horizon was indicated by high percentages of undecorated ceramics.

Subsequently, accumulating archaeological evidence for the early and widespread distribution of Lapita pottery led Green (1963a) to propose a revision of Gifford's Fijian sequence. Based primarily on stylistic change in ceramics, Green's sequence comprised four phases: the Sigatoka Phase (pre-500 BC to 100 BC) defined by a Lapita ceramic complex, including both dentate-stamped and undecorated forms; the Navatu Phase (100 BC to AD 1100), distinguished by ceramics decorated with carved paddle-impressions; the Vuda Phase (AD 1100 to 1800) marked by an increased use of incising and appliqué in ceramic decoration as well as a greater relative abundance of plain sherds; and the Ra Phase (AD 1800 to 1900), based on a second increase in the use of incising as a

ceramic decorative technique. Green (1963a, 250) proposed ceramic-culture associations in which Sigatoka materials were seen as ancestral to Polynesian cultures, Navatu was left open to question and Vuda and Ra traits were affiliated with 'Melanesian culture'.

Shaw (1967) reanalyzed Gifford's collections and offered slight modifications to Green's (1963a) revised sequence. In particular, Shaw speculated that carved paddle-impressed ceramic decoration might extend back in time to 710 BC, the date then available from the Yanuca Rockshelter (Birks 1973, 69). A more recent synthesis of Fijian prehistory by Frost (1979) essentially follows the conceptual structure offered by Green over twenty years ago.

It is important to recognize that the orthodox synthesis of Fijian culture history is based on relatively few excavated sites and published sources (see fig. 3.1). The Lapita ceramics are best known (Birks 1973; Mead *et al.* 1975; Green 1979; Hunt 1980), even though, apart from the few known Lapita sites, a relative abundance of excavated and published archaeological data date to the first century BC and later.

A common explanatory theme in Fijian prehistory relies on population intrusions in the form of 'migrations' or 'replacements' to account for cultural change and diversification that through time distinguished Fiji from its neighbors (e.g. Hale 1846; Riesenfeld 1950; Gifford 1951; Frost 1974, 1979; Bellwood 1978). Notions of Fijians as 'Melanesianized Polynesians' (Howells 1973, 96), or hybrids at the boundary of two culture areas, seem to have provided at least the tacit requirement of an exotic episodic history of 'mixing' two abstracted 'racial types'. With these predilections, some archaeologists have turned to *stylistic* change in ceramics as material manifestations of either foreign migration, intrusion, replacement, diffusion or some combination of these to explain cultural changes and human diversification. Frost is perhaps the best current spokesman for this longstanding traditional view (cf. Hale 1846, 178–9) of Fiji reflecting

> an interweaving of influences that has produced a complexity not typical of the more homogeneous cultural sequences in Polynesia. Some of this complexity resulted from the ebb and flow of Oceanic migrants who sailed to and sometimes through Fiji during the eastward populating of the Pacific Islands. (Frost 1979, 62)

Frost (1974, 1979) argues that the Fijian ceramic record, excluding Lapita, can be viewed as a continuum with significant increment of new traits at and subsequent to AD 1100. He sees migrations as the primary stimulus for change. Apparently new ceramic decorative traits correlate with the origin and development of fortified occupations throughout Fiji as Frost envisions a situation where migrants clashed with already established populations throughout the archipelago (cf. Hale 1846). Frost invokes population replacement or intrusion from the west to account for a Lapita to Impressed-ware change. Apparently Frost regards intrusions or population replacements as the most probable mechanisms responsible for ceramic as well as other cultural changes. He writes:

> Little is known of the cultural dynamics of the post-Lapita ceramic change and whether indigenous populations were *replaced* or *intruding populations* simply produced a circumstance where the Lapita ceramic complex, already moving toward plain ware, was abandoned and replaced with the Impressed-ware complex. (Frost 1979, 79, emphasis added)

Simply put, following initial colonization, cultural change over three millennia of Fijian prehistory is reduced to two events or episodes of migration, intrusion, or population replacements. It is important to stress that this model for Fiji's past is given in terms of *migration* (the movements and potential displacements of established populations) and not specifically in terms of *diffusion* (Adams 1978). Unfortunately, migrationist accounts for prehistoric change pay little attention to the relation between ceramic style and other aspects of a functioning cultural system. These accounts also fail to specify precisely what a migration might amount to, and how and why such an event would precipitate widespread cultural change. As Adams and his colleagues (1978, 483) point out, migration has never been articulated as a general principle of historical

explanation, and yet it has been invoked as an ad hoc explanation for change in countless numbers of cases. Major cultural changes are viewed as interventions from outside a particular cultural domain, and causation for such intervention remains outside the system(s) being studied. In short, migrationist accounts treat change as rapid and usually discontinuous, with mechanics of movement, interaction, and ultimate causation placed beyond investigation. Given this kind of explanatory approach, are we to conceive of Lapita potters, for example, being simply replaced by a canoe load of pottery-bearing folk from somewhere in the west who made carved paddle-impressed ware more than a thousand years after initial Fijian colonization? Did fortified occupations in Fiji really develop simply in response to western intruders who also introduced allegedly new ceramic decorative traits? It seems that conventional accounts of Fijian prehistory have used a sequence of gross stylistic change to infer cultural changes and processes of diversification that in fact have little to do with the stylistic variability of ceramics (cf. Adams 1979; Nicklin 1971).

Culture historical research underlies much of contemporary archaeology and has indeed provided much of our substantive knowledge of prehistory in Oceania. The conceptual basis of culture history lies in Worsaae's dictum of variation of form with time. The synthesis of form with time from which concepts of historical type developed made possible a *testable* method (i.e. seriation) that intoxicated early culture historians. The primary goal became limited to temporal and spatial descriptions of the archaeological record worldwide.

With emphasis necessarily placed on variation in form or style through time, culture historical accounts of change and differences focus on culture as a body of *shared ideas*. For example, shared ideas, or in the case of Fiji stylistic traits such as dentate-stamped or carved paddle-impressed decoration on pottery, have been treated as correlates of distinct cultures or ceramic traditions (e.g. Frost 1974, 1979; Groube 1971, 284). With culture conceived of as a body of shared ideas, various stylistic and functional traits ('ideas'), such as ceramic style versus fortifications, form a basis in traditional culture historical analysis to measure the 'similarity' between cultures (e.g. Gifford 1951, 236–7; Frost 1974). Accordingly, explanations for cultural change are directed toward apparent stylistic and functional similarities and based on events or processes such as diffusion, migration, intrusion, or population replacement. Such explanations of change share a common element of human contact that is quite reasonable when dealing exclusively with stylistic units of analysis usefully employed by culture historians and analysts of diffusion (e.g. Davis 1983; Hodder 1978; Kaplan 1976). In this respect, the value and necessity of culture historical research (including study of diffusion) and areal synthesis in identifying spatial and temporal patterns in the archaeological record are not at issue. Rather, the ways in which sense is made of the empirical record, or how we set out to explain the observed patterns, is the crucial problem. With this in mind, what are the limitations of conventional culture historical explanations and how has the approach structured our current view of Fijian prehistory?

Cultural historical accounts offer valuable syntheses or 'best' summary statements for a body of evidence as known, yet all too often such tentative time-space constructs and explanations become reified as fact. Inferences, interpretations, and assertions become the topics of discussion and the 'facts' themselves. In addition, a kind of regional scale sampling error or founder effect shapes and directs subsequent research and synthesis. For example, our current understanding of early prehistory in Fiji has relied too heavily on negative evidence (Hunt 1980, 1981a). In particular, the Sigatoka Dune Site (Birks 1973) with its three separated deposits containing stylistically distinctive ceramics was taken to indicate discontinuities in the cultural historical sequence, especially between the phases designated Sigatoka and Navatu on ceramic criteria (Frost 1974, 1979). The problem here is the approximate 700 year hiatus in the deposition of cultural remains at the site. Seen in this light, ceramic differences between strata at the Sigatoka Site are hardly surprising and not necessarily evidence for cultural discontinuity. As Adams *et al.* (1978, 499–500) have pointed out, it is in the earliest stages of investigation in a new area that different archaeological 'cultures' are recognized from excavation of 'pure' or single component sites. As a result, 'cultural discontinuities always appear greater in the early stages of investigation than they do when more information has come to hand' (Adams *et al.* 1978, 500). This observation no doubt applies to Fiji, as it does elsewhere.

Another area of difficulty lies in the explanatory structure and content of conventional Fijian culture history. Faced with the challenging task of studying and describing a record of things that constantly change, either gradually or abruptly, prehistorians fall back on periodization, allowing us to talk about phases, cultures, periods and so on. The problem of periodizing a temporal sequence of change or apportioning spatial diversity to culture areas is the conversion or reduction of variability into homogeneous *conceptual* units. These units then mark *differences* among one another; change and variability are reduced to the lines between such temporal and spatial units. Potentially *continuous change* or *variability* is thus converted to *differences* (Dunnell 1982a). Such temporal and spatial units of difference such as the ceramic phase sequence constructed for Fiji are explained with reference to principles involving human movement such as migration and replacement at some scale with pre-existing material or cultural entities. The conceptual structure of differences marked by episodic migrations and cultural discontinuities may in fact seriously distort our understanding of the mode and tempo of prehistoric change. In other words, the Fijian record has been conceived of, perhaps inadvertently, as punctuated by short if not instantaneous episodes of change separated by long periods of stasis. In migrationist terms, naming a *source* for change has comprised the final *explanation* for how and why change

occurred. In the case of Fiji, have the mode and tempo of prehistoric change been obscured simply because of the conceptual difficulties of dealing with the expanded temporal dimensions of prehistory (Bailey 1983; Dunnell 1982a)?

With these issues in mind, is the notion of cultural discontinuity which underlies the migrationist accounts of Fiji's past accurate? Or is it a product of an uneven sampling of the archaeological record and our research of it? Or is it simply an artifact of the way we have conceptualized and described change through time? These are crucial questions not only for prehistorians, but for all students dealing with variability in the temporal dimension (Ruse 1982).

The Yanuca evidence

Yanuca Island lies just off the coast of southwestern Viti Levu, opposite the coastal villages of Rukurukulevu and Cuvu. Archaeological investigations there began in 1965–6 when Lawrence and Helen Birks surveyed this small island and excavated over 60 m³ of ceramic-bearing midden at the Yanuca Rockshelter, designated Site VL 16/81 (Birks 1973, 1978). Subsequent excavation and analysis of the archaeological collections by the author (Hunt 1980, 1981a) have made the Yanuca site a critical locality for testing the orthodox paradigm of Fijian prehistory. The rockshelter deposits provide a wealth of varied archaeological data which span a temporal range of over 3000 years.

Radiocarbon estimates place the early use of the Yanuca Rockshelter at about 1300 BC (Hunt 1980). Deposition of archaeological remains spans an early period of time that had been a temporal gap in the record known for Viti Levu Island. The Yanuca ceramic assemblage amounts to nearly 40,000 sherds, and about 17,000 sherds from the central and deepest portions of the deposit have been analyzed. A variety of stone, shell, coral and historic artifacts were also recovered in comparatively small numbers (Hunt 1980). Given the abundance of early ceramics at Yanuca, the Lapita to Impressed-ware changes were of special concern. Ceramic evidence has been *analytically* treated as continuous, with arbitrary divisions made according to distribution of the ceramic classes being described in terms of relative change. It should be stressed that phase designations are not meant to imply *fixed* temporal spans, precise ceramic content, cultural ('racial') attributions, or applications across the Fijian archipelago. Phase designations already found in the literature (e.g. Frost 1979; Green 1963a), with my own addition (Hunt 1980), are used only as working models and for ease of discussion.

The Sigatoka Phase is defined by the presence of dentate-stamped and plain Lapita pottery. Decorated vessel forms, motifs and decorative systems have already received detailed attention (Mead *et al.* 1975; and see fig. 3.3). Undecorated body forms associated with the dentate-stamped ceramics include globular pots with everted rims, carinated bowls, flat-bottomed dishes as well as shallow, deep and small bowl forms (Birks 1973; Hunt 1980; see fig. 3.2). Some of

Fig. 3.2. Sherds of dentate-stamped Lapita flat-bottomed vessels.

Fig. 3.3. Sherds from globular vessels with appliqué band, decorated with notching or shell impressing.

Fig. 3.4. Sherds with carved paddle-impressed decoration (parallel-ribbed).

Fig. 3.5. Sherds with carved paddle-impressed decoration (cross-hatch).

these 'plain' forms do include non-dentate decorations such as red slips, notched rims, shell impressing, and appliqué (fig. 3.3). While fine temporal distinctions of Lapita plain forms, decorated forms and individual decorative traits have not yet been well segregated for the area, it does appear that dentate-stamping was 'rapidly' abandoned, in archaeological terms. This early change in Fijian ceramics resulted in 'simplification', or reduction of the ceramic forms and decorative traits comprising the assemblage.

Sherds decorated with the carved paddle-impressed technique, including both common motifs of parallel-ribbed and cross-hatched, are associated stratigraphically with the earliest Lapita ceramics at Yanuca (figs. 3.4, 3.5). Recent work in thermoluminescence dating of both dentate-stamped and carved paddle-impressed sherds suggest their separation in time (Prescott *et al.* 1982). The possibility of some apparently consistent stratigraphic mixing (downward) must be considered – a question that might be resolved with sedimentological analyses of Yanuca samples (cf. Hughes and Lampert 1977). The question of dentate-stamped and carved paddle-impressed contemporaneity at Yanuca remains unresolved (Hunt 1980, 126–36). Further research, including stratigraphic excavation in the area, should help to address this question, although a precise chronological placement of *any* stylistic form will have to be assessed independently area by area (Hunt 1980, 207; Rowland and Best 1980).

Evidence from Yanuca indicates that, at some period of time as yet undetermined, carved paddle-impressed decoration is added to the existing or familiar plain ware forms associated with, but persisting after, dentate-stamped Lapita (fig. 3.6). The sequence appears to involve first an assemblage of dentate-stamped and plain Lapita ceramics that become 'simplified' with the demise of the decorative system and its associated pot forms (Mead *et al.* 1975), leaving Lapita

plainwares ('Polynesian Plain wares' after Green 1974, 1979) to which carved paddle-impressed was subsequently *added* (figs. 3.7, 3.8, 3.9). This relatively simple addition to ceramic decoration of vessel forms already present marks what I have tentatively called the Yanuca Phase (Hunt 1980). The empirical basis *at Yanuca*, for what may prove to be a useful culture-historical phase designation, includes carved paddle-impressed forms otherwise classed as Lapita plain ware. These impressed forms include globular pots with everted rims (fig. 3.8, and Birks 1973, e.g. figs. 9(10), 13(71), 14(91), 19(37, 92, 99, 121)), shallow concave vessels (fig. 3.8 and Birks 1973, fig. 25, in particular vessels 7, 19, 20, 36, 42, 43, 45, 74) and deep bowls (fig. 3.8; Birks 1973, e.g. 28(1)). Such a transition appears to link plain wares with carved paddle-impressed ceramics that became common, with various stylistic derivations, throughout Fiji (e.g. Best 1977; Frost 1974; Rowland and Best 1980). A proposed link can be made on the grounds not only of ceramic forms (comparable vessel and rim classes) found undecorated and decorated with paddle-impressions, but also of observed technological continuity (Hunt 1980; cf. Rye 1981). While an early presence of carved paddle-impressed wares associated with dentate-stamped Lapita could become clear in some or most parts of Fiji (cf. Green and Mitchell 1983), a model for Yanuca transitional ceramics remains independent of this particular chronological problem.

What have been called Navatu Phase ceramics include, at Yanuca, high proportions of carved paddle-impressed sherds from a relatively limited assemblage of vessel forms. Globular pots with everted rims (e.g. Birks 1973, figs. 39–47) and large 'clumsy' leaf-impressed platters (e.g. Birks 1973, pl. 5A(a); Lambert 1971; Green 1963b, pl. 1) dominate the ceramic assemblage. Various additional decorative techniques such as incising, fingernail impressing, finger pinching, tool

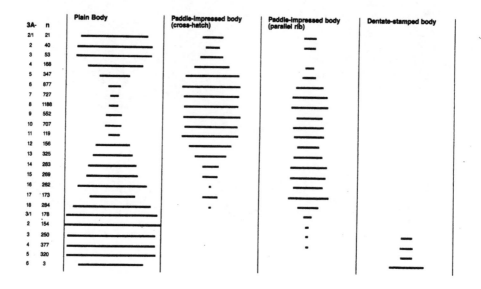

Fig. 3.6. Frequency distribution of four body sherd classes from the Yanuca Rockshelter.

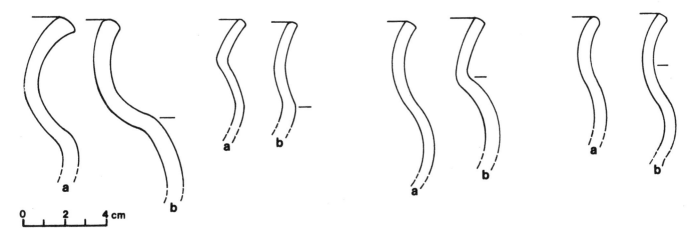

Fig. 3.7. Profiles of rim sherds showing continuity in form: (a) undecorated rim forms; (b) comparable forms with paddle-impressed decoration added to the body (below line shown on exterior of sherds).

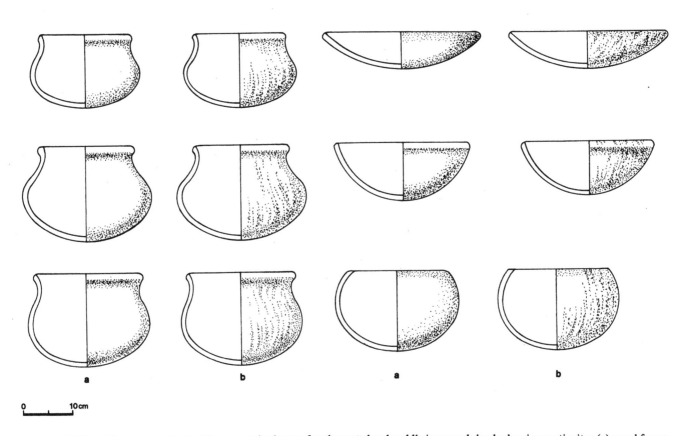

Fig. 3.8. Vessel forms reconstructed from ceramic classes of undecorated and paddle-impressed sherds showing continuity: (a) vessel forms with undecorated surfaces; (b) comparable forms with paddle-impressed decoration.

impressing, and notching are also represented on the upper bodies, necks, and rims of the globular pots.

Ceramics typical of late sequences in Fiji – the Vuda and Ra Phase ceramics – are only poorly represented at Yanuca. The only suggestion of change comparable to late sequences posited elsewhere is the relative demise of carved

paddle-impressed decoration, giving way to plain ware and pottery on which incised and tool impressed decoration continues. The little available evidence from Yanuca appears consistent with Frost's (1974), but especially Babcock's (1977) model for a continuum of ceramic variation over time.

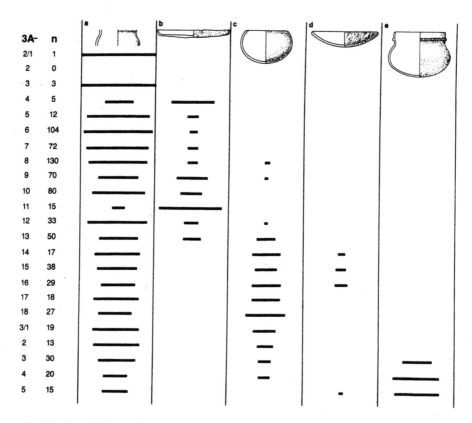

Fig. 3.9. Frequency distribution of five vessel form classes from the Yanuca Rockshelter: (a) necks of undecorated and paddle-impressed vessels with everted rims; (b) leaf-impressed ceramic trays; (c) undecorated and paddle-impressed deep bowls; (d) undecorated and paddle-impressed shallow bowls; (e) large globular pots with incised appliqué band.

Matrix analysis of the Yanuca ceramics

A primary task in assessing the orthodox view of Fijian prehistory against the Yanuca evidence is to determine how ceramic change is patterned in time. Do stylistic changes in pottery, such as those conventionally used in phase designations, occur gradually over time, or is this sequence punctuated by sudden change followed by periods of relative stasis? Paleobiologists, like prehistorians, are concerned with rates of change and their patterns over time and space. Pielou's (1979, 1983) quantitative method using an ordered similarity matrix (OSM) aimed at discrimination between patterns of continuous and discontinuous (or stepwise) change is applicable here. The OSM method has already been usefully applied in paleoecological research in Hawai'i (Kirch and Christensen 1980) and Kirch pioneered its application in modeling prehistoric change for the Tikopia archaeological assemblages (Kirch and Yen 1982).

Pielou's (1983) method offers an opportunity to model change quantitatively in ceramics at Yanuca. An OSM is a matrix whose (i, j)th element is an index that measures similarity between the ith and jth entities in a sequence where sample (case) order is retained. In other words, a pattern is graphically displayed in a similarity matrix whose elements

are pairwise similarities between every possible pair of samples (Pielou 1979, 435; 1983, 31). The similarities expressed in the matrix are proportional similarities (PS values) of the classes analyzed. The matrix constructed is necessarily symmetrical with the similarity of an entity to itself being equal to one (100%) and left blank along the cells to the lower left of the principal diagonal. Pielou (1983, 31) points out that OSMs are useful pictorial models of change. However, it is possible to do more than just judge pictorial patterns intuitively. The patterns with an OSM can be quantified and tested statistically against a model for random distributions. Pielou (1979, 1983; see also Kirch and Yen 1982, 321–3) provides a grading index, or a Q statistic that tests the *disarray* of the matrix patterning and renders matrices comparable one to another.

For analysis of the Yanuca assemblage, nine ceramic classes whose frequencies are sensitive to time and whose counts could be presumed adequate for comparative purposes were selected and analyzed by units of excavation (Trench 3A, arbitrary excavation levels; see Hunt 1980). These ceramic classes included plain (undecorated body) sherds in the first OSM analysis (fig. 3.10).[1] This run resulted in large blocks of relatively close proportional similarities that can be postulated to depict minor ceramic changes among the classes

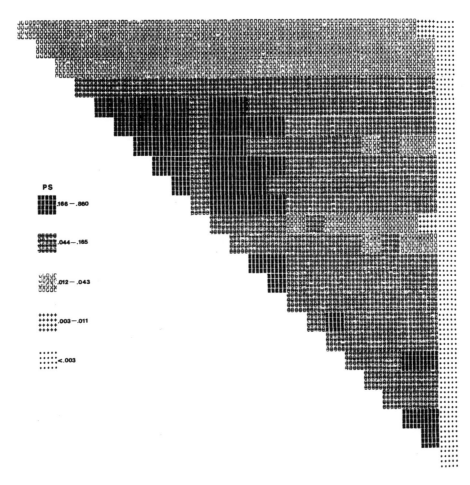

PS

.166 — .860

.044 — .165

.012 — .043

.003 — .011

<.003

Fig. 3.10. Ordered similarity matrix (using SYMAP computer graphics) of nine temporally sensitive ceramic classes, including undecorated body sherds, from the Yanuca Rockshelter (n = 24, Q/Q$_{max}$ = 0.305).

compared against a background of continuity. In the second OSM run (fig. 3.11) plain body sherds were removed from the matrix analysis, leaving time-sensitive stylistic markers that have been used in conventional phase designations for Fiji, together with classes apparently temporally restricted in the Yanuca sequence. As would be expected, the greatest temporal distinctions are made in this second analysis with plain sherds removed. This matrix, like the first, provides a pictorial representation of the postulated continuity with stepwise variability among the classes compared from Yanuca. As is graphically evident (figs. 3.10 and 3.11), the test statistics for OSM disarray (*n*, Q/Q$_{max}$, after Pielou 1983) indicate well-graded sequences, or sequential trends where pairwise similarities decrease with the distance between pairs.

The two OSM analyses provide pictorial and quantitative models of ceramic change as patterned in the temporal dimension at Yanuca. Presumably these models, like interpretation of ceramic change in general, are not grossly affected by small-scale stratigraphic mixing. Rather, the overall pattern of change is represented. The matrices illustrate how temporally variable *stylistic* classes create a strong stepped

effect (fig. 3.11) that would provide the criteria for phase designations, as indeed is the case for Fiji. However, such distinctions in the OSMs are only breaks of *relative similarities*. When the OSM analysis is run including plainwares (fig. 3.10), which comprise an important part of many Fijian ceramic assemblages, the stepped or discontinuous effect is weakened and greater continuity is clearly evident. As with any model, the variables (or classes) and the cases (Yanuca samples) used in construction will ultimately dictate its usefulness and relevance. Further research with comparable analyses on additional assemblages from throughout Fiji may prove valuable in recognizing patterns of change, especially beyond the limitations of analysis of a single site.

In sum, at least three important implications might be drawn from the OSM analyses and the evidence from Yanuca in general: (1) stylistic change takes place within a greater context of ceramic continuity; (2) recognizing patterns of ceramic variability in both temporal and spatial dimensions is necessarily linked to the analytic units (classes or types) used; and (3) periodization — albeit often necessary — may obscure continuous change and conflate rapid change and discontinuity.

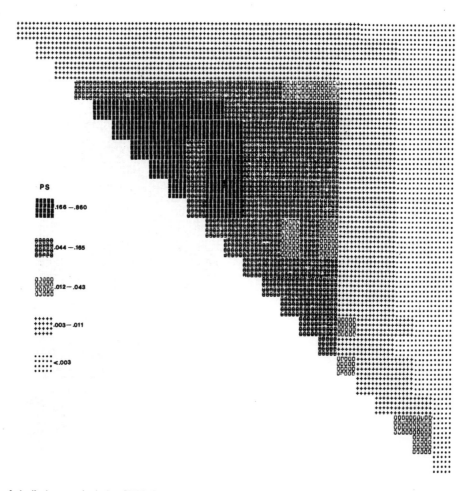

Fig. 3.11. Ordered similarity matrix (using SYMAP computer graphics) with eight temporally sensitive ceramic classes, excluding undecorated ceramics; compare with Fig. 3.10 (n = 24, Q/Q$_{max}$ = 0.285).

Rethinking Fijian prehistory

Since any single archaeological site represents a unique formation history of cultural and natural events and processes, it would be a serious error to suppose that analyses from the Yanuca rockshelter alone could resolve our general questions about how and why things happened over the course of prehistory in Fiji. However, the evidence presented for Yanuca can be treated as a model comprised of hypotheses about ceramic change to test at scales beyond a single site. In particular, questions of cultural continuity or discontinuity must be asked of regional-scale archaeological data. Presumably, if movement of a substantial number of people took place (e.g. migrations from the west) or population replacements occurred (Frost 1974, 1979), then variability resulting from such events should follow some predicted pattern of distribution over a region such as southwestern Viti Levu, for example. Regional scale research would necessarily include acquisition of various kinds of data (e.g. settlement–subsistence variation) beyond artifacts with stylistic qualities. However, it would be a serious mistake, given what we already know about human diversity in Fiji, to think that the

archaeology of one region could somehow represent what happened throughout Fiji.

While no cataclysmic events need be invoked to explain ceramic change observed in the Yanuca sequence, could *diffusion* of ideas or stylistic traits account for change? Human contact with islanders from beyond Fiji no doubt occurred with some frequency (Levison *et al.* 1973), and would have certainly enabled diffusion or transmission of stylistic traits. Accepting the potential for relatively frequent contact and diffusion, Dunnell's (1978) distinction of style from function is particularly useful. Stylistic traits can be regarded as adaptively neutral and therefore their frequencies in a population are free from environmental contingencies or selective pressures. The statistical behavior of stylistic traits might be best explained by stochastic processes. Because stylistic elements are transmitted over time and space, yet remain selectively neutral, their frequencies in populations take on a distinctive Markovian pattern (Dunnell 1978). Such patterns of distributional frequencies (unimodal seriation curves) are paralleled by the random clades biologists have constructed using computers (e.g. Gould *et al.* 1977), perhaps suggestive of a comparable neutral or stochastic component in change over time.

If stylistic traits — being adaptively neutral — follow a distinctive Markovian pattern and arise by innovation, or through diffusion, then linking stylistic change with systemic changes in culture will prove overly simplistic and very misleading. This points to perhaps *the major flaw* in the orthodox culture historical paradigm of prehistoric change in Fiji: patterns of *stylistic* change have been extended to offer 'explanations' for large-scale or processual cultural change in Fijian prehistory. For example, the emergence of fortified occupations in many parts of the Fiji Islands is not likely to relate to stylistic diffusion in a causal way (cf. Frost 1974, 1979; Hunt 1981b; Parry 1977; Rowland and Best 1980). Rather, the task of tracking environmental variables and social pressures that would select for competition among and within populations lies before us (see Kirch 1984). In short, if we wish to treat islands as laboratories for problem-oriented research, then venturing beyond the explanations tied strictly to stylistic diffusion will be essential.

Underlying much of what I have touched upon in this paper is a crucial issue of metaphysics, or ontology. This is not new and might be most widely recognized as the controversy between *typological* versus *populationist* thinking, or *essentialism* versus *materialism* (Clark and Terrell 1978; Dunnell 1980; Mayr 1959, 1982). Essentialism is the ontological position where reality is viewed as comprised of fixed, discrete things which have essential or diagnostic properties. In contrast, materialism (not to be confused with the very different conventional anthropological use of 'cultural materialism') is the ontological position where reality is considered as a continuum of variability or uniqueness. As Mayr (1959, 29) put it, 'for the typologist [essentialist] the type (eidos) is real and the variation an illusion, while for the populationist [materialist], the type is an abstraction and only the variation is real. No two ways of looking at nature could be more different.' It would be a mistake not to recognize that both essentialists and materialists acknowledge variability. The crucial distinction is the explanatory potential attributed to variation (Sober 1980). Materialists 'postulate a reality sustained by diversity' (Sober 1980, 370) and *empirical variation* rather than *abstracted essences* is the subject of inquiry (Dunnell 1982b, fn. 99). Materialists view things as *continually becoming*. Such a perspective, admittedly counterintuitive, enables us to think about *process* and time-like frames of evolutionary change.

It seems safe to argue that many ideas concerning prehistory in Fiji, as elsewhere, have been pervaded by essentialist or typological thinking. Notions of pre-existing 'pure' or ideal racial and cultural types that eventually became mixed, such as in the case of Melanesian-Polynesian hybridization, are rooted in essentialism. Other expressions of essentialism surface in treating abstractions such as inferences, interpretations, and assertions as if they were empirical facts in and of themselves.

I have attempted to outline some of the problems and limitations of conventional culture historical accounts (e.g. Frost 1974, 1979) for change in Fiji's past. In terms of archaeological data, we still know very little about what happened in Fijian prehistory. We know even less about how and why Fijian prehistory happened the way we might suspect it did. Further fieldwork together with analyses of Fijian archaeological and paleoenvironmental remains must provide the foundation for outlining basic patterns of the record. However, even a profusion of additional data will not be sufficient if we are continually bound by conceptual, descriptive, and explanatory limitations that have persisted since the earliest anthropological interests in Fiji. These problems are not strictly tied to a 'culture historical' approach, but have a pervasive ontological underpinning in typological thinking.

Where do we go from here? If migrations and intrusions do not exhaust the possible explanations for change and the human diversity we are only beginning to understand (e.g. Geraghty 1983; Ward 1967), then what kinds of events and processes led to the patterns evident today and presumably reflected in the record of the past? Going beyond culture historical analyses of style are problems of tracking changing patterns of demography, colonization, settlement and the configurations of populations over the Fijian landscape. Making sense of ecological, geographic, and human variability together with selective forces acting in adaptive change will prove essential. Coming to grips with how human impacts affected the environments of the Fiji Islands will also be necessary (see Kirch 1984). These requirements will demand interdisciplinary research at a level becoming increasingly common throughout Oceania (see Kirch 1983 for a review; but see also Hughes and Hope 1979, and McLean 1980 for examples of important work in eastern Fiji). In addition, as archaeologists we need to consider environments not only in ecological and biogeographic respects, but also in terms of where records of the past will be preserved and in what forms.

Orthodox explanations for how and why change took place in Fiji's past — ranging from Hale (1846) to Frost (1979) — have been typological to the point that the *facts* of empirical variation have been ignored in favor of abstractions or stereotypes that exist only in some imaginations. As some scholars have already shown (e.g. Geraghty 1983; Ward 1967), prehistory in Fiji is likely to be far more interesting and complex than many have allowed for. Most scholars would probably now agree that an orthodox culture history of Fiji calling upon three migrations to somehow explain change and human diversity across the Fijian archipelago is not only too simplistic, but dangerously misleading. Geraghty's (1983) recent work on linguistic variability across the archipelago clearly reveals a complex pattern of human diversity over both time and space. His careful analysis documents the evolution of 38 communalects (which Geraghty suggests approaches only a quarter of the total number in Fiji) from a potentially homogeneous parent language spoken by Fiji's first Lapita colonists. Taking Geraghty's detailed linguistic patterns as a source for models of change in Fijian prehistory it becomes clear that change and diversification probably had more to do with local processes and geographic configurations than with spectacular, romantic, or cataclysmic events (Terrell, in press). What remains is a tremendous challenge that has not yet been adequately met in constructing prehistory for Fiji. Rethinking Fijian prehistory will require paying due attention to the variability of the real world as well as how we attempt to deal analytically and conceptually with such complexity. As archaeologists have struggled with what their discipline should be, it has become increasingly clear that understanding prehistoric change will require sometimes counterintuitive concepts of *variation*, *time* and *process* (Dunnell 1982a). The added stricture of science is linking the conceptual with the empirical. In these most challenging ways, making use of

islands as laboratories and explaining change and diversification in processual terms is a formidable, yet exciting endeavour that awaits us in Fiji and beyond.[2]

Notes

[1] OSMs were generated using a FORTRAN program provided by Pielou (1983, Appendix) and run on the University of Washington's CDC 2000 Cyber computer. Graphic representations (figs. 3.10 and 3.11) of the proportional similarities comprising the matrices were produced using a SYMAP cartographic program. Class intervals for the SYMAP run follow Jermann and Dunnell's (1979, 45) geometric transformation. This particular interval arrangement places the finest graphic discrimination with the lower, or most frequent values.

[2] I would like to thank M. S. Allen, C. Benson, V. Butler, R. C. Dunnell, P. V. Kirch, P. C. McCoy, J. F. Simek, S. J. Studenmund, J. E. Terrell and M. J. Wagner for their help, comments and criticisms.

Chapter 4

Exchange systems and inter-island contact in the transformation of an island society: the Tikopia case

Patrick V. Kirch

For the archaeologist, the study of trade is central to the study of society. (Renfrew 1984, 89)

For many years the prevailing, if often unstated, working model of island societies among Oceanic anthropologists and especially culture historians has been that of the *closed system*. Despite a keen interest on the part of Pacific archaeologists in the initial origins of various island populations, the basic assumption has been that once settled by a founding group, the subsequent historical development of most island societies was largely a matter of local process. If external forces were invoked at all in discussions of island prehistory, it was usually in terms of subsequent discrete 'migrations', after which local ('closed') development again held sway (see Hunt, this volume, for example, on the Fijian case). This idea of islands and island societies as closed systems is reflected in frequent references to insular 'laboratories' (e.g. Suggs 1961, 194; Clark and Terrell 1978; Kirch 1980a; Friedman 1981, 275). While I would be the last to deny that Oceanic ecosystems offer a number of 'laboratory-like' conditions that are valuable for the control they offer in investigations of island prehistory (Kirch 1984, 2), it is one aim of this paper to suggest that the closed system model has been overextended. Even in the more geographically remote islands of Eastern Polynesia, the notion that island societies

developed *in vacuo*, as it were, deserves on recent evidence to be seriously questioned.

The significance of inter-societal networks or linkages over often substantial geographic areas or regions has become an issue of considerable anthropological interest (see for example, Wolf 1982; Eckholm 1978), owing something to the influence of Wallerstein (1974) but also reflecting a long-standing concern with exchange systems. The perspective is potentially a productive one in Oceania where, after all, the ethnohistoric and ethnographic corpus is replete with instances of elaborate inter-island exchange networks, not to mention other forms of irregular but repeated inter-island contact, such as drift voyaging. Among the ethnographically well-documented inter-island exchange networks we may cite the famous *kula* 'ring' of the Massim, the Vitiaz Straits system, and the red-feather money exchange network of the Santa Cruz Islands (Malinowski 1922; Leach and Leach 1983; Harding 1967; Davenport 1962). In Micronesia, many of the Central Carolines were similarly linked in an elaborate system of ceremonial exchange operationalized by a sophisticated voyaging technology and navigational knowledge (Alkire 1965). The Polynesian islands have not been touted as a region in which inter-island exchange was highly developed, yet the triadic linkages between Tonga, Samoa, and Fiji were highly complex (Kaeppler 1978; Kirch 1984). Similarly, there is sufficient evidence to suggest that regularized inter-societal links were at one time tightly forged between the central Polynesian archipelagoes of the Societies, Tuamotus, Mangareva, and Marquesas, even though this has received scant attention in the classic ethnographic literature. In short, an ethnographic overview is, in itself, sufficient to suggest certain inadequacies of the closed system model of Oceanic societies.

The former extent and nature of prehistoric exchange systems linking island societies has begun to attract archaeological attention, especially in the Melanesian area, where exchange has long been regarded as a key factor in social process. Of particular note has been the investigation of two fairly elaborate maritime exchange systems along the southern Papuan coast, centered around Mailu and Motupore respectively (Irwin 1978; Allen 1977; White and Allen 1980). These and other studies hint that unraveling the cyclical development of interlocking local exchange systems will prove a key to an understanding of the whole of southern Papuan prehistory. Similarly, most recent interpretations of the Lapita Cultural Complex (which appears to represent the 'founding' human populations throughout eastern Melanesia and west Polynesia) also stress the importance of continued long-distance transfer of a range of materials over the considerable geographic extent of the Lapita distribution (Green 1982).

In a provocative article, Friedman (1981) outlines a model for the transformation of Oceanic societies which puts great stress on the role of exchange systems, particularly long-distance, 'prestige-good' exchange. Friedman's model, which is offered in opposition to certain prevailing 'evolutionary' approaches, clearly focusses on the issue of closed and open systems, for it suggests that the possibilities of external, prestige-good exchange were central to the transformation of an ancestral Oceanic social system into the 'big-man' type societies of Melanesia on the one hand, and the 'theocratic feudalism' of Polynesia on the other (Friedman 1981, fig. 4). If Friedman's model is to be put to serious archaeological test, then the role of external contacts in the historical development of island societies must become a major subject of archaeological inquiry.

In the following pages, my aim is more modest: specifically, I will focus on the evidence from one island society, Tikopia (perhaps the most anthropologically famous island in the world), and address the issue of whether the development and transformation of this society can meaningfully be treated in terms of a closed system model. On the face of it, Tikopia comes as close to a cultural 'laboratory' as one might wish: a small (4.6 km^2), isolated high island whose population was even noteworthy for its fierce independence. Certainly, the classic ethnographic monographs of Sir Raymond Firth, which have lent Tikopia its anthropological fame, stressed the self-contained aspects of the Tikopia social system (Firth 1936; 1939). Tikopia lay outside any of the well-known inter-island

exchange systems of eastern Melanesia (including the Santa Cruz network), and its subsistence and economic system could effectively be characterized as 'closed' (Kirch and Yen 1982, 25). In such a microcosm, one might expect (according to the prevailing model of Oceanic culture history) that endogenous processes of population growth, environmental change, agricultural intensification, and the like would be the dominant factors shaping the course of prehistory. Indeed, such processes *were* significant, as the island's rich archaeological, geomorphological, and ethnobotanical records testify (Kirch and Yen 1982). Yet, to presage the argument, such internal processes do not provide a *sufficient* model of prehistoric change, for the archaeological and ethnographic signals of external contact in Tikopia are not only abundant, but prove to be key in understanding and interpreting the prehistoric sequence.

Ethnographic considerations

A brief review of certain ethnographic and historical evidence pertaining to Tikopian links with surrounding island societies in the nineteenth and early twentieth centuries

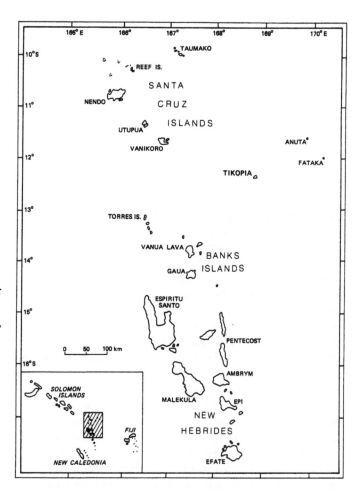

Fig. 4.1. Map of the Santa Cruz Islands, the Polynesian Outliers of Tikopia and Anuta, and northern Vanuatu.

provides a useful starting point for this inquiry. Figure 4.1 frames the geographic setting, with Tikopia forming one apex of a triangle comprised also of Vanikoro (in the southern Santa Cruz group) and Vanua Lava on the Banks Is. (the distances from Tikopia are 228 km to Vanikoro, 210 km to Vanua Lava). Somewhat closer is diminutive Anuta, 137 km to the NE (Fataka Is. is an uninhabitable volcanic pinnacle). Stretching NW beyond Vanikoro are the other islands of the Santa Cruz group (Utupua, Nendo, the Reef Is. and Taumako), while S of Vanua Lava lies the extensive Vanuatu archipelago (formerly called the New Hebrides). The prevailing winds and ocean currents in this part of the Pacific generally sweep from E to W (or SE to NW); hence, the up-wind archipelagoes of Fiji, Tonga, Samoa, and the Ellice group, though lying between 1170 and 2025 km distant, are also relevant to our problem.

In 1928–9, the date of Firth's ethnographic fieldwork, the Tikopia had virtually ceased to voyage overseas on any regular basis, partly because of recent government interdictions and partly since they could travel on the Melanesian Mission vessel, *The Southern Cross*. Nevertheless, the Tikopia regaled Firth with extensive oral traditions of overseas voyages made by Tikopia, and of the arrival of foreign immigrants in drifting canoes from various points. As to the magnitude of Tikopia voyaging, Firth 'reckoned that over a period of approximately four generations before [1928–9], more than 100 men went on overseas voyages' (1961, 151). These oral traditions provide a valuable source of data on external contacts, even though a number of the traditions would generally be classed as 'myths' rather than accounts of actual historical events. Additionally, however, there are several historical documents from the nineteenth century, such as those of Dillon (1829) and Dumont D'Urville (1833), which offer further details on links between Tikopia and its neighboring islands in the recent past.

An exhaustive presentation of the full corpus of oral traditions and historical evidence would go beyond the scope of this paper.[1] Here, I will simply review the patterns of regular and irregular external contact that can be reconstructed for the past few centuries of Tikopia history.[2] These patterns can be divided into two basic kinds of external linkages: (1) two-way voyaging initiated by the Tikopia to islands known to them, where regular economic or kinship relations had formerly been established; and (2) the arrival in Tikopia of foreign canoes from a variety of sources (usually to the E), whose crews were sometimes hospitably received as immigrants, sometimes met with hostile actions. The evidence for regular two-way voyaging is confined, perhaps expectably, to the three islands closest to Tikopia: Anuta, Vanikoro, and Vanua Lava (see fig. 4.1). I will discuss these in turn, and afterwards consider of the drift-voyaging situation.

Anuta Using classic anthropological definitions, it would be fair to say that the populations of Tikopia and Anuta share more or less the same *culture*, at the same time that they constitute distinct, autonomous *societies*. Both groups speak mutually intelligible Samoic-Outlier languages (Green 1971),

and their economic and socio-political structures, as well as their belief systems and ritual activities, are highly similar in structure and content. These similarities were reinforced by regular contact between the two populations, and inter-island voyages were initiated by Anutans as well as Tikopia.

The relationships between these two societies went beyond mere economic transactions, although exchange and trade were aspects of the relationship. There have always been a certain number of marriages between Anutans and Tikopia, in part a consequence of the very small size of the Anuta population (less than 200 individuals) and the frequent unavailability of suitable mates within the local population there (see Feinberg 1981 for a recent ethnographic description of Anuta). Thus at any time there are apt to be a few Tikopia living on Anuta and vice versa. Each Tikopia lineage has a corresponding lineage in Anuta, with which it has 'ancestral kinship or bonds of friendship' (Firth 1954, 98); this relationship is designated by the term *tauranga*, literally 'anchorage'.

Exchange relationships between Anutans and Tikopia are usually conducted along these *tauranga* lines. As Firth remarks, 'part of the reciprocal importance of Anuta and Tikopia lies in the opportunity each community offers to the other of supplementing its resources by trade' (1954, 108), a relationship Firth has termed 'symbiotic'. Material items sought by the Tikopia in Anuta include sennit cord, coconut water bottles, strong digging sticks, canoes, special kinds of fish nets, and decorated ceremonial mats known as *kie*. In return, the Tikopia usually offer barkcloth, their island having a much greater supply of the raw material (derived from cultivated stands of the *Antiaris* tree). It is worth noting that none of these items is restricted from either island by ecological or environmental constraints. Firth notes, however, that 'the principles of economic advantage are followed out by retention of specialization in crafts and most effective utilization of differences in natural resources' (1954, 109).

Oral traditions place the beginnings of contact between the two islands at about twelve generations B.F. (before Firth!), which on the independent evidence of archaeological materials from the main stratified site on Anuta (Kirch and Rosendahl 1973; Kirch 1982) may be fairly close to historical reality. Over the past few hundred years contact has been fairly frequent; Firth refers to more than twenty voyages recounted by his Tikopia informants.

Vanikoro The historical evidence for two-way voyaging between Tikopia and Vanikoro is bound up with one of the more fascinating episodes in early Pacific exploration: the disappearance and subsequent discovery of the fate of La Perouse, the French explorer whose ships were shipwrecked at Vanikoro sometime in 1778. The first clues to La Perouse's fate came when the colorful trader Peter Dillon called at Tikopia in 1826, and was shown a variety of metal, ceramic, and glass artifacts 'all of French manufacture', which the Tikopia had brought from Vanikoro in one of their regular voyages. Dillon correctly guessed that these artifacts derived from La Perouse's ships, and mounting a second expedition to Vanikoro in 1827, revealed the fate of the French navigator (see Davidson 1975).

In Dillon's account of the 1827 expedition, he remarks upon the regular 'trade' that existed between Tikopia and Vanikoro. The principal items obtained from Vanikoro consisted of 'an inferior kind of pearl shell, shell ornaments for the arms, head and neck, also necklaces of a shell resembling the cowry shells of the Maldives . . . and the bows and arrows' (1829:II, 170). In exchange, the Tikopia provided fine mats, presumably of *Pandanus*, and 'tappar', presumably barkcloth, though whether of *Broussonetia* or *Antiaris* is uncertain (see Kirch and Yen 1982). Although not specifically referred to by Dillon, there is reason to believe that the Tikopia also obtained pigs in Vanikoro, having ceased to husband these animals themselves (see Kirch and Yen 1982, 26, 52, 353, 358).

On the basis of the oral traditions given him, Firth (1961, 151) described the relations with Vanikoro as 'a kind of rudimentary trade by gift-exchange', and believed that it operated 'only spasmodically and with very long intervals'. Some Tikopia, however, evidently voyaged to Vanikoro repeatedly, as with the Ariki Taumako, Matakai II, who 'broke the ocean path' to Vanikoro ten times, and is credited with introducing the *Canarium* almond to Tikopia (Firth 1961, 158–9; 1939, 84; Kirch and Yen 1982, 37, 306, 362).

It is worth remarking that while Vanikoro was integrated into the 'red-feather money' exchange system of the Santa Cruz Islands (Davenport 1962, 1964), Tikopia lay outside of this network. The Santa Cruz network was maintained by the long-distance voyaging of the Duff Islanders with their *te puke* canoes. Tikopia exchange with Vanikoro was effected in Tikopia canoes; as far as we know, the Vanikoroans did not themselves voyage to other islands.[3]

Vanua Lava Ethnographic and historical evidence for two-way voyaging contacts between Tikopia and the Banks Is. is far more skimpy than for Anuta or Vanikoro. Indeed, the bulk of the available oral tradition would be regarded as myth, specifically dealing with the magical origins of an ancestor of the Tafua chiefly line, Tisasafa, in Varuka (or Valua), the Tikopia name for Vanua Lava (Firth 1961, 71 passim). Some historical confirmation, however, is provided by the missionary Codrington, who reported, 'I have myself witnessed the arrival of eleven canoes from Tikopia among the Banks' Islands. The men said they had come to see the islands, and were hospitably received' (1891, 6 n). Evidently, no voyages had been made in the two or three decades prior to Firth's 1928–9 fieldwork, for he records no instances of such. Nevertheless, the memory of connections between the two islands is not lost, for in 1977 I was told by the present chief of Tafua that he still held ancestral rights to land in Vanua Lava; in fact, he expressed regrets that the government ships calling at Tikopia were not permitted to make the southerly trip to the Banks, so that he might visit his lands![4]

Recently, a population genetic study by Blake *et al.* (1983) has provided additional evidence for contacts between Tikopia and the Banks Islands. Specifically, the Tikopia population exhibits several rare genetic markers of Melanesian origin, and in a genetic distance matrix based on data for eleven polymorphic loci, links closely with several Banks Islands populations (see Kirch, 1985b, for further discussion of these data).

In short, the available ethnographic and historical data for two-way voyaging between Tikopia and adjacent islands in the last one or two centuries suggests regular contacts with the three geographically proximal islands, with the frequency of contact rapidly declining with voyaging distance. Between Tikopia and Anuta, only 128 km apart, contacts were very regular and relationships between the two communities included intermarriage and long-term kinship links, as well as economic transactions. Voyaging between Anuta and Tikopia was initiated by both groups. With Vanikoro, the relationship was strictly economic, the Tikopia exchanging mats and barkcloth for items not otherwise manufactured on their home island. The nature of the relationship between the Tikopia and the occupants of Vanua Lava is almost impossible to specify on the available data. Codrington's brief statement would hint at voyaging simply for the sake of adventure (not unknown to the Tikopia, see Firth 1936, 1961), but some form of exchange or trade may well have underlain the apparently infrequent two-way voyages made by Tikopia between these points.

I turn now to the second kind of external contact recorded in the ethnographic record (primarily in Tikopia oral traditions), that of the arrival of drift voyagers from other islands. The documentation of such drift voyager arrivals in Tikopia has been extensively provided by Firth (1936, 1961), who notes that many of the major lineages trace their origins to ancestors who arrived in this fashion. Among the origin points for drift voyages to the island, the Tikopia cite Tonga, 'Uvea, Rotuma, Samoa, Taumako, Luanguiua, Anuta, Pukapuka, Somosomo, and Valua (Firth 1961, 86). The origins of one of the four chiefly lines is itself said to be a Tongan chief, Te Atafu, who was blown off course (see Kirch and Yen 1982, 342–3). Although some of the immigrants recorded in oral tradition hailed from the nearer Melanesian islands, the majority were of West Polynesian derivation. This is not surprising since, as Firth writes, 'the trade winds, blowing for half the year steadily from the NE–SE quadrant which the Tikopia call the *tonga*, have facilitated the coming of Polynesian canoes blown out of their course in inter-island travel or while fishing' (1961, 160). Indeed, the computer simulations of drift voyaging probability by Ward, Webb, and Levison (1973) demonstrated the likelihood of canoes from West Polynesia and Fiji making landfall in Tikopia. In his speculations on Tikopia culture history, Firth stressed the importance of these immigrant groups in framing the structure of contemporary Tikopia society, and wrote of the 'galvanising influence of immigrants from overseas' (1961, 165).

To return to the main problem, a review of the ethnographic and historical evidence clearly suggests that Tikopia society as constituted in the past two centuries or so was heavily influenced and affected by a variety of external contacts. 'The use of bow and arrow, plaque neck ornaments, fish designs on canoes, and betel apparatus, and the use of croton, cycas and cordyline in ritual' were all aspects of culture with suspected Melanesian origins, owing perhaps to the two-way voyaging links with Vanikoro and Vanua Lava (Firth 1961, 158). On the other hand, the typical (and dominant) Polynesian traits, and the Samoic-Outlier language itself, clearly imply strong influence from Western Polynesia. Firth summed up the situation succinctly: 'Tikopia society is the result of a fusion of a number of elements from a variety of islands — mainly Polynesian but probably some Melanesian also. Hence Tikopia culture, and presumably language, are complex products' (1961, 167). What Firth could not know, lacking the benefit of archaeological materials, was the time depth of such external contacts, and their changing nature over the course of prehistory.

Archaeological evidence of exchange and external contacts

Survey and intensive excavations carried out on Tikopia in 1977–8 yielded a large body of stratified materials, including 5939 artifacts and more than 35,000 faunal remains, which provided the basis for a reconstruction of the island's prehistoric sequence (Kirch and Yen 1982). This sequence has been subdivided into three main phases:

Kiki Phase	900 to 100 BC
Sinapupu Phase	100 BC to AD 1200
Tuakamali Phase	AD 1200 to 1800

These phases can be distinguished on the presence or absence of one or both of two distinctive ceramic wares, although a great many other changes in material culture and faunal traits also correspond with phase boundaries. For purposes of finer temporal analysis of change, these three phases are subdivided into eight subphases which correspond to minimal 'stratigraphic-assemblage' units (Kirch and Yen 1982, 317–23).

To briefly synopsize the sequence in culture-historical terms, Tikopia was initially settled early in the first millennium BC by a population which produced largely plain-ware pottery of the Lapitoid Series. The non-ceramic material culture of this initial phase shows close resemblances to other Lapitoid assemblages in Eastern Melanesia and Western Polynesia, and it is likely that these colonists were of an Austronesian (probably Eastern Oceanic) language group. They were horticulturalists who also husbanded pigs, dogs, and fowl, and who exploited the island's reef and marine resources with a variety of techniques.

The most abrupt change in the sequence occurs at about 100 BC, with the sudden disappearance of the locally produced Lapitoid plain ware from the stratigraphic column,

and its replacement by low frequencies of a non-local ceramic decorated in the characteristic Mangaasi style. Other changes occur at the same point, such as the sudden dominance of a particular style of *Tridacna* shell adz, the disappearance of various ornament types, and the absence in the faunal record of turtle and shark. Despite these changes, there are a significant number of material culture and faunal traits which persist across the phase boundary. Yen and I have argued (1982) that the Kiki-Sinapupu phase boundary does not represent a 'replacement' of one local population by a new 'invading' group (as has sometimes been argued for certain of the Polynesian Outliers), but certainly some degree of immigration and/or increased external contact is implied.

The final prehistoric phase, the Tuakamali, is marked by the absence of any ceramics, and by the appearance of a number of characteristically 'Polynesian' material culture traits. Faunal changes include the presence once again of turtle and shark. This phase overlaps in time with the oral traditions of numerous drift voyage immigrants from various West Polynesian sources. Although the island was sighted by the Spanish explorer Quiros in 1606, significant contact with Europeans did not begin until after about AD 1800.

Turning to the problem of external contacts, and the degree to which Tikopia was ever a 'closed system', there are three classes of archaeological data to be considered. The first of these consists of material items of clearly exotic origin, where the raw material is not present on Tikopia. Included in this class are ceramics and several kinds of lithic objects (polished stone adzes, obsidian and volcanic glass, cherts and chalcedonies). The great value of these materials is that they can, given sufficient geological information for the Eastern Melanesian region, be traced to specific origin points. The second class of materials consists of artifacts whose stylistic features appear to be closely linked with assemblages known from other islands. Such stylistic comparisons have, of course, always underlain reconstructions of migration routes in Oceania, but they are a far more *subjective* data set than the first class. Third, there are a limited number of floral and faunal materials (primarily domestic or anthropophilic species) which were transported to the island by man, and for which approximate origin points can be delineated. I will briefly review the evidence for each of these classes below; full details on all of these materials are provided in Kirch and Yen (1982).

Exotic materials

Ceramics The Lapitoid plain ware of the Kiki Phase appears to have been locally manufactured, since the dominant calcareous and microcrystalline volcanic temper grains incorporated in the paste are entirely consistent with placer sands derivable locally (Dickinson, in Kirch and Yen 1982, 370–1). However, the ceramics from the Sinapupu Phase, which carry incised and punctate designs typical of the Mangaasi style (known primarily from Vanuatu) contain a markedly different temper. Particularly distinctive are vesicular glassy grains of palagonitic or pumiceous appearance, although volcanic rock fragments, plagioclase feldspars, and pyroxene grains are also present. Judging from our current petrographic knowledge of Tikopia and of the surrounding archipelagoes, a non-local source appears highly likely, and these Tikopia sherds compare closely with ceramics observed from Santo Island in northern Vanuatu. They also compare closely with a small suite of Mangaasi-style sherds excavated by Kirch (1983) from the Emo site on Vanikoro. Geologically, Vanikoro is not likely to be the source of this distinctive temper, and both the Tikopia and Vanikoro ceramics (which on archaeological criteria would be classed as the same ware) presumably derive from a northern Vanuatu source, possibly Santo, or another island with andesitic-arc petrography.

A single distinctive sherd from the Sinapupu Phase stands out from all other ceramics in the Tikopia collection. This paddle-impressed piece has a temper which appears to match that of Navatu-Phase ceramics from the central basaltic-temper province of northern Viti Levu in Fiji (Kirch and Yen 1982, 206).

Stone adzes The breccias, tuffs, and weathered lavas that comprise Tikopia's volcanic base are not suited to the manufacture of stone adzes; a number of these tools which were recovered from the excavations, and others recorded ethnographically by Firth (1959), are clearly of rock types exotic to the island. Petrographically, the adzes fall into two groups which also have discrete temporal distributions in the prehistoric sequence. The first set includes three oval or plano-convex sectioned adzes, of amphibolite, diabase, and a weathered andesite, respectively. The two metavolcanic specimens probably derive from the central or western Solomon Islands, where pre-Miocene basement rocks are exposed. All three specimens in this first set are from the island's initial settlement, Site TK-4. The second set, which includes all of the ethnographic specimens as well as several surface finds and sixteen adz flakes from excavated contexts, is petrographically uniform, of fine-grained, gray or black oceanic basalts. The source of these tools has to be from one or more islands east of the andesite line, and the most likely candidates are 'Uvea and Samoa. Typologically, the diagnostic specimens fall within the formal variability defined for West Polynesian adzes, which further supports the attribution of a Samoan or 'Uvean source. These basalt adzes are all temporally associated with the final prehistoric phase, the Tuakamali.

Obsidian Fourteen flakes of a clear, gray, highly isotropic obsidian were excavated, all but one from the island's earliest site, TK-4 (the odd specimen is believed to be in an intrusive context). Although analysis of major and minor element composition has yet to be performed for these artifacts, standard petrographic sectioning and measurement of specific gravity suggest that the probable source of this material was Talasea in New Britain, a major quarry known to have supplied much of the obsidian distributed throughout the Lapita network (Ambrose and Green 1972).

Volcanic glass Far more common throughout the Tikopia sequence than the obsidian are cores and flakes of relatively opaque and banded volcanic glass with SiO_2 content of less than 68%. A number of these flaked artifacts were examined petrographically, and they exhibit a fair range of variation (for example, in flow structure, bandedness, predominance of feldspars, and presence of phenocrysts), suggesting more than one local source. As a suite, however, these artifacts fall within the range of variation known for the Vanua Lava and Gaua sources in the Banks Islands, from whence they are believed to have derived. These volcanic glass artifacts are present throughout the Tikopia sequence, but in low frequencies until the Tuakamali Phase, when they become very common (table 4.1).

Cherts and chalcedony Also present in modest numbers throughout the Tikopia sequence (table 4.1) are cores and flakes of siliceous rocks which can be divided into three groups: (1) fine-grained, highly isotropic, 'creamy' cherts; (2) microcrystalline 'chalcedony' characterized by numerous impurities and inclusions, including frequent vugs with quartz crystals; and (3) macrocrystalline, or coarse-grained cherts. The latter two categories tend to grade into each other, and the distinction between them is somewhat arbitrary. Our knowledge of Southwestern Pacific chert sources unfortunately remains quite imperfect, making it difficult to go beyond the statement that these artifacts are unquestionably exotic to Tikopia. Specimens of the first category, 'creamy' cherts, appear to closely match cherts from Ulawa Island in the eastern Solomons, where extensive quarries are known archaeologically (Ward 1976). The chalcedony and macrocrystalline cherts, however, are probably of marine origin, and could conceivably be associated with uplifted

Table 4.1. *Exotic materials in Tikopia sites by phase*

Materials	Kiki Phase	Sinapupu Phase	Tuakamali Phase
Ceramics			
Probable Vanuatu temper		152	
Probable Fijian temper		1	
Adzes			
Metavolcanic	3		
Oceanic Basalt		1	15
Volcanic glass			
Obsidian	8		
Basaltic glass	15	4	568
Siliceous rocks			
Fine-grained chert	11	1	3
Chalcedony	70	4	70
Coarse-grained chert	2	2	
Stone image – oceanic basalt			1[*]

[*] Ethnographic context, probably assignable to Tuakamali Phase.

limestones in any number of islands, including Santa Cruz (Nendo), and several of the northern Vanuatu Islands.

Stone image A final exotic artifact was not excavated, but obtained from a senior member of the Taumako clan. This is an image of a fish deity (Kirch and Yen 1982, fig. 109), sculpted from the same fine-grained oceanic basalt used for the stone adzes mentioned earlier. As with the adzes, this artifact probably derives from one of the West Polynesian islands, quite possible 'Uvea or Samoa. Traditionally, the image was associated with the chief of the Kafika clan.

Artifact styles with external correlates
The exotic materials just reviewed clearly provide the most unambiguous evidence for external contacts. A number of other material culture items also suggest external relations, however, particularly certain artifact styles which appear abruptly in the sequence at various times, and which can clearly be correlated with identical or highly similar styles in the sequences of neighboring islands and archipelagoes. In the case of the Sinapupu Phase ceramics, the Mangaasi decorative style, which can be correlated with ceramics throughout the Vanuatu archipelago, appears on materials of exotic origin. Other styles, however, are reflected in materials available locally (although the artifacts could have been produced outside of Tikopia). Of particular note in this regard is a distinctive style of *Tridacna* shell adz, Type 4 in the Tikopia adz typology (Kirch and Yen 1982, 221–30), characterized among other attributes by a sharply pointed, ground butt. The distribution of this adz appears to be closely correlated with the Mangaasi ceramic series, and is thus far known from Vanikoro, the Banks Islands, and Mangaasi-bearing sites in the central Vanuatu area (see Kirch 1983). It appears quite abruptly in the Tikopia sequence at the beginning of the Sinapupu Phase along with the exotic Mangaasi ceramics, and becomes the dominant adz form throughout this phase. Other distinctive artifact styles possibly reflective of external contact include the West Polynesian form of pearl-shell trolling lure point, which appears in the Tuakamali Phase, bi-convex *Spondylus* shell pendants of the Sinapupu Phase identical to Caroline Islands specimens, a single surface find of a *Cassis*-shell whorl adz also of Caroline Islands type, and the use of quarried coral conglomerate slab uprights in structures of the Tuakamali Phase, a possible West Polynesian trait.

Floral and faunal items
Several species of plants and animals represented in the floral and faunal collections from the Tikopia excavations were doubtless human introductions to the island. The domestic dog, pig, and fowl, as well as the Pacific rat (*Rattus exulans*), all of which appear at the beginning of the sequence, were widely distributed throughout Oceania beginning with the Lapita incursion, and do not point to any particular island or archipelago as immediate source area. However, a larger rodent which first appears at the end of the Kiki Phase does not appear to have been an indigenously distributed species.

This is probably one of the mosaic-tailed rats of the genera *Melomys* or *Uromys* naturally distributed through the Solomon Islands; it may have been purposively introduced as a food item. Christensen and Kirch (1981) reported on anthropophilic land snails from Tikopia archaeological deposits, all of which are of species known to have been distributed throughout parts of the Pacific through human agency, especially with cultivated plants (either adhering directly on the plant cuttings, or in associated soil). While several of these anthropophilic species were evidently introduced with the island's initial Lapita colonizers, several other species appear in later deposits, and provide evidence of additional inter-island contact and, presumably, of the transport of plant materials. Finally, we note the presence in Sinapupu and Tuakamali Phase deposits of carbonized endocarp fragments of the *Canarium* almond. The several domesticated species of this genus are differentially distributed through the Solomon Islands and Vanuatu (Leenhouts 1955), but unfortunately the fragmentary nature of the Tikopia specimens does not permit a confident attribution to species, thus precluding a precise identification of source area. It should be noted that Tikopia oral traditions attribute the introduction of the *Canarium* almond to the chief Matakai II, who is said to have obtained the plant in Vanikoro.

Summary
The archaeological evidence for external contacts can now be summarized in terms of the Tikopia phase sequence (fig. 4.2). In the Kiki Phase, the majority of exotic materials point to westerly sources, primarily in the Solomon Islands and New Britain, although some Banks Islands volcanic glass is also present. The metavolcanic adzes and obsidian flakes, however, are confined to early settlement site TK-4, and may therefore represent items brought to the island on an initial colonization voyage. In contrast, the fine-grained chert and volcanic glass are found in low frequencies throughout all three stratigraphic-assemblage units of the Kiki Phase.

With the Sinapupu Phase, an abrupt change in the type and source of exotic materials occurs. The only westerly source material which continues to be represented is a small quantity of the fine-grained chert. Replacing the locally manufactured Lapitoid plain ware are Mangaasi-style ceramics from one or more source areas in northern Vanuatu; volcanic glass flakes from the Banks sources also continue. A single sherd of probable Fijian origin also appears during this phase. Also corresponding with the exotic Mangaasi ceramics is the sudden dominance of the Type 4 *Tridacna* adz, again suggesting some form of contact or relationship with Vanuatu.

In the Tuakamali Phase no items of westerly source are present, and the Mangaasi ceramics are also absent (not surprisingly, since they disappear from the central and northern Vanuatu sequences as well by about AD 1200–1300). However, the quantity of Banks Islands volcanic glass in deposits of Tuakamali Phase increases dramatically (table 4.1) indicating that contacts with the northern Vanuatu archipelago by no means ceased. Appearing in the Tuakamali Phase for the

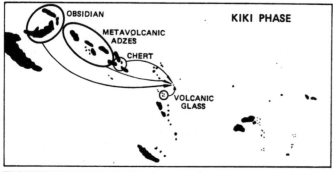

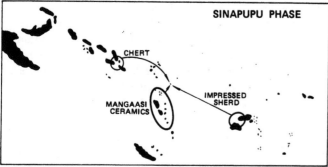

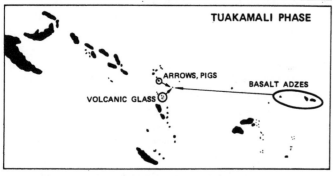

Fig. 4.2. Origins of exotic materials in Tikopia, by period.

first time are substantial quantities of oceanic basalt adzes, and several material culture traits also indicative of West Polynesian sources (fishing gear, structure forms).

Discussion

Various kinds of archaeological evidence having been presented, what can we infer regarding the nature of external contacts between Tikopia and other southwest Pacific islands and archipelagoes over the course of its three-millennia-long sequence; and what significance have such contacts had for the development or transformation of Tikopia society?

First, it is obvious that Tikopia has never been a 'closed system' in any meaningful sense, that contacts with external populations and communities have continually played a role in its prehistory. Second, the nature of such contacts has shifted substantially over time. The infrequent two-way voyaging with Vanikoro, Varuka, and Anuta known from the ethnographic and historical records does not provide a sufficient model for Tikopian external relations in prehistory.

While recognizing that archaeological evidence provides an uneven and often insufficient basis for reconstructing the nature of inter-societal relations, let us briefly press the evidence for what it suggests of Tikopia's changing position in the 'world system' of the southwest Pacific.[5]

Judging from the archaeological data, Tikopia would appear to have been least influenced by external communities during the first few centuries following initial colonization, or what we have designated as the Kiki Phase (Kirch and Yen 1982, 325–7). Yet even if the putative Talasea obsidian and the metavolcanic adzes of probable Solomon Islands origin (occurring primarily in Site TK-4) are ascribed to the cargo of the initial colonizers, low frequencies of fine-grained chert, chalcedony, and volcanic glass occur throughout the Kiki Phase deposits, and attest to some degree of external contacts. It is difficult and probably impossible to discriminate among several competing models for the kind of inter-societal relationships represented by these materials. The main possibilities would seem to be: (1) Tikopia was minimally connected to the larger Lapita exchange network which extended, for a time at least, from New Britain to New Caledonia (Green 1979). The various items of westerly derivation would have been received as a result of 'down-the-line' exchange (Renfrew 1984). Such a link could have been maintained by two-way voyaging initiated by either Tikopia, or neighboring groups, or both. (2) Alternatively, the low frequency exotic materials of the Kiki Phase could have been carried to the island by occasional drift voyagers from one or more of the nearby Santa Cruz or Vanuatu islands, who were themselves directly connected into the Lapita exchange network.

The archaeological record of external contacts changes abruptly with the boundary between Kiki and Sinapupu Phases.[6] The regular and continuous importation of Mangaasi-style ceramics, volcanic glass, and chalcedony over the ensuing thirteen centuries can be taken as signals of Tikopia's incorporation into a regional exchange network which extended into the northern Vanuatu group, and also included Vanikoro of the southern Santa Cruz Islands (Kirch 1983). The archaeological data are mute as to whether this link was established and maintained by Tikopian navigators, or by voyagers from the south. Nevertheless, the effects on Tikopia culture and society were considerable, as reflected for example in various artifact styles (such as the distinctive Type 4 shell adzes). More will be said of the possible *social* significance of this relationship shortly. There is also evidence in the Sinapupu Phase of the arrival of at least one drift voyage from the east, notably Fiji (the paddle-impressed sherd of putative Viti Levu origin).

The boundary between Sinapupu and Tuakamali Phases is not abrupt, as with that between the Sinapupu and Kiki Phases, but rather appears to have been more transitional.[7] Although Mangaasi ceramics ceased to be imported to Tikopia after about AD 1200, this does not necessarily signal a diminution of contacts with the northern Vanuatu Islands, since in fact the frequency of volcanic glass in deposits of the Tuakamali Phase increases dramatically (table 4.1). Rather than the sundering of the older exchange connections to the south, the Tuakamali Phase appears to mark the addition of a second kind of external contact, that of drift voyagers arriving from the east. The direct archaeological indicators are the stone adzes of oceanic basalt, and several new material culture traits (e.g., fishing gear, house types) of 'Polynesian' form. These are joined by the oral traditions of numerous immigrants from Samoa, 'Uvea, Tonga, Rotuma, and other easterly islands, summarized earlier. Based on the evidence from Anuta (Kirch and Rosendahl 1973; Kirch 1982), the link between this island and Tikopia was also established during the later centuries of the Tuakamali Phase.

Sometime during the late Tuakamali and Historic Phases, the long-standing exchange link with northern Vanuatu weakened to the point where, by Firth's visit in 1928–9, it was largely an aspect of 'memory-culture'. It is tempting to suggest that the arrival of Europeans on the scene, and the availability of steel tools after the early 1800s (from whalers, traders, and so on), played a critical role in this by obviating the Tikopian need for volcanic glass. Drift voyages from the east continued well into the Historic Phase, however, witnessed for example by John Maresere of 'Uvea, who became Rivers' principal informant on Tikopia culture (Rivers 1914, 299). Similarly the close 'symbiotic' relationship with Anuta has remained a key element in Tikopia external relations even to this day.

In short, Tikopia has throughout the course of its nearly three-thousand-year-long history been linked in a variety of ways with other southwest Pacific communities, some more than 2000 km distant. While the implications of these connections for Tikopia material culture are substantial, and well reflected archaeologically, what can be said of their broader significance for social change? As Sahlins has remarked of 'primitive exchange' generally, 'the material flow underwrites or initiates social relations' (1972, 186), a reflection of the 'embeddedness' of the economy in non-capitalist societies. In fact, the incorporation of Tikopia into a regional exchange network during the Sinapupu Phase appears to have been accompanied by significant transformations in the local subsistence system (the beginning of a dominance of arboriculture), and even in Tikopian concepts of the edibility/inedibility of several marine species (notably turtle and elasmobranchs). The latter, involving emic concepts, might appear to be a tenuous reconstruction on archaeological evidence, but as we argue at length elsewhere (Kirch and Yen 1982, 355–9), the sudden and continued absence of turtles and elasmobranchs from the Tikopia faunal record throughout the Sinapupu Phase seems unexplicable on environmental or ecological grounds. Rather, given the close totemic associations between these animals and various social groups in eastern Melanesia, it is not at all implausible that

what we see in the Tikopia faunal record is a reflection of the imposition in Tikopia of an external lineage system. Likewise, the subsequent reappearance of these food items in the Tuakamali Phase may mark another transformation of the local lineage system effected by the dominant Polynesian drift-voyager immigrants, who did not share in the eastern Melanesian gastronomic aversion to turtles, sharks, and rays. Such interpretations are, admittedly, far from ironclad, and some will doubtless take issue with the scenario advanced above (and presented in considerably greater detail in Kirch and Yen 1982). Nonetheless, the example points to the sort of fundamental social, and cultural, changes which external contacts may have effected in Tikopia.

Certainly, the dominantly *Polynesian* character of Tikopia culture and language as known ethnographically can now be shown on the archaeological evidence *not* to be the product of strictly local development from an ancestral Lapita community, but rather the result of successive drift-voyage immigrants who rapidly achieved social and political dominance over the island's original population during the Tuakamali Phase. Despite the unquestioned importance of internal changes in the subsistence system, of demographic pressures, and of environmental transformations (both natural and human-induced), the origins of *the* Tikopia culture and society known so well to anthropology can only be understood when Tikopia is set in its wider regional context.

Notes

1. Firth (1961) presents an exhaustive study of Tikopia oral tradition.
2. How far back in time the oral traditions extend is a matter of some debate. On standard genealogical reckoning, most of the traditions probably refer to the period after about AD 1400. For further discussion of the significance of oral traditions in the interpretation of Tikopia prehistory, see Kirch and Yen (1982).
3. It is just possible, however, that these two seemingly separate exchange networks did have a material intersection at Vanikoro, for some of the shell ornaments traded to the Tikopia may have had their origin in Nendo. Shell ornaments manufactured in Nendo were exchanged by the Duff Is. voyagers in Vanikoro for the *Myzomela* bird feathers essential to the manufacture of the red-feather money.
4. One further minor indication of former contacts between Tikopia and Vanua Lava lies in a shared placename, Ravenga, a district of Tikopia and the name of a small offshore islet in Vanua Lava.
5. I use Wallerstein's term here not without reservation, since with Renfrew (1984, 82), I regard it as misleadingly general. The alternative, 'global system', used by Ekholm (1978) and others does not offer much of an improvement.
6. This boundary, it should be pointed out, is archaeologically discrete, marked by the stratigraphic break between Zones C and B of the Sinapupu site (Kirch and Yen 1982).
7. This is reflected statistically in a matrix analysis of the stratigraphic assemblages (Kirch and Yen 1982, 318–24).

Chapter 5

**The role of competition and cooperation in
the evolution of island societies**

George J. Gumerman

Athenians (to the people on the island of Melos): From our
opinion of the gods and from our observation of men we
conclude that it is a constant and irresistible law of nature to
use power wherever one is superior. We did not make this law
ourselves, nor were we the first to use it once it had been
enacted. But as we found it already in existence, and expect
to leave it in existence for all time, we are making use of it.
                                        Thucydides, *Historiae* V.105

Renfrew refers to the above quote by the world's
earliest known political historian as 'apparently the first
recorded statement of what today might be called a "law of
cultural process"' (1982, 264). While not necessarily believing
that the 'law' of exploitation has sacred sanctions, many
anthropologists subscribe to the causal role of competition
and conflict in the evolution of complex societies. Often
anthropologists relinquish the role of the gods to the natural
environment, which they usually view as influencing or even
determining the form that conflict or cooperation takes.

For anthropologists, islands are a special subset for
analyzing the role of cooperation and competition in the
development of complex societies. The island as a circumscribed
natural and cultural laboratory has been repeatedly touted
as a controlled test situation (Clark and Terrell 1978; Kirch
1980b) and, furthermore, the role of conflict in island societies
has been the subject of many anthropological studies.

This paper examines the role of cooperation and

competition in the evolution of social complexity in island
societies within the context of the natural environment. The
archipelago of Palau in Micronesia will be used as an example
of a place where the interplay of competition and cooperation
within an island environment is related to and partially explains
the evolution and persistence of hierarchical social forms. The
study tends to confirm those theories, such as Carniero's
(1970), which view the social evolution of complex forms as
the result of population pressure and, therefore, competition
over the resources of a circumscribed environment. There is
no presumption that the model presented is a universal one,
relevant to all situations, but insights about the role of the
reciprocal forces of competition and cooperation in
circumscribed environments do have cross-cultural
applicability.

Most of the currently accepted explanations for the
evolution of complex societies in any environment are derived
from ecological models – and with good reason. First and
foremost, evolution is a biological concept which by analogy
or homology has been often utilized effectively to understand
the nature of cultural adaptation. Second, as archaeologists
who deal with prehistoric societies often point out,
nonindustrial societies interact more directly with their
natural environment than do industrial societies. Third, most
archaeologists have found the techno-economic aspect of
culture and its articulation with the environment the easiest

aspect of a cultural adaptive system to reconstruct.
Furthermore, some archaeologists consider the techno-economic
system to be the driving force in culture change.

Systemic models of culture change commonly view the
environment as only one of three variables in explaining major
adaptive change, the other two being demographic and
behavioral variables (Dean, Euler, Gumerman, Hevly and
Karlstrom 1985). In most models significant change in any
one of the three variables would result in systemic culture
change. Environment and demography are usually considered
by archaeologists to operate independently. In other words,
changes in them that exceed certain thresholds create
conditions that require adaptive behavioral response.
Behavioral variables, on the other hand, are considered
dependent, although under certain conditions they too can
impose constraints on the system which result in major
systemic culture change.

Problems in the use of ecological models

The very general model of culture change described
above is used by archaeologists in a variety of forms to explain
both specific and general forms of cultural evolution. As a
general framework the model is adequate to explain culture
change, but difficulty arises in operationalizing the model and
attempting to test it empirically. Especially difficult are
problems of measurement in the archaeological record. Even
such basic determinations as 'carrying capacity' are very
difficult to determine empirically (Hassan 1981; Hayden
1975). Archaeologists with the aid of their natural science
colleagues have felt most comfortable about reconstructing
past environments, but a recent retrodiction of environments
in southwestern North America, where conditions for
paleoenvironmental studies are better than in most regions, has
demonstrated that past environments are extraordinarily
difficult to characterize (Dean *et al.* 1985).

The southwestern study also demonstrated the great
suite of critical environmental conditions that required adaptive
behavior given the permutation of the numerous environmental
variables which impinged on human populations. The large
number of environmental variables which affected human
behavior and the numerous combinations of these variables
demonstrated that there was not a single fifty-year period
in the last two millennia that was comparable to any other.
In short, given the broad range of demographic, behavioral
and environmental variables and their various combinations,
every fifty years was essentially a unique situation.

The single most important fact of the southwestern
study is that generalizations archaeologists usually make about
the environment are seldom detailed enough for explaining
systemic culture change. Although island environments have
been highly touted as amenable for the measurement of
environmental variables, there are drawbacks. It is true that
island terrestrial environments are relatively easy to quantify
and to describe, principally because of territorial
circumscription. But the usually critical marine environment

is often more important to the island populations and is also
more difficult to quantify and describe, requiring skills that
few, if any, archaeologists command. R. E. Johannes, a marine
biologist, has demonstrated in a study of marine lore and
fishing in the Palau islands that few members of his own
discipline command the basic knowledge of fish behavior
which was vital to traditional Palauans (1981). He details
the problems of using modern marine biology studies to
attempt to understand humans' utilization of marine life,
demonstrating that Micronesian fishermen have a considerably
greater understanding of fish behavior in relationship to
their use of it as a food resource than do modern Western
scientists.

In addition to the problem of archaeologists not
adequately understanding the natural environment, there is
the counter problem of assuming island populations know
all that it is necessary for them to know about their
environment. Archaeologists often assume that decision
making about the economic conditions of the environment
is based on some sort of omniscient rationality on the part
of individuals striving for economic optimization. They have
consistently failed to recognize that decision making takes
place within a social context, and it may or may not be based
on accurate information about the environment. Further,
models assuming that decision making is geared to economic
optimization ignore the fact that optimization may not be
the actual goal. As Moore has noted, 'In reality decisions [in
response to the environment] are based on a mix of
information, ignorance, error and lies' (1983, 183). In short,
archaeologists cannot expect a one-to-one correlation between
environmental change and human behavior as if humans had
perfect knowledge of their environment and were seeking to
take maximum economic advantage of environmental
conditions.

Related to this problem is the assumption made by a
majority of archaeologists that evolutionary processes lead
almost inevitably to beneficial adaptations and positive
functions (Diener 1982). It is, after all, possible for evolution
to lead to a decrease in long-term efficiency although there
may be relative reproductive advantages in the short term
(Kirch 1980a, Rappaport 1978). Archaeologists cannot
therefore take their usual stance that observed behavioral
change necessarily results in long-term evolutionary benefits.

Another problem with the use of ecological models
arises with our inability to develop sufficiently accurate
chronological controls. This is especially true for most tropical
and subtropical islands with developed chiefdoms, which
makes it difficult to correlate behavioral, demographic, and
environmental change. The correlation of events is a prerequisite
to understanding the relationship between the variables
considered in an ecological model.

I do not mean to paint an entirely gloomy portrait
of attempts to explain the evolution of complex societies
through traditional models of culture change, especially
those based on ecological models, because there are some

advantages in this when studying island societies. Because most island environments with developed complex societies do not have the heterogeneous environment of larger land masses, environmental spatial variation is easier to measure. Another difference is that most islands with complex societies are situated in the tropical latitudes where rhythmic environmental changes are less severe, although they are still difficult to measure.

There are two means by which archaeologists may be able to use ecological models for understanding culture change which avoid the need for very detailed description of an entire ecosystem. First, archaeologists can attempt to be less global in the scope of research questions, and second, archaeologists can pose questions which focus more on behavior as a variable and use only general ecological and demographic data.

The first method narrows the scope of the research question asked, thereby limiting the data that are needed to address the question. The restricted focus of questions in ecological anthropological research has made the potential for answering those questions much greater. For example, rather than asking a general question, such as, 'How did Polynesian settlers from the Tonga–Samoa region adapt to the quite different environment of the Marquesas Islands?', Kirch (1980b) narrowed the inquiry to, 'Given the subsistence importance of marine life to the Polynesians, how did the Marquesan colonizers adapt their angling techniques to a different marine environment?' Quite obviously the potential for answering the latter question is much greater than for the former. By narrowing the scope of the investigation Kirch was able to devise a evolutionary explanation for a portion of Marquesan adaptive behavior. Unfortunately, however, this approach does not permit an understanding of total behavioral sets.

The second solution to the problem is to seek explanation for the evolution of complex societies only in the broader context of environment, focusing more on aspects of social integration than on details of the total ecosystem. This is an approach favored by Flannery (1972), Wright and Johnson (1975), and specifically for island environments Cordy (1983a, b) among others, while Kirch and Yen (1982) and Cordy (1981) have attempted to test these theories. These scholars feel that greater attention has to be paid to social interaction and especially to how information is obtained, processed, and distributed within the matrix of a social and natural environment. The mechanisms and processes by which societies evolve to greater complexity are viewed as the result of social conditions which are influenced by general environmental parameters.

Cooperation and competition

As indicated earlier, the social conditions most commonly cited for the causes of complex social development are a consequence of conflict, competition, and warfare (Haas 1982; Adams 1975). This view is a more specific perspective of the general one that treats conflict as but one aspect of

many that regulate a variety of social relationships in a continuing and predictable fashion (Corning 1983, 310).

Patterns of cooperative and competitive behavior are opposing processes for regulating behavioral relationships (Sanders and Price 1968; Service 1975). Conflict and competition are conflicting social options to alliances and cooperation, although conflict and competition seldom exist without cooperative agreements such as alliances. Social grouping for defensive coordination or offensive collaboration involves networks of cooperation for competitive or conflict oriented goals. Competition in many instances may actually be a major stimulus for cooperation. The adaptive advantage of competition, therefore, has to be modeled with some form of cooperation.

Most theories which cite warfare as a causative factor in the development of complex societies or the origin of the state assume that environmental or social circumscription becomes a critical factor as population increases. Some anthropologists argue that competition ensues over limited resources in these situations, resulting in conflict; weakened groups are subdued until all groups within the circumscribed boundary are under the control of a single polity (Carniero 1970). Other anthropologists subscribe to the theory that circumscribed environmental and demographic pressure conditions result in social complexity, but instead of seeing the state as a result of larger and larger conquests, in this situation they view it as the consequence of the increasing solidification of power of the war leaders (Fried 1967; Harner 1970; Webb 1975; Webster 1975). In either case, the argument is made that hierarchical social forms are necessary in these circumstances to provide long-range tactical planning, subdue populations, and efficiently monitor information flows and administrative resources. Military sophistication is highly correlated with the level of political centralization (Otterbein 1970, 106). Highly coercive and authoritarian social and political forms may be more efficient in these instances than are those which are highly consensual or participatory, as any drill sergeant will attest.

Flannery (1972) has criticized this view of competition and cooperation as a cause for social complexity. As he points out, if competition and cooperation *per se* resulted in more complex societies, bands and tribes would be extinct because competition and cooperation are ubiquitous. He groups 'competition and cooperation' with other examples of 'linear' causality, such as trade and symbiosis (Rathje 1972; Wright and Johnson 1975) and irrigation (Wittfogel 1957). In place of models of linear causality, he proposes a model of multivariant causality in which numerous causal variables have complex interrelationships with feedback between them.

Flannery's comments are well taken, but he ignores the role of environment, which all advocates of the importance of the role of competition and cooperation in cultural evolution include as a factor in their models. Recent studies suggest that it is the character of the environment that determines the evolutionary fitness of strategies of cooperation and competition (Axelrod 1984; Axelrod and Hamilton 1981).

Adaptation based on cooperation and competition has been modeled using methods of game theory and computer simulation based on the game of iterated Prisoner's Dilemma. Game theory explains optimal behavior by modeling situations involving conflicting interests. It has been demonstrated that the adaptive value of decisions involving choices between cooperation or competition are as applicable to bacteria as they are to tribes, bureaucracies, and nation states (Axelrod 1984; Axelrod and Hamilton 1981). In several international tournaments by game theorists from many disciplines a strategy which combines cooperation with other entities, retribution when acted against, and then a rapid return to cooperative behavior when the other entity cooperates proved most successful against competing strategies when run for many generations of encounters. Interestingly, the cooperation–retribution–cooperation strategy did not defeat a single rival in the many generations of encounters which have been run; the best result it produces is a tie and often it loses to competitors by a slight margin. In other words, it is not necessary to beat the other player, but rather to elicit behavior which permits both to do well. The important element is not trust, but rather the durability of the relationship, expressed in terms of the belief that there will be an indefinite future to the interaction.

It is important to stress that cooperation (operating in a behavioral relationship with coordination of goals) is quite different from altruism (self-sacrifice of an individual or group for others). This distinction is important because of sociobiologists' emphasis on the role of altruism which by definition reduces personal fitness and is a form of self-destructive behavior (Wilson 1975). Cooperation is a form of mutualism that attempts to effect benefits to both parties.

Another interesting point brought out by the Prisoner's Dilemma simulation is that those strategies which were exploitative and aggressively tried to take advantage of more cooperative programs often did well for several generations of encounters. However, in a closed system environment the process is self-defeating in the long run if the aggressive strategies depend on less adaptive programs, because it eventually eliminates the weaker programs on which it depends for its existence.

The character of the environment in which the game is played is vitally important for understanding the adaptability of any specific strategy. The cooperation–retribution–cooperation strategy's strength is its ability to adapt to, and solicit cooperation from, a great variety of environments.

One environment in which the cooperation–retribution–cooperation strategy does not do well is a zero-sum world where there is, or appears to be, a limited number of resources. The situation is compounded when there is the knowledge that there will be a finite number of encounters, meaning that the end of the game is known to the players because one or both participants will no longer deal with one another or

because the resources will be exhausted. In these zero-sum games losses on one side always represent gains for the other side. In a zero-sum game it is useful to apply deception and aggression where any efficiency on the part of an opponent results in an adaptive advantage to a player. The game of chess is an example of a zero-sum game. Winning must result in the defeat of the opponent. In the environmentally circumscribed situation of a zero-sum game with limited resources the soundest evolutionary strategy is one of defection and aggression. In the iterated Prisoner's Dilemma game this situation equates with the kinds of social and natural environment that islands provide.

The strategy of defection and aggression in a zero-sum game is a stable one. If it is known that an opponent will always act in an aggressive fashion, there is no point at all in ever cooperating (Axelrod 1984, 63), so a situation of stability by means of competition ensues. In island environments where there are a perceived finite number of encounters in a zero-sum world a competitive strategy may be most adaptive and could result in a stable situation.

A stable situation does not mean that individual social entities do not rise and fall. As Wright has observed, chiefdoms and simpler states exist in networks constantly changing in scale, intensity and direction, regulated by both competition and alliance (1977, 385). That is, while the evolutionary stages tend to be thought of as relatively stable, individual chiefdoms and states come and go.

There are some major objections to the use of the iterated Prisoner's Dilemma game to understand group human behavior in island societies. Most obvious is the fact that real life situations are usually more complex than the Prisoner's Dilemma model can consider. The Prisoner's Dilemma does not take into consideration interaction with three or more parties as allies, foes, or neutrals. Among other things, there can be degrees of cooperation or aggression that can modify the results of action, negotiation that may color the results, co-operative and competitive behavior that may be misinterpreted, and there simply might be difficulty in pursuing a desired course of action (Axelrod 1984, 19). Despite these problems, the simplicity of the model and its help in understanding many forms of human interaction suggest that it will provide insight into the evolution of island societies.

A major question regarding the use of the Prisoner's Dilemma game to understand the evolution of island social complexity is, 'What is the appropriate unit of analysis for examining patterns of cooperation and competition?' The classic Prisoner's Dilemma game is based on the actions of two individuals. In fact, Axelrod and Hamilton contend that the role of cooperation has been neglected in evolutionary studies because scholars have traditionally focused on adaptation above the individual level (1979, 1390). Ecological anthropologists, such as Ruyle (1973, 212–14) and Richerson (1977, 21) have also suggested the most appropriate unit of analysis is the individual. Others, such as Vayda and McCay (1975), feel that the role of both the individual and the group must be considered. Nevertheless, as Kirch (1980a, 118) has pointed out, in many instances social units larger than the individual provide for greater understanding of adaptive processes.

Kirch notes four factors favoring the role of groups larger than the individual as the appropriate unit of analysis for adaptive studies: (1) cultural adaptation permits rapid sharing of adaptive information; (2) culture in the sense of a shared pool of ideas and concepts is never controlled by a single individual; (3) social groups usually act as functional units in decision making and in interacting with the environment. Therefore all members of the group face the same selective pressures; and (4) individual behavior is constrained by the group (1980a, 118).

Therefore, while a focus on the individual has underscored the role of cooperation in evolutionary studies, the examination of larger social units is necessary to understand the reciprocal roles of cooperation and competition.

Axelrod suggests that 1000 individuals may be an appropriate number (1984, 75–6). It is large enough to be perceived as responsible for competitive or cooperative behavior over a specific geographical unit and yet it is small enough so that most people know others by sight and individual behavior can be controlled by a variety of formal and informal means.

The Palauan example

A brief look at Palauan patterns of competition and cooperation, as one example of the island chiefdom model, may make an understanding of the evolutionary trajectory of this socio-political form more clear.

The Palau archipelago in the Western Caroline Islands consists of about 250 islands extending 150 km along a north–south trending arc. It is some 900 km east of Mindanao in the Philippines and a similar distance north of Irian Jaya. The island system is environmentally quite diverse as compared to most others in Micronesia. It is dominated by a large volcanic island whose 306 km^2 area is three-fourths of Palau's total land mass. The rest of Palau consists of three volcanic islands, two atolls, and many uplifted coralline limestone islands, known as 'rock islands'. An extensive barrier reef extends along the western side of the central islands enclosing a prolific lagoon of more than 1200 km^2. The volcanic islands consist of eroded hills up to 250 m above sea level, while the atolls and rock islands vary from sandy beaches a few meters above sea level to jagged limestone hills more than 200 meters high. A mixed tropical forest covers all the islands; the volcanic islands have, in addition, broad, fire-maintained savannas and coastal mangrove swamps.

The traditional subsistence base was a mix of terrestrial and marine resources. Both 'dry' and 'wet' taro were grown as were bananas and coconuts. Although slight evidence of domesticated pig and possibly goat is found in the archaeological record (Osborne 1979, 66), no large mammals were noted at the time of first contact and it was even mentioned that

the Palauans did not have pigs (Keate 1788, 97). A species of pigeon was a delicacy but was of little significance to the total caloric intake since its flesh was restricted to a few members of the highest class. There is no doubt that the bulk of the protein came from the incredibly rich Palauan marine resources. Marine biologists (Clark 1953; Johannes 1981) and anthropologists (Kubary 1895; Masse, Snyder and Gumerman 1983) alike have attested to both the richness and the diversity of marine life in the Palau waters and the skill of Palauans in exploiting it.

Traditional Palauan settlement had two major integrated settlement units above the household level (Gumerman, Snyder and Masse 1981; Masse, Snyder and Gumerman 1984). The first was the village settlement system which consisted of a population of about 100 or more people usually situated in a defensive position and which included all the resources of a strip of land from forested interior through a mangrove swamp (if possible) including an area of lagoon to the ocean outside of the reef. Each village traditionally had seven or ten clans. Clans and villages were rank ordered by status based mostly on wealth, especially land.

Many ethnographers have remarked on the competition, accumulation, and manipulation theme so pervasive in Palauan society (Barnett 1949, 1960; Force 1960; Force and Force 1972; McKnight 1960). Because there was considerable flexibility in determining kin group membership, there was a great deal of manipulation to gain economic and political advantage (McKnight 1960; Smith 1983). This means that within villages kin groups developed alliances for prestige and power at the expense of other kin groups.

Palauan villages were grouped into a number of larger alliances, called *districts*, for political, social, and economic functions. These districts consisted of variable numbers of villages, with one village being the most powerful and most highly ranked. On the basis of early European observations (Keate 1788; McCluer 1790–2) it appears that these districts formed four rival matrilineal chiefdoms, each controlled by a paramount chief. Each of these chiefdoms had three, and perhaps four, levels of administrative hierarchy, with these positions being filled on the basis of heredity. The lowest level in the hierarchy consisted of each individual village chief, a position filled by the highest ranking member of the most highly ranked clan of the village. The next level consisted of district chiefs who controlled the village chiefs within their districts. The highest level of the hierarchy was that of the paramount chief, a person who could organize military expeditions, who exercised the power to demand tribute from subject districts and villages, and who required various tokens of deference from commoners and lesser chiefs.

Dualistic organization from the clan to the village level on up through the division of the archipelago itself in a north and south dichotomy ordered the pattern of cooperation and competition. This meant that not all individuals and kin groups were in competition with one another, but rather that competition was ordered along two lines, resulting in what McKnight calls 'controlled conflict' (1960, 18). Clans were divided into two competing divisions for power and wealth as were the villages themselves. Above the village level the most powerful village divided the cluster of satellite villages into two parts, one part on either side of the controlling village. The largest dual competing social units were the north and south geographic division of chiefdoms which divided the entire archipelago into two traditional enemies in a state of constant warfare.

Individual chiefdoms were in actuality weakly organized and unstable, and the power of the paramount chief may not have been absolute. Oral traditions indicate that prior to contact district boundaries, ranking villages, and ranking clans were commonly in a state of flux due to the endemic warfare.

How far into the past this pattern extends is unknown, although archaeological evidence suggests that the village structure, if not the social forms associated with it at the time of European contact, goes back perhaps as early as AD 1200 (Masse *et al.* 1984). Since many of the early villages were obviously positioned for defense it can be assumed that warfare was prevalent at these early dates also. Osborne succinctly describes Palauan warfare as follows:

> Village-district battled with village-district, far or near. Treachery, atrocities, surprises, and sneak attacks, and the making and breaking of alliances were accepted aspects of war. Campaigns appear to have been well thought out and to have often involved complex plots and counterplots. Conquest of land and domination of the defeated were the logical and apparently usual outcome of large-scale warfare. Defeats in battle that did not and probably could not end in wholesale domination of the defeated group's territory or popu-lation were usually settled by indemnity. (1966, 30)

In sum, Palauan society from the level of clans to the dual division of the archipelago itself was a balanced system of cooperation and competition, of alliances and conflict. The flexibility of this relationship, the resultant limited ability to manipulate status, and the vagaries of war made the network of cooperation and competition a fluid one.

Population and the environment

There are a number of aspects of the environment and demography that make a detailed understanding of the interaction between the two difficult. The problems have mainly to do with site formation processes, preservation – especially in the acidic soil of the volcanic islands – and measurement of both the cultural materials and the natural environment. Because of these difficulties an attempt will be made simply to demonstrate that at times there was population pressure on critical resources. A demonstration that this condition existed is sufficient for purposes of this discussion.

Estimates of population at time of contact have ranged from a low of 20,000 to 25,000 (Krämer 1919, 292) and a high of 40,000 to 50,000 (Semper 1982, 289–90). None of

these figures are derived from reliable data nor are they presently confirmable, although the lower figures appear more realistic.

The important fact is that prior to historic contact much of the rock island group was densely occupied (Masse *et al.* 1983). By and large these islands are less desirable for human occupation than are the larger volcanic islands. The poor soil development, small area, extremely rough terrain, scarcity of canoe landing sites, and relatively lesser amounts of fresh water make the rock islands less suitable for both habitation and terrestrial based subsistence. Despite these conditions, surveys have shown that many of these miniscule fragments of rock poking above the ocean surface are covered with the remains of permanent prehistoric villages. Although chronological control is poor, in at least some instances it can be demonstrated that village systems extending over much of an island's land surface are contemporaneous. Stone covered paths link the various villages, suggesting that they were occupied contemporaneously (Masse *et al.* 1983, 14). In short, it appears that at some time the population of the archipelago was sufficiently large to require the habitation of the most undesirable land in the Palau Islands. This does not necessarily indicate that there was a shortage of subsistence goods, only that habitable land may have been in short supply, or perhaps even that defensive considerations required a dispersed population and the use of the scattered rock islands.

There are other indications that there may have been a population–resources imbalance. Despite the rich marine resources, Johannes (1981) indicates that there was a bewildering range of rhythmic availability of marine resources. Good fishing clustered around the new and full moon, correlated with spawning runs. There were also seasonal rhythms of fish availability due mainly to changing currents and wind direction. Even daily changes in fish behavior and movement affected fish availability. Turtles and a species of land crab, both important food resources, were also seasonally variable in abundance and accessibility. McCluer even notes that famine was a common motif on carved beams in men's club houses (1790–2, 66).

In spite of the rhythmic availability of protein, Johannes feels that there is no evidence in the oral history that there was ever a shortage of food (1981, 63). He does indicate, however, that laws restricted the catching of certain less desirable fish to periods of bad weather when fishing was poor; and sea cucumbers and giant clams were not eaten in order to conserve their use for when fish were unavailable (Johannes 1981, 66). He also points out that today Palauan consumption of canned fish (especially Japanese canned mackerel) and meat accounts for one-third of the animal protein consumed (1981, 71). Modern political and economic conditions have, of course, helped contribute to the great reliance on imported protein.

The most dramatic evidence that food, or at least land, was in short supply at times is the extensive system of terraces that cover the larger islands (Osborne 1966, 1979; Lucking

1981). Many thousands of acres of land have been greatly modified by cutting and filling, creating a 'manicured' cultural landscape. The function of the terrace system has been greatly debated. However, the consensus is that some forms of terraces may have been used for defense and that others were used for agriculture. Brian Butler, on the basis of a survey of terraces and villages on the western part of the largest island (1984), feels that agricultural terraces are associated with specific villages, and defensive structures related to terraces appear to be located in critical topographic situations between individual village-agricultural terrace systems.

In short, considerable energy was marshalled in order to terrace the landscape, probably for both agricultural and defensive purposes. Given the high percentage of land which was terraced and the amount of effort expended in terracing, the need for these land forms must have been extraordinarily high. There was arable land on the interior of the largest island, Babeldaub, which from cursory archaeological investigation appears to have been unused for permanent habitation (Masse *et al.* 1983). This is probably a result of the need to have ready access to marine resources. Most of the interior of Babeldaub is rugged, jungle covered terrain, and travel on foot is extremely slow, making access to the lagoon difficult. In all probability, at certain times the amount and nature of suitable natural landscape was probably not sufficient for the precontact Palauan population.

Alkire has commented on how the limited amount of land has pervaded Micronesian culture:

The generally high population density common to the area, especially in precontact times, meant that nearly all potentially productive land in Micronesia was either directly or indirectly exploited for subsistence purposes (and more recently commercial ones). The scarcity of such productive land in most areas naturally increased its value and consequently man's adaptation to this limited resource not only shaped the subsistence economic systems but other social, political, and religious institutions as well. In Micronesia one can not only say that land is life in the sense that land provides the basic sustenance for survival, but also that land is a way of life, since throughout Micronesia the basic social institutions have been molded by adaptation to the concept and reality of limited land.

In pre-European contact times, the Micronesian islands were isolated from the epidemic diseases that effectively controlled and reduced populations in other regions of the world. Consequently, on many of these islands, natural population growth eventually placed strains on available resources. The near universality of land disputes in the societies described are witness not only to present conditions but also, in many cases, to these former conditions. (1977, 87–8)

It appears, therefore, that as population increased to the point of putting pressure on available resources, a perception of a zero-sum situation would necessarily develop.

This situation in turn would make competition the most appropriate strategy and a hierarchical social order evolutionarily most fit. In Palau a combination of high population, scarcity of critical resources, and perhaps the requirements for defense necessitated the use of the less desirable rock islands for habitation in addition to a massive effort at agricultural intensification. The population vied for the scarce and finite resources by means of the controlled ordering of competition and cooperation through the social networks and nested hierarchies of settlement relationships.

Of this hierarchy, it would seem that the village district is a unit of analysis most conducive for the study of the role of competition and cooperation in Palauan society. While, as has been stated earlier, population figures for Palau at the time of contact are difficult to determine, chiefdoms apparently ranged from 1000 to 3000 individuals (Cordy 1983a, b; Masse *et al.* 1983). Population figures are therefore at least approximately appropriate for the individual chiefdom to be used as the unit of analysis. Furthermore, chiefdoms are unified in their cooperative and competitive behavior; i.e., while individuals, clans, moieties, and villages may compete for status, it is the chiefdom which makes formal alliances and wages war. It is the formal social unit which is responsible for competitive and cooperative behavior which is territorially defined. Social units smaller than the chiefdom do not permit as clear an understanding of the reciprocal forces of cooperation and competition because the interaction among units is more difficult to interpret; social units larger than a chiefdom contain too many individuals for on-sight recognition and social control.

Palauan society was a combination of cooperative behavior and competition between clans, villages, districts, chiefdoms, and the north and south division of the archipelago, competing for limited resources — economic, political, and social. In spite of the richness of the Palauan reef system the vast amount of energy expended on the complex system of terraces on the larger island and the dense occupation of the smaller and less productive corraline islands indicate that Palauan society was near the limits of its carrying capacity. This means that the most effective strategy was one of aggressive defection and competition since the end of the 'game' could be predicted and, as in Prisoner's Dilemma, this is the best strategy for that environment. According to the simulations of the iterated Prisoner's Dilemma, the strategy of aggression was a stable one even though the fortunes of individual social entities would rise and fall. The most effective way to organize that competition was through a social hierarchical ordering which controlled both cooperation and competition. An egalitarian society in which there is equal access to resources and information is not an efficient means of ordering networks of cooperation and competition. Warfare (as opposed to feuding) on a large and continuing scale is most efficient when there is a hierarchical arrangement of participants to effect long-term planning and coordinated strategy. The essential element of hierarchical organization is that it has the potential for enhancing the value of the component parts of a system so that goals of the entire system may be facilitated (Johnson 1978).

The model proposed here states that as an increasing population approaches carrying capacity in a circumscribed environment, patterns of warfare and alliances within a hierarchical social order become the most effective adaptive strategies. A detailed knowledge of the past environment is not a requirement to test the model. Unfortunately, the cultural history of Palau is not well enough known to document the development of the relationship between (1) population increase, (2) resource scarcity, (3) social hierarchies, and (4) warfare and alliances. And finally, this model begs the question which generations of anthropologists have pondered, 'Why does population grow in the first place?'

Conclusion

Modeling the complexities of human behavior on the basis of the abstract formulation of a computer simulation game masks many potentially important variables. The iterated Prisoner's Dilemma game does not take into consideration features such as negotiation, the influence of third parties or allies or foes, uncertainty about what the other party did, and problems involved with implementing a choice of action. Analysis without the complicating factors, however, can help to clarify some of the results of social interaction. As with all attempts at modeling to understand real situations, the need for simplicity versus the need to include relevant variables are conflicting requirements. The crucial decision in model building is where to draw the line between on the one hand, simplicity for clarity, on the other hand, complexity which includes relevant variables.

The simple model of the iterated Prisoner's Dilemma has provided some insights into the role of cooperation and competition in circumscribed environments with a relatively complex form of social order. Especially important is the fact that it is not necessary to retrodict the environment in great detail in order to understand the articulation between the development of complex social forms and the natural environment. The model needs to be refined to provide a better understanding of the complicating effect of third party alliances. This is especially crucial for testing the relationship between hierarchical social orders and competition and cooperation.

The conclusion to this essay is that theoretical constructs, such as Carniero's (1970), which view the development of the state as the result of increasing and variable population in a circumscribed environment seem to be appropriate. Competition does not directly result in more complex social forms but in a zero-sum world with limited resources it provides certain adaptive advantages.

The lessons from the iterated Prisoner's Dilemma may also help explain why in band societies, such as those in Australia and Africa, evolutionarily stable egalitarian societies existed for millennia based on cooperation and extensive social and economic networks. The now well-documented amount of leisure time, and their ability to increase their resource base if necessary in the very heterogeneous and uncircumscribed environment, favored a strategy of cooperation (Berndt and Berndt 1977; Lee 1979; Lee and DeVore 1968; Maddock 1972). It was essential that in this sort of environment the information flow was largely unrestricted with an equal access to critical resources. Institutionalized cooperative social relationships in these egalitarian societies mediated the effects of environmental variability and potential differential access to resources due to their spatial variability. Ethnographic accounts underscore that these people did not perceive their world as a zero-sum situation with cooperative behavior eliciting cooperation in others and all reaping the rewards.

On the other hand, it seems that the reciprocal forces of cooperation and competition in a circumscribed environment were the mechanism by which at least some hierarchical social and political societies evolved as carrying capacity was reached. It also meant a stable situation even though individual polities did not stay in power long. In circumscribed environmental situations, as opposed to more open systems, nice guys do indeed finish last.[1]

Note

1 Assistance in the writing of this article was provided by Brian Butler and Worthen Hunsaker. Editorial help was provided by Barbara E. Cohen and the typing was done by Terri Mathews.

Chapter 6

Some basic components of the Ancestral Polynesian settlement system: building blocks for more complex Polynesian societies

R. C. Green

. Cultural reconstruction or 'culture history' has in recent decades fallen into theoretical disfavor as an interpretive enterprise, especially among some North American archaeologists. Often it is dismissed, as in a recent review of Oceanic archaeology, as consisting of little other than a series of speculative scenarios aimed at constructing nothing more than historical narratives of uncertain veracity (Clark and Terrell 1978, 300–1). Such views are reminiscent of an earlier generation of social and cultural anthropologists with respect to the value of previous historical reconstructions in ethnology. Often pejoratively labelled 'conjectural history' (Radcliffe-Brown 1952, 49–50), their excessive reliance on diffusion and migration plus a lack of methodological rigor brought historical anthropology into disrepute and rendered it unfashionable (Goodenough 1983). Only in historical linguistics, with its explicit comparative theoretical framework based on the well-established principle of the regularity of sound change, has historical reconstruction continued without serious challenge (see, for example, Dyen and Aberle 1974). In the Pacific, especially among the Austronesian languages and particularly those of the Oceanic branch, the application of the comparative method has in recent decades been greatly extended. This has led to better lexical reconstructions, subgroupings, and postulated relationships within the Austronesian Family. The results, moreover, have provided critical information for interpretation of the prehistory of the whole region.

The present essay is an unapologetic exercise in culture history or cultural reconstruction of a methodologically rigorous type. Its publication is encouraged not only by the advances of the last decades in Polynesian and Oceanic linguistics, but also by two other papers in another symposium held at the same Congress at which this paper was delivered. In one of these, Aberle (1983), drawing on comparative linguistic methods, sought to reestablish the value of historical reconstruction in ethnology, distinguishing such reconstructions with their testable implications from those of conjectural history. He saw the *proto-speech community* as a primary focus in which to undertake such a careful kind of historical reconstruction. In the other paper Goodenough (1983), again drawing on linguistic models, suggested that by searching for homologous or cognate cultural traditions within societies possessing phylogenetically related languages whose cultures were probably also similarly related, it was possible to devise a successful and productive strategy for discovering historical relationships. He argued that Oceania is such an area, where one can apply the strategy of the comparative method of historical linguistics to cultural traditions. Following Goodenough, this paper focusses on the Oceanic area with its phylogenetically related cultural traditions, and following

Aberle, on the proto-speech community of the Polynesians. It attempts to integrate linguistic, ethnological, and archaeological data bearing on a reconstruction of some of the main structural components of the Ancestral Polynesian settlement pattern. Clearly, the successful reconstruction of these structural components (along with other aspects of Ancestral Polynesian society) will provide a critical baseline on which to chart the subsequent development and transformation of descendant island societies.

Strategies for cultural reconstruction

Three main strategies appear possible for reconstructing Ancestral Polynesian settlement and social systems. One has long been with us, the comparative ethnological approach practiced by several generations of Polynesian scholars from Hale, Fornander, and Smith in the nineteenth century, through Williamson, Burrows, and Handy in the first half of the twentieth century, to Goodenough, Goldman, and Sahlins in the 1960s and 70s (Kirch 1984). Each generation produced studies with quite different theoretical stances and methodologies, but the underlying procedure has always been the same. From the ethnographic observations of the range of Polynesian societies at the time of European contact and shortly thereafter (the traditional form supposedly little altered by cultural contact with Western societies), one postulated according to a given methodology (often not explicit or rigorous) the ancestral form from which the present variety of ethnographic societies and their material manifestations arose. Usually there was an attempt to explain the variation by the operation of one or more of a small set of factors: migrations, diffusion, cultural peaks, status rivalry, or ecology. Such historical reconstruction has always had its critics, and the difficulties are numerous and widely recognized.

The second approach has only recently been applied in Oceania. It is based on reconstructions of the lexicons of proto-languages using the comparative method of historical linguistics. For Proto-Polynesian the lexicon now numbers around 3000 items, for Proto-Oceanic nearly 2000. In this strategy the reconstruction of the proto-forms is more certain than their presumed semantic meanings. Regularity of sound change and rules for the same, combined with a subgrouping hypothesis, yield relatively secure phonemic shapes for the reconstruction obtainable from a given cognate set. However, unless the meanings in the set are highly uniform, some kind of what Dyen (ms.) calls a 'semantic history hypothesis' has to be formulated to identify the original content of the semantic category and account for the range of meanings that has subsequently developed in each of the daughter languages (cf. Dyen and Aberle 1974, 15—22 for some formal procedural methods). In the Polynesian and Oceanic subgroups of Austronesian, the establishment of the lexical forms for the proto-language has been fairly well advanced by Biggs (1979, with subsequent additions) and by Grace (1969), Blust (1972a, b), Lincoln (1979), and others. However, sophisticated

semantic history hypotheses identifying the original meanings of many of the terms are lacking. Rather, the items judged to be cognate are identified only by very loose or general meaning glosses. Still, for Oceania, following some isolated studies of specific areas like kinship, Pawley (1982a, b, in press), his students, and some others (Clark 1982) have begun to explore this problem for a number of discrete linguistic domains such as terms for people, for fish, for gardening, or for birds.

Other recent arrivals on the scene of reconstructing the ancestral culture from which the traditional societies of Polynesia developed are the archaeologists. Largely they have dealt with the later prehistoric to early historic end of a given island sequence, and often operated within a spatial or settlement pattern approach. Green (1967, 1970a, in press a) and Bellwood (1979) on the settlement pattern method, and Cordy (in press) on the development of more complex societies in Oceania provide overviews resulting from such studies. Archaeologists undertaking settlement pattern studies have also tended to work within the more detailed framework set up by their ethnological colleagues in Polynesia, and in so doing have contributed much valuable information to correcting a notable bias in the ethnographic data. This bias deals with the often rapid change in Polynesian societies that took place during the early period of European cultural contact, such that the incomplete ethnographic observations (and even later memory ethnographies) of these societies failed to reflect accurately their state at the time before sustained western contact in the late eighteenth century.

Archaeologists have been much less successful, however, in the recovery of data, and in the reconstruction of society and settlement, for the much earlier period. The only in-depth attempt for 'Archaic' or 'Ancestral' Polynesian culture is the recent work by Kirch (1984). His efforts suggest that there are now enough data available, provided one is willing to draw on all three major strategies, for archaeologists to attack this problem with new insight and hypotheses. Even where one cannot archaeologically document ancestral Polynesian cultural items of more than 2000 years ago, one can often triangulate back to them from much earlier time frames than those of the ethnologist. One also has the supporting help of the historical linguist to suggest various lexical categories and items for which one can seek to find material evidence. This approach is multi-faceted and not strictly archaeological, but it provides a rigorous means for achieving a robust reconstruction of early forms of island societies.

An example of reconstruction: fishing gear

An example from the domain of technology will further illustrate the 'triangulation' approach to cultural reconstruction. On the basis of museum collections and ethnographic accounts, Anell (1955) surveyed the fishing methods and fishing gear of the Pacific. This comparative survey revealed the widespread distribution of the trolling lure in various characteristic forms in Polynesia, in Micronesia, and in parts of Melanesia, but the general absence of one piece or simple fishhooks in Eastern Island Melanesia or Western Polynesia. Various theories could be offered to account for the historical development of these discontinuities in the distribution of fishing gear.

The problem was given additional focus by Proto-Polynesian lexical reconstructions of the 1970s suggesting that both the simple fishhook, PPN *ma(a)ta'u*, and the trolling lure, PPN *paa*, are Ancestral Polynesian forms. Both items were quickly attested in the earliest archaeological levels of Eastern Polynesia by initial archaeological excavations of the 1960s and 70s, but contrary to expectations, neither was initially recovered from those of the West Polynesia–Fiji area presumed to have been the Polynesian homeland. No lures, and only a single simple fishhook, were recovered from an early level in Tongatapu, and another incomplete simple hook from a later level in Samoa, while close study revealed the historic rather than the prehistoric nature of the supposedly typical 'West Polynesian lure type' common in museum collections (Green 1974). A rather different form of lure proved to be more characteristic of West Polynesian examples from the late prehistoric period.

Against this initially confused and enigmatic picture, subsequent excavations in early Lapita and slightly later Lapita-related levels in West Polynesia and Eastern Melanesia began to yield one piece fishhooks from sites in a number of regions, and ultimately the existence of an entirely new early form of trolling lure was demonstrated as a possible ancestral form for the later Polynesian examples (Green, in press b). The material used for manufacture was not the pearl shell so common in ethnographic museum collections, but other shells such as *Trochus*. Our understanding of fishing gear development was at the same time further clarified by ecological explanations for the numerical increase and development of a variety of one piece fishhook forms in Eastern Polynesia, especially the Marquesas (Kirch 1980). Correlation of fishing gear with faunal assemblages indicating the range of species taken (or lack thereof) showed that in the early Lapita assemblages of West Polynesia and Eastern Melanesia, other methods (such as spearing, netting, trapping, and poisoning) were the preferred methods of taking lagoon fish, while pelagic fish — generally taken on lures — were only being caught occasionally (Kirch and Dye 1979; Green, in press b). In sum, when the varied data from ethnography, historical linguistics, and archaeology were finally brought to bear on the problem, a quite different evolution of Polynesian fishing gear from that proposed solely on the basis of Anell's museum data, or from historical linguistics, resulted.

Structural components of Ancestral Polynesian culture

The association of an Ancestral Polynesian culture with the last stages of the archaeologically recovered Lapita cultural complex (characterized by a type of Polynesian plain ware pottery) has been demonstrated in West Polynesia (Kirch 1979, 1984). Its highly probable correlation with the Proto-

Polynesian language has also been argued in detail (Pawley and Green 1973; Green 1981). The derivation of Ancestral Polynesian culture from the earlier stages of the Lapita cultural complex, widespread in island Melanesia as well as in West Polynesia, has also been shown archaeologically (Green 1979a). Again, the correlation of this widespread Lapita cultural complex with the Remote Oceanic subgroup of the Oceanic languages, if not with Oceanic itself, is a reasonable inference (Pawley and Green, in press). Also, as Pawley (1981, 285, 297–8) has in several places remarked, as comparative linguistic work has progressed within the Austronesian family, it has become more and more evident that the Polynesian societies derive most of their common technology not just from Proto-Polynesian, but from Proto-Oceanic. Thus both sets of lexicons, internal and external witnesses so to speak, bear on the Proto-Polynesian, Ancestral Polynesian culture problem, and relate to the Lapita cultural complex in its various earlier and later, Eastern and Western manifestations.

Recently, Pawley (1982b) using linguistic data for Proto-Oceanic and Proto-Polynesian has argued that at an early stage these were already ranked societies with chiefs as well as various specialists, and were even then to some extent weakly stratified. Hayden (1983), reviewing the data and models for the Lapita cultural complex, has considered whether an egalitarian or stratified incipient chiefdom model better fits the available evidence. Through use of economics, and especially the labor investments of a sea-going society involved in making and sailing large ocean-going canoes over considerable distances plus a society involved in the trade and transport of primitive valuables between elites in the Lapita communities, Hayden comes down firmly on the side of the Lapita cultural complex representing an already stratified society. Further support for his argument seems possible to me from a study of the elaborate pottery and its distribution within Lapita sites, but this has not yet been formally attempted. If these arguments from linguistics and archaeology are accepted, the probability of a Polynesian society being some form of an incipient chiefdom from its initial stages seems highly likely, as Kirch (1984) also argues in his recent study of the evolution of Polynesian societies. The question I ask in the remainder of this paper is, 'What range of material structural features, recoverable archaeologically, might we expect Ancestral Polynesian sites to contain?'

Comparative ethnological studies have long suggested the household as one of the basic structural units throughout Polynesia. Such households are largely identified in social and economic terms, but often have explicit material manifestations in the early ethnographic accounts. Not surprisingly, archaeological settlement pattern studies in Polynesia have recently identified what have variously been termed *household units* (HHUs), *household clusters*, or *residential complexes*, especially in settlement pattern work in Samoa (Jennings, Holmer, and Jackmond 1982), Easter Island (McCoy 1976), Hawai'i (Cordy 1981, in press; Weisler and Kirch, 1985a), and New Zealand (Prickett 1982). The archaeologically demonstrated antiquity of these residential complexes in the respective islands is no more than 700 to 900 years, but the ethnographic and archaeological sources of data suggest to me that the household unit or residential complex are an Ancestral Polynesian type, potentially recoverable through excavation.

Household units have no exact or reconstructable linguistic equivalent that I can discover, but the proto-form *kaainga comes fairly close (Pawley ms.). Widespread meanings associated with the term are 'to be related' as of a family or line, and 'home' or 'dwelling place', or in Eastern Polynesia 'the portion of the land where one makes a home'. Certainly in Eastern Polynesia the meaning of 'homestead' is well attested, and it is a plausible reconstruction as part of the probable range of meanings for the Proto-Polynesian form also. The term in its initial element may be cognate with the Proto-Oceanic terms *kai or *kai(n), and Proto-Polynesian *kakai which referred to the people of a place, the inhabitants, the local community, and the Proto-Polynesian and late-stage Proto-Oceanic term *kainanga for the land-holding descent group (Pawley 1982b, 43–4).

The structural composition of the Ancestral Polynesian household unit also seems reasonably well indicated. From an ethnographic, ethnohistoric, and late prehistoric settlement pattern point of view, the dwelling, cook house, and canoe shed are consistent features everywhere (Green 1970). Linguistically, the house, *Ruma, and the building (possibly for public use), *pale, are well attested Proto-Oceanic forms. In Proto-Polynesian only, *fale meaning house is retained. Associated with it are a term for the ridge pole (*ta'ufufu), three terms for rafters (*fatunga, *hoka, *kaso), post (*pou), thatch (*rau), inner room (*loki), gravel floor (*kilikili), floor covering (*faaliki), outside pavement (*paepae), outside earth oven (*'umu), and storage shelf (*fata) inside or outside the house (Pawley and Green 1971). Besides the cook house (*fale 'umu), the canoe house or shed (*folau) is designated linguistically.

Archaeologically, a few house structures with both straight and curved sides are indicated from posthole patterns in early Western Lapita sites in the Reef Islands and New Caledonia (Green 1979a; Green and Mitchell 1983). Round-ended houses are known from early contexts in Western Samoa (Davidson 1974), the Society Islands (Emory 1979; Green, Green, Rappaport, Rappaport, and Davidson 1967, 166–7), Easter Island (McCoy 1979), Hawai'i (Kirch 1975), and perhaps the Marquesas (Sinoto 1979). Straight-sided houses are known from early contexts in the Marquesas (Sinoto 1979), Easter Island (McCoy 1979), Tahiti (Emory 1979), and New Zealand (Prickett 1979). Both types frequently occurred contemporaneously in the same communities as in the Society Islands, although other island groups often favored either one form or the other at any given point in the cultural sequence. Ethnographically, where the two types occur together, they are functionally differentiated either by status of the occupants, or into dwelling and cooking/storage shed categories.

It is my view that both house forms are Ancestral Polynesian, and probably Lapita in cultural origin. However, archaeological documentation for the rectangular house form in West Polynesian sequences at all periods, and in Lapita site contexts generally, is at present weak. The water-sorted gravel spread on the floors of houses and the associated stone pavements are attested to archaeologically throughout Polynesia for the later periods and have at least a 2000 year time span in Western Samoa (Davidson 1974). Stone-kerb outlined fireplaces are also found widely throughout Polynesia, with later examples best known from New Zealand, Easter Island, Hawai'i, and Samoa (Green 1979b). They have also been found in early Lapita contexts in New Caledonia (Frimigacci 1970). The earth oven is even better documented, from Lapita contexts (Green 1979a) on up to the present throughout Polynesia, although the association with a cook house near to the dwelling is not yet well demonstrated archaeologically. Still, examples of prehistoric cook houses excavated in several island groups of Polynesia suggest that the number of finds will increase and their time depth grow longer. Only in Hawai'i has the canoe house (in stone) any well-established antiquity based on archaeology (Cordy 1981, 82–3), largely because seaside situations elsewhere which might have demonstrated this have not been explored so as to reveal its presence.

While on the domestic level some success is beginning to attend the archaeological identifications of ethnologically and linguistically expected categories, this is less so on the community level. From comparative ethnographic and ethnohistoric accounts, and from late period settlement patterns, one would expect the following community structures to have been present in Ancestral Polynesian settlements: a community house for guests, assemblies and entertainment; a god house; and a 'Polynesian style' men's house where unmarried males gathered (Green 1970). The god house (PPN *fale aitu) is reconstructed linguistically, but I have as yet not found Proto-Polynesian terms for the community house or men's house. *Fale karioi is certainly a probable Proto-Central Eastern Polynesian term for the community structure. Archaeologically, each of the above categories has been demonstrated as fully prehistoric in some Polynesian societies, but with only limited distribution and time depth. Community houses with a 600 year antiquity in the Society Islands (Green et al. 1967) and several hundred years in Samoa (Davidson 1974) are known, god houses have tentatively been identified as prehistoric in Samoa and the Society Islands, and structures with a similar antiquity have been classified as men's houses in Hawai'i (Green 1980, 68; Cordy 1981, 82–3). Not yet sufficient data from which to infer an expected archaeological age of several thousand years indicated by the linguistic and more recent comparative evidence.

Other communal structures to be anticipated based on ethnohistoric evidence are a Proto-Polynesian linguistic term *tafua, or platform for various secular or council meetings and similar events, and the *mala'e, a public meeting place with apparently strong religious connotations. The *tafua* is probably to be associated with the Proto-Polynesian term *fono*, for the deliberative assembly. Linguistically the term for *tafua* as a platform is present in Tonga and Niue, but it is lacking throughout the Samoic Outlier subgroup, where the *fono* in a meeting house is the evident alternative. *Tahua* as a council platform comes to the fore again in Central Eastern Polynesia, and is known in Hawai'i and New Zealand with related though more specialized meanings. Platforms designated by forms cognate with *tafua* are known archaeologically from the Society Islands (Emory 1979) and the Marquesas (Suggs 1961) as well as Niue (Trotter 1979). The *fono* houses of the Samoic Outlier area are presumably the structural equivalents in social and political terms. They are not yet securely identified archaeologically.

The Proto-Polynesian *mala'e* presents more of a problem. It (or its equivalent) as a formal structure is well known linguistically and archaeologically from Eastern Polynesia for the last 600 to 700 years, where it has strong religious connotations. This is less so for West Polynesia, where it is more often something of an open space with little or no easily identified structural content to reveal its presence in archaeological surveys and excavations. An ancestral form may be strongly posited on the linguistic and ethnographic evidence, but its origin, shape, features, and function may prove difficult to demonstrate by means of archaeology.

In this respect Goodenough's (1983) speculations on the symbolic layout of Malekulan villages in Vanuatu as a structural homologue of the Tahitian *marae* on the one hand and the Maori *marae* on the other are perhaps not so far-fetched as they might at first seem. What he was suggesting is that the Malekulan dance ground and the way it was organized as a ceremonial place is a cognate institution with the Tahitian and Maori *marae*. He thought them also presumably cognate with ceremonial grounds associated with communities in other Oceanic societies, which made me recall the village layout and its symbolism recently described for the Kwaio of Malaita in the Solomons (Keesing 1982, 60–74). The components, in various arrangements of meeting house, open space, uprights, images, and their symbolic arrangements in terms of male/female, sacred/secular, up/down, etc., are all part of an old Oceanic Austronesian religious complex which we are only just beginning to understand.

The last structural feature is the *afu*, a raised place made for a house or religious structure. It is closely associated with the *mala'e*. The evidence from Easter Island (McCoy 1979) plus that of Central Eastern Polynesia give the cognate *ahu* form there an antiquity of 1000 to 1200 years and a marked religious connotation. This connotation is also true for some island groups in West Polynesia, such as the Ellice Islands. But elsewhere in Fiji—West Polynesia the term has largely secular associations, as in the Fijian *yavu*, the foundation mound of a house. Thus the antiquity of the *afu* in the West Polynesia—Fiji area is as yet uncertain and its function — secular, religious, or both — unknown.

In summary, using a 'triangulation strategy' which combines archaeological, ethnological, and historical linguistic evidence, I have tried to identify some of the probable Ancestral Polynesian structural categories and social and material manifestations. Detailed histories still need to be written for each of the categories identified. The degree to which culture historians can currently reconstruct typical early Polynesian society as reflected in its structure is still fairly limited, although evidence continues to get better all the time. It is from the probable various ancestral forms and categories that have been identified, however, that the more complex highly stratified societies of Hawai'i, Tonga, the Society Islands, and Samoa with their more elaborate structural features have evolved. Thus the archaeological excavation of the earlier, if not ancestral, forms is a crucial task in any evolutionary approach to the problem, if our theories are to have a firm grounding in prehistory.

Chapter 7

Social evolution in ancient Hawai'i

Robert J. Hommon

When Captain James Cook established contact between
Hawai'i and the non-Polynesian world in AD 1778, the
Hawai'ian archipelago was divided among four relatively large,
complex polities generally considered to have been highly
developed chiefdoms or incipient states. This paper explores
aspects of the evolution of these polities using archaeological,
documentary and traditional sources.[1]

The eight major Hawai'ian islands total 16,706.5 km²
in area and range in size from 116.5 km² Kaho'olawe to
10,458.4 km² Hawai'i (fig. 7.1). At contact, the Hawai'ian
polities included territories ranging from about 2253 km² to
10,618 km² with populations estimated at 25,000 to 100,000
(Schmitt 1971; Hommon 1975, 70–95; 1976, 22, 23, 139–48).
These polities were divided into about thirty named districts
such as Kona, Hilo and Kohala of the island of Hawai'i, with
populations ranging from roughly 4000 to 25,000.

The ahupua'a

Each district consisted of an average of about thirty
and as many as 100 named territorial units called *ahupua'a*,
each of which formed the primary social and economic sphere
of a local community. Most *ahupua'a* were long, narrow land
sections extending perpendicularly from the coast several
kilometers inland to altitudes of at least 500 m. Boundaries
of typical *ahupua'a* cut across the succession of regional
ecozones formed by variation in altitude, rainfall and other
environmental factors so that each community had direct
access to the entire local range of available resources. These
resources typically included, fish, shellfish, salt, coral and
other resources of the inshore and littoral zones; potable
water sources, habitation areas and garden areas in the coastal
zone; agricultural lands in the inland zone and products such
as wood, fibers and tool quality basalt from the forests and
mountain slopes of the uplands beyond the field systems.

Ahupua'a varied greatly in size, population, quality
and quantity of resources and in other respects. Those of the
larger islands varied from about 10 to 26 km² in area, and
included about 0.8 to 1.6 km of coastline; those of the
smaller islands (Ni'ihau, Lana'i and probably Kaho'olawe)
averaged at least 29 km² in area and included at least 4 km of
coastline. The average *ahupua'a* population at contact is
estimated to have been roughly 200 (cf. Hommon 1976, 23,
table 1). *Ahupua'a* may be divided into two broadly defined
types: the wet and the dry, that is, those with irrigated
agricultural systems dependent on permanent streams and/or
springs, and those without such systems. Irrigated pondfield
systems, in which the staple was taro (*Colocasia esculenta*),
commonly were situated on the terraced floors of geologically
mature valleys (cf. Kirch and Kelly 1975; Earle 1978). Most
such valleys are on north to northeastern coasts that face the

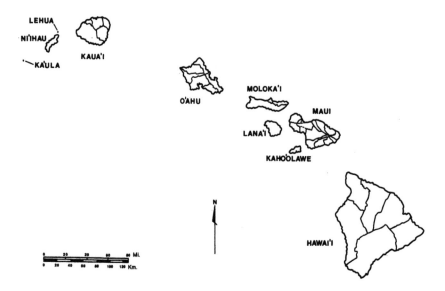

Fig. 7.1. The Hawai'ian Islands, showing ancient district boundaries.

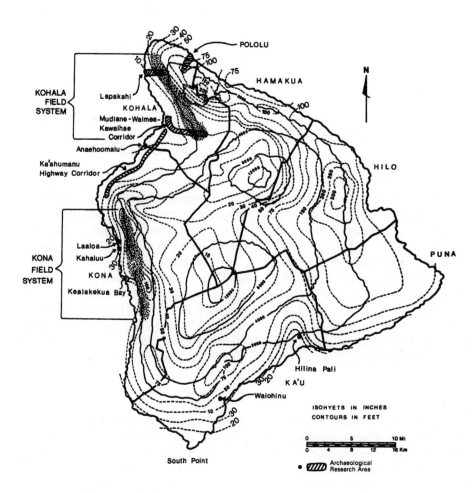

Fig. 7.2. The island of Hawai'i with ancient districts (in capitals) and archaeological research areas.

prevailing trade winds, though a number of leeward valleys such as Makaha and Waianae, Oahu, also contain ancient irrigated systems (cf. Green 1980).

The staples grown in the dry agricultural systems, dependent on rainfall, and to a lesser extent on occasional flood-water irrigation, included the sweet potato (*Ipomoea batatas*), dry land taro, and yam (*Dioscorea* spp.). The most extensive known dry agricultural complexes were two field systems in the inland zone of the Kona and Kohala districts of leeward Hawai'i (Kirch 1984, 181–92). The Kona Field System measures about 29 km long by 3.2 to 4.8 km in width and the Kohala Field System to the north is about 24 km long and 0.8 to 4.8 km wide (fig. 7.2). The upper boundaries of these and other dry agricultural complexes are usually between 610 and 1000 m in elevation. It should be noted that unlike the typical irrigated field system, which was limited to a single *ahupua'a* bounded by a valley's sides, each of the dry-land complexes such as the Kona Field System was composed of field complexes of numerous contiguous *ahupua'a*.

The Hawai'ian polity

Mid-nineteenth-century land records and other sources indicate that at European contact each *ahupua'a* community was self-sufficient to a marked degree, both economically and socially. A few instances of intra- and inter-district exchanges of food and other items are documented in the nineteenth century and preliminary archaeological evidence indicates fairly wide distribution of basalt adzes and possibly other stone tools from localized quarries. However, it appears that most *ahupua'a* were capable of producing sufficient quantities of goods both for most local subsistence needs and for the support of the chiefly hierarchy.

Sahlins's analysis of documentary data pertaining to the late eighteenth and early nineteenth centuries, and Earle's related archaeological and ethnohistorical research focussing on the Halele'a District, Kaua'i, indicate that at contact the *ahupua'a* community commonly consisted of an assemblage of ego-based bilateral kindreds (interrelated to varying degrees by marriage) rather than corporate kinship units, and that communities displayed a strong tendency toward endogamy (Sahlins 1973, 1974; Earle 1978). Most members of the self-contained *ahupua'a* community were *maka'ainana*, a term that referred at the time of contact to the general class of non-chiefs or commoners, who were fishermen, farmers and craftworkers. The apparent absence among the commoners of kinship-based units existing beyond the life of an individual, and the pronounced tendency to *ahupua'a* self-sufficiency, are factors that are essential to the investigation of socio-political evolution in precontact Hawai'i.

By the time of contact, the cleavage between Hawai'ian commoners and *ali'i* or chiefs was distinct and profound. Chiefs served as managers and administrators and were seldom directly engaged in production. In contrast with commoners, whose bilateral kindreds were evidently seldom reckoned beyond two ascending generations, chiefs customarily maintained genealogies at least ten ascending generations in length. An individual chief's social rank was determined during the *hale naua* ceremony at the accession of a paramount chief by ascertaining, through a series of explicit questions, the number of ascending generations that separated him from the new paramount's ancestral line. In general, rank varied inversely with the number of generations required to link the two ancestral lines. According to the early nineteenth-century Hawai'ian scholar David Malo (1951, 192), the interrogation customarily extended to the tenth ascending generation. As the genealogical requirements shifted with the accession of each paramount, and rank tended to diminish with each passing generation, hypergamy was a major chiefly concern. The desire for high-ranked marriage partners was undoubtedly responsible in part for the relatively cosmopolitan, or more accurately, archipelagic, outlook of the higher-ranked chiefs that was in marked contrast to that of the community-centered commoner (cf. Malo 1951, 61). A study of 319 high-ranked chiefs in traditional and historical sources, for example, shows that more than half were within one generation (as participant, parent or offspring) of a marriage between individuals identified with different islands (and often, different polities) (Hommon 1975, 27–48). Available evidence indicates that the economic, political and social advantages of marriage among chiefs had, by the time of western contact, resulted in a high degree of class endogamy.

The political structure of Hawai'i at contact paralleled the chiefly kinship pyramid, but was not identical with it. This structure included, in its simplest outline, the paramount chief or *ali'i nui*, who was of high but not necessarily the highest possible rank; a body of powerful chiefs associated with each of the districts under his control, and the numerous administrators of the constituent *ahupua'a* community units. It was customary for the paramount chief, on coming to power, to redistribute the various administrative posts of the realm to those whose kinship positions had been ratified during the *hale naua* ceremony. According to Malo (1951, 192), these posts were assigned in a way that was consonant with their respective ranks as established by this ceremony. The redistribution of administrative posts at the accession of a new paramount was undoubtedly a complex procedure, given the intricate interweaving of ancestral branches, the shifting factional rivalries among the *ali'i* and the circumstances surrounding accession (i.e., whether it took place by peaceful inheritance, by usurpation or by conquest), as well as other variables such as the social and political relationship between the old paramount and the new.

The primary responsibility of the local *ahupua'a* administrator, termed the *konohiki* in the nineteenth-century records, was to ensure the provisioning of the governmental bodies at the district and supra-district levels with food and craft goods. The contribution of goods during the annual Makahiki festival season has sometimes been likened to redistribution characteristic of a chiefdom. However, the collected goods were divided among the chiefs only. 'No share of this property . . . was given to the people' (Malo 1951, 143). The commoners, then, participated in a dual economy: a local economy satisfying the needs of the community, and a 'public economy' for the support of the administrative hierarchy.

Paralleling the two contrasting social structures and the double economy were two religious systems manifest, on the one hand, in the rituals surrounding subsistence and family affairs as performed by commoners in small local shrines; and, on the other, in the supra-community ceremonies performed by priests of high chiefly rank at major temples to ensure universal fertility and success in large-scale endeavors such as war (Malo 1951; Hommon 1976, 109–20).

The social fabric of each Hawai'ian polity at the time of western contact was rent by fissures both horizontal and vertical. The social strata or classes were separated by distinctly different economic functions, social norms, marriage patterns, political potentials and ritual duties. The commoner class was itself fragmented by the centripetal tendency of each *ahupua'a* to operate as a self-sufficient economic and social unit. The actual degree of fragmentation within these polities was probably even greater than is depicted here. For example, space does not allow discussion of: (1) the *kauwa*, apparently a small endogamous slave class; (2) stratification within the *ali'i* class; and (3) at least two additional administrative levels made necessary by the occasional presence of land units interposed hierarchically between the *ahupua'a* and the district. The language, cultural history and chiefly genealogical web shared throughout the archipelago certainly acted to ameliorate the effects of fragmentation, but such factors cannot account for the form or boundaries of the polities that existed at the time of western contact. The archipelago had never been united as a single polity, nor were the precontact polities necessarily coterminous with any island, district, *ahupua'a* or any other economically or socially based land unit. Further, while an understanding of chiefly genealogies is essential to an analysis of Hawai'ian political history, politics was no longer simply a function of the kinship system, and political boundaries were in no sense equivalent to those of any corporate kinship unit's territory.

As we have seen, no such society-wide corporate unit existed. Instead, politics itself had become the organizing principle of the maximal social unit. Within political boundaries, respect and tribute were due to the ruling chief not as senior relative but as occupant of the paramount political office. By the time of western contact, this office and, by extension, all administrative posts redistributed by the paramount were often attained by the application of military force rather than through inheritance (Hommon 1976, 140–8, passim) a process that would tend to weaken perceived kinship between residents of local communities and members of the administrative hierarchy. The most extreme demonstration of this political fact of life was conquest warfare as practiced in Hawai'i by the eighteenth century. Following conquest, surviving resident commoners ordinarily remained in their *ahupua'a* to produce

for local needs and for the newly established officials. Traditional and historical sources make it clear that the explicit purpose of war in ancient Hawai'i was often increased tribute for the government (cf. Kamakau 1961, 45–6, 62, 106, 185, 198; Hommon 1976, 153–60).

In summary, each Hawai'ian polity at the time of western contact was large, populous and complex and included two distinct social classes. These classes as well as the constituent self-contained communities were linked not by kinship but rather through the operation of a political apparatus that held the monopoly of power within well-defined and well-defended boundaries. Phenomena such as endogamous socio-economic classes, a specialized governmental apparatus, conquest warfare and the absence of large-scale corporate kinship units are very rare in stateless societies and are common in state societies. Whether, as I have argued elsewhere (Hommon 1976), the precontact Hawai'ian polities were incipient states or had reached but not exceeded the limits of the stateless society (Sahlins 1974, 5), it is clear that they represent a crucial stage in the evolution of complex society.

The archaeological data
Given the indisputably Polynesian roots of Hawai'ian culture and the absence of evidence for the imposition of the peculiarly Hawai'ian socio-political system summarized above from outside, it is reasonable to suggest that this system evolved in the Hawai'ian Islands from an antecedent resembling the non-egalitarian Polynesian conical clan or ramage (Hommon 1976, 74, 174–6; Sahlins 1974, 23, 39, 48; Kirch 1984). Cognates of the Hawai'ian term *maka'ainana* (i.e. the commoner class) elsewhere in Polynesia usually refer to a conical clan or a segment thereof (Kirch 1984, 65–6). Such units tend to be land-holding groups. I have suggested elsewhere that such corporate groups ('archaic *maka'ainana*') once existed in Hawai'i and that their original territories were the districts such as Kona and Kohala of the island of Hawai'i (Hommon 1976, 74–5, 174–6, 233–4).

Only a few of the potential archaeological approaches to the study of the evolution of Hawai'i's socio-political system have as yet produced significant results. Earle's use of nineteenth-century ethnohistoric records to supplement archaeological data has already been mentioned (Earle 1978). Recent intensive research at Kawela, Moloka'i, promises to contribute significantly to an understanding of architectural and spatial correlates of *ahupua'a* social structure (Weisler and Kirch 1985). Only preliminary results of this research are available at present. The study of the monumental architecture of temple foundations and administrative centers has thus far contributed relatively little to an understanding of the rise of complex society in Hawai'i. Very few temple structures have been investigated (cf. Ladd 1973) and further work in such structures is unlikely in the near future. While power was highly centralized in Hawai'i, this tendency was not reflected in marked settlement pattern nucleation. The largest settlements appear to be no more than large villages.

The absence of larger settlements is in part due to the fact that the entourages and administrative apparatus of the paramount chiefs, while large, were highly mobile, moving from place to place throughout the realm at intervals of a few weeks to a few years. Most of the sites favored as temporary seats of government by ancient chiefs are no longer available for archaeological study, having been expunged from the landscape by twentieth-century development. The two settlements of Ka'awaloa and Kekua on Kealakekua Bay, Kona, Hawai'i, the only relatively intact major administrative centers in the islands, have not yet been investigated in depth.

This brief review of archaeological research addressing the evolution of the Hawai'ian polities would be incomplete without reference to the recent study by Ross Cordy (1981), which is based primarily on inferences drawn from investigations of house foundations and other stone structures. Unfortunately, space does not allow an extended discussion of this ambitious approach. A note concerning one problem in the interpretation of the data must suffice.

Cordy has given insufficient consideration to alternatives to the general proposition underlying much of his study that the size and massiveness of a precontact habitation site varied directly with the social rank of its residents (Cordy 1981, 50, 86, passim). One of the important alternative explanations for variation in site size is the reuse or continued use and enlargement of sites during the post-contact period. Stone structures along Hawai'ian coasts such as the north Kona area which is central to Cordy's study often display structural and artifactual evidence of nineteenth- and twentieth-century use. In one instance, at least fifteen of 106 structures that Cordy lists as examples of precontact sites of various functional types yielded post-contact artifacts during test excavations, yet he ignored age and duration of use as possible alternatives to functional variability in explaining size and massiveness (Cordy 1981, 155, table 53, Appendix D).[2]

The present approach to the problem of the evolution of complex Hawai'ian polities from postulated pre-existing archaic *maka'ainana* focusses on large-scale demographic, economic and social processes inferred from an archipelago-wide body of archaeological data.

The last two decades have seen the rapid growth of archaeological research on all major islands except Ni'ihau. Most of this work has been financed by public agencies and private firms complying with Federal, State and County historic preservation statutes. A comprehensive collection of archaeological reports amassed recently by the Society for Hawai'ian Archaeology includes more than 1000 items from these twenty years (Matthew Spriggs, personal communication). Unfortunately few attempts have been made to summarize or synthesize this vast body of material and very little of it has appeared in published form (see, however, Kirch 1985a).

Among the subjects addressed by the reports of these twenty years have been stone technology at the large basalt adze quarry complex near the 4205 m summit of Mauna Kea,

Hawai'i (McCoy 1977, Cleghorn 1982), the highly developed Hawai'ian aquacultural system of fishponds (Kikuchi 1973) and the exploitation of marine resources at coastal sites (Kirch 1979b). Given the importance of the ways in which Hawai'ian sites were distributed throughout the various ecozones of the *ahupua'a*, an essential element in most recent research has been the study of the complexities of the typically dispersed Hawai'ian settlement pattern. The larger archaeological projects of recent years have included surveys of entire *ahupua'a* (Green 1980; Kirch and Kelly 1975; Weisler and Kirch 1985a), of the entire island of Kaho'olawe (Hommon 1980), and of sections of several adjacent *ahupua'a* (Clark and Kirch 1983).

Perhaps the most important general inference to be drawn from research in a number of areas in the last few years has been that the ancient Hawai'ians witnessed and were probably in part responsible for major environmental change before western contact (Kirch 1982). For example, presently available evidence indicates that the large marsh of Kawainui behind the town of Kailua, Oahu, may have been formed in part by human-induced siltation in what had previously been a marine embayment (Kelly and Clark 1980). In another case recent archaeological and historical research suggests that the relatively extensive dry-land forest existing on the island of Kaho'olawe when its inland zone was first brought under cultivation (c. AD 1400) had been replaced by grassland by the time of western contact (AD 1778), and that this process was largely the result of agricultural clearing and the collection of firewood (Hommon 1983).

Virtually the entire range of archaeological data is relevant to the study of as broad a subject as the evolution of Hawai'ian society. Essential to such a processual study is chronological control. The development of a Hawai'ian chronological framework has been hampered by the absence of pottery or any other time-sensitive artifacts useful in developing detailed sequences and by the shortness and recentness of the precontact history. The latter two factors reduce the utility of radiocarbon age determinations, whose chronological ranges often span major portions of the precontact sequence and may include much of the post-contact period as well. During the 1970s, development of the analysis of alteration and hydration rinds on artifacts of volcanic glass, which are often plentiful in Hawai'ian sites, appeared to provide the much needed chronometric control with multiple, inexpensive, relatively narrow age ranges. The apparent benefits of this chronometric tool led to its enthusiastic adoption by researchers, often to the exclusion of radiocarbon analysis (Barrera and Kirch 1973, Cordy 1981, Hommon 1976, Kirch 1979, Morgenstein and Riley 1974 Morgenstein and Rosendahl 1976, Tuggle and Griffin 1973). During the last few years serious questions have been raised concerning the rates of hydration and alteration, and other aspects of this chronometric technique (Olson 1983). It seems likely that while the date range of a single sample may be unreliable to an unknown degree, clusters of volcanic glass age ranges are of value when considered in conjunction with other relevant data.

The chronological framework of the original version of the present evolutionary model (Hommon 1976) depended primarily on volcanic glass data. That presented here is based solely on radiocarbon age determinations. The primary focus here is upon the last four hundred years of precontact history, the period during which, it is suggested, ancient Hawai'ian society underwent major transformation.

The calendrical year ranges used here were derived from radiocarbon age determination data according to calibration tables in Klein *et al.* (1982), which represent a consensus of attempts during the past twenty-five years to correct for long-term variations in the radiocarbon content of atmospheric carbon dioxide. The resulting AD date ranges are considered to include relevant calendrical dates at the 95% confidence level.

The settlement pattern of most Hawai'ian *ahupua'a* at contact included a relatively narrow coastal zone, usually no more than about 400 m wide, in which were found most permanent habitations, and an inland zone, where the most extensive agricultural fields were situated. While exploitation of such resources as game birds and tool-quality basalt extended the pattern of intermittent use to the forests and beyond to the summits of the highest mountains, the focus here is on those portions of the inland zone that contained the extensive agricultural systems upon which both the domestic and public economies were markedly dependent at contact.

The evolutionary model

This model, based on inferences drawn from a broad range of archaeological and ethnohistoric information, is a tentative explanation of the evolution of the unique Hawai'ian polities. The model has been designed to summarize a body of data and observations, to present a number of propositions about ancient Hawai'i, and to generate archaeologically testable hypotheses that may be as useful to the conduct of further research in Hawai'i as were those generated by the first version of this model (cf. Green 1980, 71–9; Hommon 1980, item 8, pp. 7–10. passim; Kirch 1983, 14–15; Schilt 1984, 289–92).

For present purposes, the Hawai'ian archaeological data support a division of precontact history into three phases. Phase I (c. AD 500–1400) encompasses the initial colonization by Polynesian voyagers from islands (possibly the Marquesas) to the south and the establishment of coastal settlements throughout the island group. Phase II (c. 1400–1600) sees the initial large-scale expansion into the inland zone, the development of the *ahupua'a* system and the disintegration of the archaic *maka'ainana*. Phase III (c. 1600–1778), begins with the formation of polities resembling those described in the early written accounts and ends with Western contact.

Phase I

Available evidence indicates that the Hawai'ian Islands were first settled between about AD 400 and 600 (Kelly and

Clark 1980, 52; Kirch and Kelly 1975, 163; Pearson *et al.* 1971, 230). Though this time-frame (now commonly accepted by archaeologists working in Hawai'i) is adopted here, colonization during the period AD 1 to 400, as recently suggested by Kirch (personal communication) on the basis of recent reanalysis of data from South Point, Hawai'i, would not materially affect the essential elements of the model.

The assignment of eight hundred years or more of Hawai'ian prehistory to but a single evolutionary phase should not be taken to suggest cultural stability. Undoubtedly these centuries witnessed major change in many aspects of human existence as the Polynesian colonists and their descendants settled into and began to alter a wide variety of previously unoccupied environments. To indicate the profound changes that took place during this time, it is necessary only to note that a handful of settlers in a single colony had, by the end of Phase I, become several thousand people thinly distributed along some 1207 km of coastline. However, from the standpoint of the evolution of complex society, this long period is considered a single phase in that it preceded and set the stage for the Phase II inland expansion and its consequences, as discussed below.

The exploration and settlement of the coastal zones of the eight major islands were undoubtedly in large part responses to the subsistence needs of a burgeoning population. The study of paleodemography, particularly the expansion of a human population into a large, isolated, environmentally varied and previously unsettled archipelago is essential to the analysis of Hawai'i's socio-political evolution (Cordy 1981; Hommon 1976; Kirch 1979b, 1984). In the absence of an archipelago-wide model of population growth based on a general survey of archaeological data, it is assumed here for simplicity that population grew at a steady rate throughout the precontact period, a rate that would result in a doubling of population about once every 107 years.

Given this steady rate of growth, the Hawai'ian population would have reached roughly 1/16th of its size at western contact by about the year AD 1350. For example, if the population figures at contact were 225,000 for the Hawai'ian archipelago, 100,000 for Hawai'i island (Schmitt 1971) and 25,000 for the Kona district of Hawai'i, then the figures in AD 1350 would have been 14,000 for the archipelago, 6250 for Hawai'i and 1600 for Kona.

The fragmentary archaeological data seem to indicate that by the fourteenth century the Hawai'ian population was distributed sparsely and discontinuously, in small settlements, along the coasts of all the major islands. The paucity of inland archaeological sites before about AD 1400 appears to indicate that marine resources and the agricultural production of the coastal zone were sufficient to meet nearly all the subsistence needs of the Hawai'ian population throughout Phase I.

Cordy (1981, 176–81) has noted regions he calls 'buffer zones' in northern Kona district adjacent to the boundary between Kona and Kohala districts and in southeast Kohala adjacent to the Kohala–Hamakua boundary. These zones appear to have remained unoccupied until the fifteenth century. Cordy suggests that these buffer zones represent boundaries between 'societies', a term that he equates roughly with polities (Cordy 1981, 3). He goes on to suggest that the establishment of settlements in the formerly unoccupied buffer zones signals the unification of previously separate adjacent entities into a single society (Cordy 1981, 181).

In the present model, these boundary regions, two of which are the geographical equivalent of Cordy's buffer zones, are viewed as phenomena of socio-economic history rather than as politically imposed borderlands. A cursory inspection of environmental variables in the regions of the ancient Hawai'ian district boundaries is sufficient to show that districts were often bounded by uninhabitable mountain ranges or by arid and/or marginally productive lands. Examples of mountain boundaries are those between the windward and leeward districts of both Oahu and Moloka'i. More significant for present purposes, however, are non-mountainous boundaries for which archaeological data are available: Cordy's Kona–Kohala example and the Waianae–Ewa boundary on Oahu. It is reasonable to infer that sparse rainfall, absence of permanent water courses, and a general lack of conditions conducive to agriculture were in large part responsible for the absence of settlements in these regions throughout most of the precontact sequence.

The boundary information sketched here indicates that at least some of the island subdivisions that have come to be known as districts evolved as territorial units whose geographical limits were determined by environmental factors that discouraged or prevented settlement. It seems reasonable to suggest that each of these proto-districts was the homeland of an archaic *maka'ainana*, originally established by settlers arriving from an already established community. Although contact was undoubtedly maintained with the other proto-

districts, most day-to-day interactions were probably contained within the geographical, social and economic boundaries of the local archaic *maka'ainana* once it had grown to sufficient size to be relatively self-sufficient.

Ahupua'a as they existed at the time of western contact had not yet formed before the end of the fourteenth century. The Phase I archaeological data indicate the absence of both factors essential to the development of the *ahupua'a*: a local community of sufficient size to allow the high degree of social self-sufficiency documented in the early post-contact literature, and inland agricultural complexes of sufficient size and productivity to support such a population.

Phase II

The volcanic glass chronometric data used in the original version of the present model of Hawai'ian socio-political evolution (Hommon 1976) indicated that large-scale expansion into the inland zone did not begin until the fifteenth century. The lateness of this phenomenon in the Hawai'ian sequence, its archipelagic scale, the heavy dependence placed on inland agriculture at contact, and most importantly the implications for Hawai'ian socio-cultural evolution required that re-examination of the inland expansion hypothesis be an essential element of the present study.

For this purpose radiocarbon age determinations were assembled from all available reports of archaeological research in the inland zone during the past fifteen years. The 163 radiocarbon samples from 132 archaeological sites and features in nineteen inland areas on six islands (figs. 7.2–6) reported in twenty-three literature sources are summarized in the Appendix and represented graphically in fig. 7.7. With the exception of twelve samples from four features in the Mauna Kea adze quarry complex, all samples are directly or indirectly associated with agricultural activity in the inland zone. The

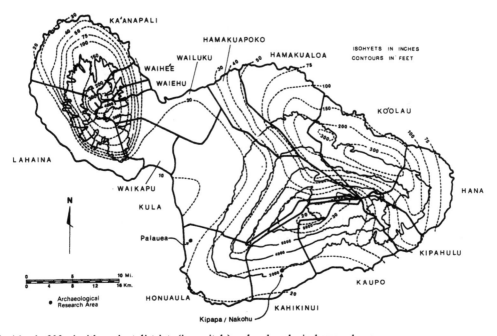

Fig. 7.3. The island of Maui with ancient districts (in capitals) and archaeological research areas.

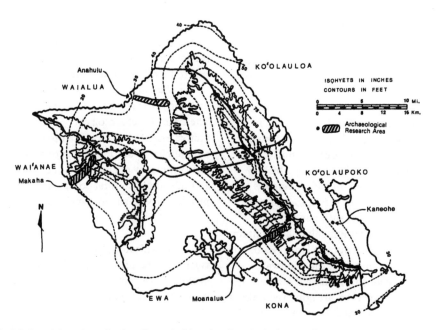

Fig. 7.4. The island of Oahu with ancient districts (in capitals) and archaeological research areas.

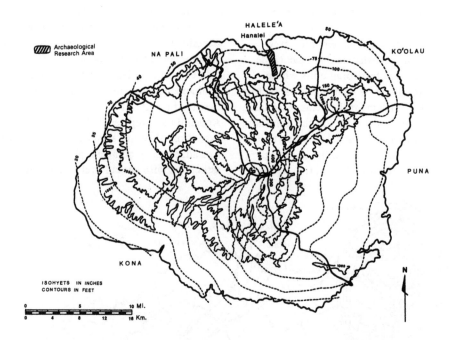

Fig. 7.5. The island of Kaua'i with ancient districts (in capitals) and archaeological research areas.

four samples that were split in two parts and subsequently analyzed by different radiocarbon laboratories are presented here as eight entries. Age determinations reported by laboratories as 'modern, less than *x* years' are represented in fig. 7.7 as dashed lines symbolizing radiocarbon years. All other data are symbolized by solid lines representing calibrated ranges of calendrical years. Ranges labeled 'R' have

been rejected by the authors reporting them as being inconsistent with associated chronological data.

Precise quantification of the inland expansion phenomenon is precluded by the fact that the event 'dated' by the radiocarbon-based data (such as the cutting of firewood) may have occurred at any point along the indicated calendrical range with equal probability. Given the distribution of ranges,

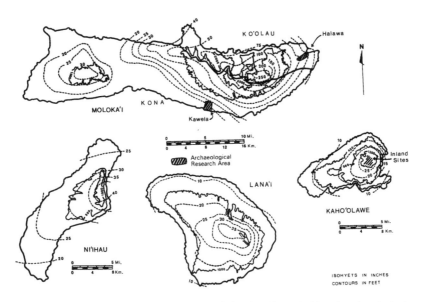

Fig. 7.6. The islands of Moloka'i, Ni'ihau, Lana'i and Kaho'olawe with districts (in capitals) and archaeological research areas.

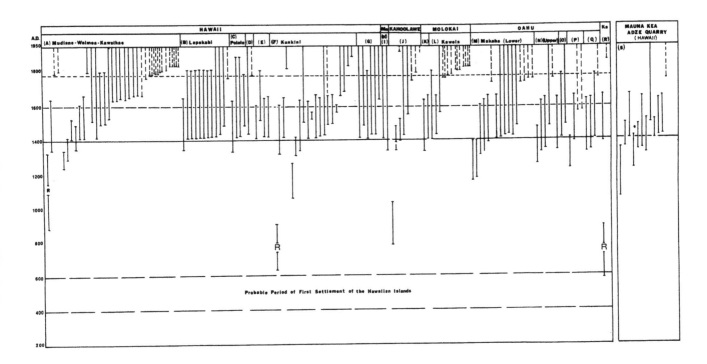

Fig. 7.7. Date ranges of Hawai'ian inland archaeological sites and features based on radiocarbon age determinations. The solid vertical bars represent calibrated calendrical ranges (cf. Klein *et al.* 1982). The dashed bars represent uncalibrated ranges of age determinations reported as 'modern, less than *x* years'. The letter 'R' in the center of a bar indicates that the date range was rejected by the author reporting it.

however, a statement that 90–95% of all events dated by samples from Hawai'ian inland zone sites probably occurred after AD 1400 would be in agreement with available data. The primary inference to be drawn from this chronological pattern, then, is that extensive agricultural use of Hawai'ian inland zones post-dated c. AD 1400, some nine hundred years after the initial colonization of these islands.

It should be noted that throughout the precontact period a wide variety of resources including stone, wood, fiber and other craft materials as well as medicinal herbs and some wild food items were probably collected in the inland areas. With the exception of quarrying for adze-quality basalt, these activities were evidently ephemeral and left little in the way of archaeological evidence. The 'inland expansion' that distinguishes Phase II from Phase I refers specifically to the development of large-scale permanent agricultural complexes. It is reasonable to speculate that beginning with initial settlement the inland zone was considered to be part of the territory of the archaic *maka'ainana*. Though the self-contained Phase I archaic *maka'ainana* may have been ancestral to the self-sufficient *ahupua'a*, an essential aspect of the present model is that the multi-*ahupua'a* district differed qualitatively from its predecessor and that the new pattern could have developed only after the inland expansion was well advanced.

The array of calibrated radiocarbon data from sites in the Mauna Kea adze quarries is quite similar to that of data from the inland zone agricultural complexes. If we assume that an increase in the number of utilized sites varies directly with the level of activity at the quarries, it is reasonable to suggest that production of basalt adzes increased significantly after AD 1400 in response to the need for tools for clearing agricultural fields of vegetation.

At this juncture a brief consideration of the present radiocarbon-derived chronology as compared with that based on volcanic glass analysis used in Hommon (1976) is instructive. The volcanic glass data from fifty-one sites in the coastal and inland zones of Hawai'i (figs. 7.8a and b) indicate initiation of a large-scale inland expansion about AD 1400, after at least 400 years of coastal development in the areas being dated. The similarity of this volcanic glass-derived chronology to that based on calibrated radiocarbon data suggests that, considered as a whole, the former may approximate calendrical chronology about as accurately as the latter.

The need for additional food for a continually growing population appears to be the simplest explanation for the inland expansion initiated about AD 1400. Among the alternate hypothetical engines of change, the one that is perhaps the most interesting and amenable to investigation is mid- to long-term climatic variation. Effectively, the most significant climatic variable in Hawai'i is rainfall. The 1983–4 drought in Hawai'i, in many regions the most severe in recorded history, appears to be a manifestation of the recent world-wide

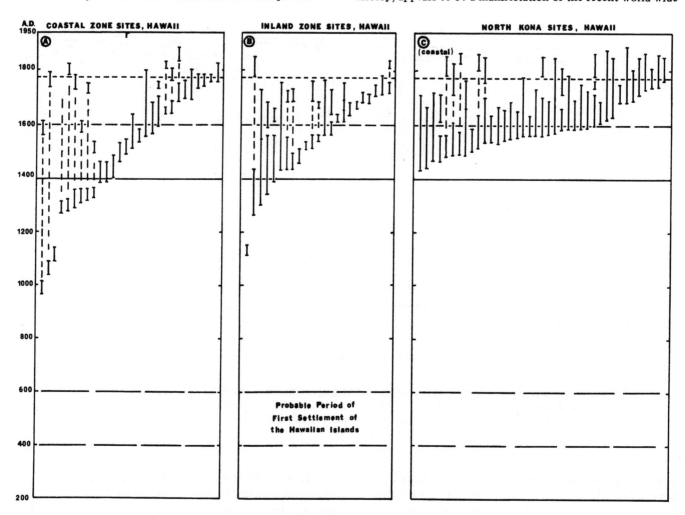

Fig. 7.8. Date ranges of Hawai'i Island sites and features based on volcanic glass age determinations. Sections A and B represent data summarized in Hommon (1976, 181–205). Section C represents data published in Cordy (1981, Appendix E).

'El Niño' phenomenon. This is but an extreme demonstration of the fact that Hawai'i's weather pattern is a small integral element in the global meteorological system. A study of the relationship between recent Hawai'ian weather patterns and those of other regions of the world might generate hypotheses concerning the effects of large-scale climatic variation in the past (such as the 'Little Ice Age' of the mid-second millennium AD) on Hawai'i's weather.

An essential element of the present model of socio-political evolution is that the Phase II inland expansion initiated the development of the *ahupua'a* as a socio-economic unit. It is suggested that the high degree of economic self-sufficiency evident at contact developed as most local communities discovered that the quantity and variety of resources available within the boundaries of their own *ahupua'a* were sufficient (from the standpoint of simple subsistence) to satisfy all community needs. Further, in most areas of Hawai'i exchange of goods between neighboring communities was probably obviated by the fact that the array and quality of goods varied little from one *ahupua'a* to the next. Two factors that may have led toward the high degree of *ahupua'a*-community endogamy evident in the early historical records are, first, the reduction in inter-community contacts that had previously accompanied exchange of goods; and second, the growth of the local population to the point that eligible marriage partners could be found with relative ease within the community.

Admittedly, such statements are highly speculative and for the most part untestable. They are attempts to explain the disintegration of the archaic *maka'ainana* which probably existed during the early centuries of Hawai'i's existence but had apparently disappeared by the time of western contact.

The nature of the process by which *ahupua'a* were formed may be hinted at by two observations that can be made concerning *ahupua'a* in the early nineteenth century. First, *ahupua'a* in relatively dry areas of marginal agriculture tended to be unusually large, suggesting that size was to some extent inversely related to productivity and resulting population density. Examples of this apparent correlation are the large *ahupua'a* of Lana'i, Ni'ihau and (probably) Kaho'olawe (all relatively dry islands with sparse populations) and of several of the arid district boundary regions of Hawai'i and Oahu. The second observation is that certain *ahupua'a* in some regions were divided lengthwise (along the coast to inland axis) following the unification of the islands by Kamehameha (AD 1753–1819). Though the latter case appears to have been a political act related to the distribution of lands among relatives and supporters, the process of multiplication of *ahupua'a* by territorial division may have been rooted in ancient tradition as a response to growing population within an *ahupua'a* community.

Phase III

Two disparate bodies of evidence suggest that the third and final phase in the evolution of the ancient Hawai'ian polities began around AD 1600. First, traditional historical accounts pertaining to the late sixteenth and early seventeenth centuries for the first time contain several references to the establishment and expansion of political boundaries and the succession to the office of *ali'i nui* (paramount chief) by force of arms (Hommon 1976, 279–80, 315–31). Second, the archaeological evidence appears to indicate that about AD 1600 the continued development of previously occupied inland agricultural complexes was accompanied by a significant increase in the occupation and use of arid, marginal regions including those at the boundaries of some districts.

The chronometric evidence for the initiation of Phase III is considerably more ambiguous than that for Phase II. It consists primarily of data from radiocarbon samples reported as 'modern less than x years' and on analyses of volcanic glass samples. The volcanic glass-derived chronology of thirty-nine sites and features along the arid coast of northern Kona district, Hawai'i (Cordy 1981, 156–7) suggests that this region was not extensively settled until roughly AD 1600 (fig. 7.8). According to Bertell Davis (University of Hawai'i, personal communication), the same is probably true of Barbers Point (the arid southwestern point) of Oahu, where Davis has conducted research for several years. Age determinations from 111 recently collected radiocarbon samples from Kaho'olawe (kindly provided by Paul H. Rosendahl, who is currently analyzing their chronometric significance) indicate that the most extensive use of this island may have post-dated AD 1600. As in the case of the other areas mentioned above, Kaho'olawe, the smallest and most arid of the main Hawai'ian islands, was only marginally suited to cultivation.

The archaeological and traditional historical data appear to be consistent with the following account of the years AD 1600 to 1778, Phase III of the present model.

As the first two centuries of inland expansion drew to a close, an increase of at least four-fold in the Hawai'ian population had accompanied the development of large, productive agricultural complexes in the salubrious core regions of the districts. Throughout much of Phase II as well as III, two general processes were probably increasing production within the district cores to meet the demands of the domestic and public sectors of the economy. First, it is likely that the large inland agricultural complexes continued to grow (though perhaps at a diminishing rate) as previously unused land within and at their environmentally determined borders were brought under cultivation (Hommon 1976, 294–6). The second process would have been the application of various intensification techniques such as the increased use of flood-water irrigation and mulching and the reduction of fallow periods.

Though the district cores included fully developed *ahupua'a* well before the end of Phase II, the sparsely populated boundary regions may have lacked both *ahupua'a* and clearly defined inter-district boundaries until the late sixteenth century. With continued population growth in the core regions it appears that settlement expanded into areas of diminishing agricultural potential. The settlement of Kaho'olawe and the boundary regions noted above seems to mark the final stage in this lateral expansion.

For the most part these areas contain no permanent watercourses and are agriculturally marginal by reason of their low annual rainfall. In the context of the present model this factor is particularly significant because of the susceptibility of these marginal areas to drought. In the Hawai'ian Islands both the departure from the mean annual rainfall value and the duration of droughts vary inversely with that mean (Nakamura 1933; Ripperton and Hosaka 1942, 10–11). Thus, with the expansion of population into marginal regions came an increase in the frequency and intensity of the adverse socio-political effects of crop failure and famine resulting from drought.

Accounts in the traditional literature and early post-contact historical sources indicate that famine was known to accompany drought in regions of low rainfall such as the Kula district of Maui (Kamakau 1961, 23–4) and the island of Ni'ihau (Vancouver 1967, II: 230; Portlock 1968, 184) that were dependent on dry-land agriculture. The fact that a part of the common knowledge was which wild plants were 'famine foods' suitable for consumption in times of emergency (Kamakau 1961, 23–4, 105; Malo 1951, 22, 43; Schmitt 1970, 110) suggests that famine was not a rare occurrence in ancient Hawai'i (Hommon 1976, 293–4).

The archaeological data at hand indicate that by the beginning of the seventeenth century a significant portion of the Hawai'ian population was dependent on agricultural production in regions where drought was relatively frequent. Despite the fact that population was probably sparse in such regions throughout the precontact period, their settlement has major ramifications because these regions form a substantial portion of the occupied zones of all islands. For example, regions averaging less than 30 inches of rain annually, where (if we assume a meteorological pattern similar to that of present-day Hawai'i) drought would have been a frequent problem, include nearly all the inhabited zones of Kaho'olawe, Ni'ihau and Lana'i and substantial portions of all the larger islands (Figs. 7.2–7.6).

A growing body of evidence indicates that human-induced environmental change reduced agricultural productivity in ancient Hawai'i. Post-contact accounts describe Kaho'olawe as an island entirely devoid of trees (Hommon 1980, Item 7, pp. 9–12), yet the botanical identification of charcoal samples from excavated precontact fireplaces on Kaho'olawe demonstrates that a variety of shrubs and small trees typical of the Hawai'ian dry-land forest once existed on the island (Hommon 1983, 95–8, 150–1; Murakami 1983). The presence of fireplaces estimated to have numbered several thousand in the inland zone of Kaho'olawe suggests that deforestation may have resulted from the collection of firewood as well as the clearing of agricultural land. Originally the Kaho'olawe evidence appeared to indicate that the massive erosion that has stripped the soil from about one quarter of the island

was well advanced by the end of the precontact period (Hommon 1980, item 7, pp. 60–5). On the basis of additional research, Spriggs concludes that precontact settlement of Kaho'olawe probably resulted not in catastrophic degradation but rather in the replacement of forest by grassland. He notes that while the development of grassland would not have precluded agriculture entirely, it would have reduced the amount of ground water available to sweet potatoes and other crops (Matthew Spriggs, personal communication). Kaho'olawe is sufficiently similar to other arid regions in Hawai'i, in terms of environment, general archaeological inventory and the apparent problems faced by the settlers, to support the contention that its history is in broad outline typical of such regions in Hawai'i (cf. Kirch 1982).

Following the Polynesian pattern, chiefs throughout Hawai'i's precontact history funded prestige and wielded power through control of the public economy. It is in the area of the public economy that archaeology can make its most valuable contribution to an understanding of the last major step in the evolution of complex society in Hawai'i. Archaeological evidence supports two significant observations concerning the quantity of goods and services available to the chiefly establishment in the late sixteenth century. First, the increase in land under cultivation and in population during the first two centuries of inland expansion brought a corresponding several-fold increase in the production of most if not all districts. Second, irregular and unpredictable oscillations in the amount of goods available to chiefs increased in magnitude with the increase of agricultural lands that were susceptible to drought, soil exhaustion resulting from insufficient fallow periods, increased soil erosion, the effects of deforestation, and other factors that reduced the capacity of the land to produce.

By the late sixteenth century the archaic *maka'ainana* had disintegrated as the growth of population within the districts had led to the development of the largely self-sufficient *ahupua'a*. While the chiefs may have been recognized in a distant and metaphorical way as senior relatives of the commoners, the genealogies that once demonstrated the relationship were being lost. The legitimacy of rule of the emerging chiefly class was increasingly based on the exercise of political power, which continued to be a chiefly monopoly, rather than senior kinship status itself.

It is during the late sixteenth to early seventeenth centuries, in the context (according to the model) of developing power-monopolizing governments whose tax revenues were varying unpredictably in magnitude and frequency even as they increased in the long term, that we find the traditional historical accounts cited above telling of the resolution of jurisdictional disputes by military force rather than by the application of the prerogatives of senior kinsmen. In view of the fact that, as noted in an earlier section, increased revenue was often the stated purpose for war in precontact and early post-contact times, it seems reasonable to suggest that these early instances of conquest, usurpation, and rebellion may have been precipitated by shortages resulting ultimately from the inland expansion as described here.

An additional note in regard to the environmental effects of the inland expansion concerns the 'Spriggs Hypothesis', which stresses a factor that has so far received little attention here: the windward–leeward dichotomy. Spriggs (1981) has suggested that in various island groups of Oceania, including Hawai'i, the apparent prehistoric human-induced degradation of uplands resulted not in catastrophic loss of agricultural potential but in the significant growth of fertile alluvial flats where intensive agriculture was practiced. While this hypothesis may apply in Hawai'i to those districts with permanent streams, the benefits of upland degradation would have been limited in drier leeward areas.

The traditions of the island of Hawai'i speak of a long-standing rivalry, punctuated by armed conflict, between windward and leeward polities. Though various episodes of conquest, rebellion and other mechanisms of unification and disintegration during the seventeenth and eighteenth centuries varied the constitution of the polities, they usually consisted of the windward districts of Hamakua, Hilo and Puna allied against a union of the leeward districts of Kohala, Kona and Ka'u (Kamakau 1961, 62, passim; Hommon 1976, 318–21). It is possible that the long-lived competition between these two polities was rooted in disparate economic histories.

The great majority of radiocarbon data used in the construction of the present model derive from leeward areas lacking perennial water sources, because most research has been done in leeward areas. The data from the windward valleys of Pololu (Hawai'i), Halawa (Moloka'i), and Hanalei (Kaua'i), appear to agree with the general body of data from the leeward areas concerning the history of the inland expansion. However, the windward data probably do not date the single most important process in the windward valleys: the growth of the irrigated agricultural systems. The presence of apparently optimal conditions for early settlement along permanent windward watercourses, together with archaeological evidence, supports the commonly held idea that such areas were favored by the early Polynesian settlers (Green 1980, 71). For the present it seems reasonable to surmise (in the absence of a body of chronometric evidence) that at least some windward valleys were extensively cultivated and densely populated well before the initiation of inland expansion in the leeward districts.

If we add to this suggestion the observation that arid marginal lands formed a much smaller proportion of windward than of leeward districts then we may speculate that the economic history of the former differed in important ways from that of the latter during Phases II and III. The rivalry described above may in fact have been a competition between an alliance of windward districts whose wealth and power were based on a long-established stable productive economy on the one hand and, on the other, the upstart *nouveaux riches* leeward districts with their rapidly growing but somewhat unstable economies.

Summary

The model outlined here summarizes evolutionary processes inferred from archaeological and ethnohistorical information, that may have resulted in the transformation of an Ancestral Polynesian society into the complex Hawai'ian polities documented in the ethnohistoric literature of the late eighteenth and early nineteenth centuries. The absence of substantial evidence for introductions after initial settlement of population, material goods, social practices, or cultural concepts of significance to the current problem supports the contention that the evolution of these polities can be explained by reference to locally identifiable variables.

Some 800 to 1000 years following initial settlement the Hawai'ian population was thinly scattered in small communities along the coasts of all major Hawai'ian islands. Multi-community non-egalitarian corporate kinship groups, here termed archaic *maka'ainana*, occupied the most productive coastal areas (the core regions of what would come to be called districts) that were often separated from each other by mountain ranges and relatively unproductive lands. During the fifteenth and sixteenth centuries the *ahupua'a* pattern developed as settlements in the salubrious core regions established major inland agricultural complexes that, together with abundant marine and upland resources, came to support communities that were sufficiently large and productive to be markedly self-sufficient both economically and socially.

Though the archaic *maka'ainana* were disintegrating as kinship ties among the self-sufficient *ahupua'a* community gradually diminished in number and strength, the developing chiefly class maintained their superior social, ritual and political status even as their position as senior relatives passed from being genealogically demonstrable to metaphorical. By the end of the sixteenth century the quantities of agricultural goods available to fund the chiefly establishment was varying unpredictably from year to year with the increasing dependence on marginal, drought-prone and, possibly, exhausted lands. Whatever its origin, the *hale naua* ceremony that maintained the clear distinction between chief and commoner at the time of contact had the effect of limiting the number of recipients of goods collected from the society at large. Redistribution had become tax collection.

The divorce of politics from the kinship structure was manifest at the time of contact in the degree to which accession to political office and establishment and maintenance of political boundaries were based on application of force rather than exercise of genealogical prerogative. Accounts of attainment of political power through force of arms can be traced in the traditional literature as far back as the time of 'Umi, a late sixteenth-century paramount chief of Hawai'i identified with Waipi'o valley on the windward Hamakua coast. 'Umi's most renowned descendant was Kamehameha, who, supported by an alliance of chiefs from Hawai'i's leeward districts and with an assist from western technology, succeeded in uniting the Hawai'ian Islands by the year 1810.

APPENDIX: RADIOCARBON SAMPLES
FROM PRECONTACT HAWAI'IAN
ARCHAEOLOGICAL SITES OF THE
INLAND ZONE

This appendix provides sources of radiocarbon samples whose AD date ranges are represented graphically in fig. 7.7 by island and research area. Research areas are alphabetically keyed as in fig. 7.7.

Hawai'i Island

A. Mudlane–Waimea–Kawaihae Road Corridor. Thirty-eight samples from twenty-six charcoal deposits, ten fireplaces, one cremation and one pig bone in thirty-two sites and features (Clark 1983, table 9.1, pp. 319–20). One sample with a calibrated range of AD 880–1325 was rejected as too early on the basis of other chronometric and stratigraphic data at the site and in the research area as a whole (Clark 1983, 320).

B. Lapakahi. Twelve samples from ten fireplaces and two charcoal deposits in twelve sites in the Kohala field system (Newman n.d. [1970], 141; Rosendahl 1972, table 53, pp. 428–9).

C. Pololu. Four samples from charcoal deposits in four agricultural sites in a valley with irrigated field systems (Tuggle and Tomonari-Tuggle 1980, table 1, p. 307).

D. Hilina Pali. Two samples from charcoal deposits in one site (Cleghorn 1980, table 4, p. 20).

E. La'aloa. Four samples from three charcoal deposits and one fireplace in three sites at the edge of the Kona field system (Hammatt and Clark 1980, table 7, p. 81).

F. Kuakini Highway Realignment Corridor. Twenty-two samples from six fireplaces and ten charcoal deposits in seventeen sites and features at the edge of the Kona field system (Schilt 1984, table 1.30, p. 264).

G. Ka'ahumanu Highway Corridor. Six samples from four fireplaces in four sites (Rosendahl 1972, table 12, p. 102; Rosendahl 1973, 41; Ching 1971, 91).

Maui island

H. Palauea. One sample from a fireplace (Kirch 1971, 76).

I. Kipapa/Nakohu. One sample from a charcoal deposit (Chapman and Kirch 1979, table 3, p. 35).

Kaho'olawe island

J. Inland Zone. Ten samples from eight fireplaces in seven sites and features (Hommon 1983, table 19, p. 123).

Moloka'i island

K. Halawa. Two samples from charcoal deposits in two sites (Kirch and Kelly 1975, table 41, p. 163).

L. Kawela. Fourteen samples from about fourteen sites and features (Weisler and Kirch, in press).

Oahu Island

M. Makaha, Lower. Sixteen samples from thirteen fireplaces and one charcoal deposit in fifteen sites and features (Green 1970b, table 1, p. 99).

N. Makaha, Upper. Six samples from four charcoal deposits in an irrigated field site (Yen *et al.* 1972, table 4, p. 89) and one charcoal deposit (with a calibrated date range of AD 1395–1650) in the platform of the *heiau* (temple) of Kaneaki (Ladd 1973, 30).

O. Anahulu. Two samples from a fireplace and a charcoal deposit in one site (Kirch 1979a, table 4, p. 42).

P. Kaneohe. Four samples from four charcoal deposits in one site (Rosendahl 1976, table 6–12, pp. 6–44).

Q. Moanalua. Four samples from two fireplaces and two charcoal deposits in four sites (Ayres 1970, 66).

Kaua'i island

R. Hanalei. Three samples from two charcoal deposits in two sites in an irrigated field system (Schilt 1980, 57). The sample with the earliest date range (calibrated at AD 585–900) rejected as too early on the basis of additional data (Schilt, personal communication).

Upland Hawai'i island

S. Mauna Kea Adze Quarry Complex. Twelve samples from four sites and features (Allen 1981, table 8, p. 59).

Notes

1 In general outline, this paper is a synopsis and revision of my 1976 doctoral dissertation (Hommon 1976) incorporating the results of recent research.

2 A further comment on a related matter is based on a personal observation. Cordy (1981, 182) states that site 42 at Kaloko, Kona 'merits interpretation as a high chief's household, at least'. He appears to base this statement primarily on the massiveness of the base of site 42 which he refers to as a 'stone terrace', $1000\,m^3$ in volume, on which were built several stone walled structures (Cordy 1981, 132–5). A recent inspection of the site convinced me, however, that the 'terrace' is little more than an area of a clinkery aa lava flow that had been crudely leveled by redistribution of the surface fragments. Such pavements are common features in sites on aa flows, are usually found in locations that were fairly level before modification and probably required relatively little labor to construct. Certainly this structure is an unsubstantial foundation on which to build a hypothetical high chief's household.

Chapter 8

The socio-political structure of the southern coastal area of Easter Island: AD 1300–1864

Christopher M. Stevenson

Easter Island is one of the more intensively studied islands in southeast Polynesia, but the difficulties in acquiring large data sets and the inability to routinely date archaeological sites have hampered attempts to reconstruct the island's prehistoric socio-political system. Intensive site surveys by McCoy (1976) and by the Centro de Estudios Isla de Pascua (Cristino, Vargas, and Izaurieta 1981; Cristino and Vargas 1980), and a re-evaluation of the hydration rates for the island's obsidian sources (Michels *et al.* 1984) now make it feasible to begin an examination of the settlement pattern on a temporal basis.

This paper offers a preliminary reconstruction of the island's prehistoric socio-political structure. It is argued that corporate descent group identity, under conditions of moderate resource competition, is frequently expressed through ritual construction. It is also proposed that shrines or temples are focal points for corporate groups and serve to distinguish structural components of the population. Differences in size and elaborateness of ritual structures may also reflect differences in the size of a social group which patronizes a specific shrine. Consequently, an analysis of the coastal ritual centers, termed *ahu* in the Rapanui language, and of mortuary facilities, can result in the identification of particular corporate units.

All structures located along the southern coast between Hanga Hahave and Runga Va'e (fig. 8.1) constitute the sample of ritual centers and interment locations considered in this paper. Each of the platform *ahu* (N = 57) has been dated using the obsidian hydration method to determine the period of construction. *Ahu* within the study area are analyzed to determine if there exist regularly occurring site types which may be socially meaningful in terms of their spatial distribution. Above ground burial structures (N = 24) have been classified into morphological types and assigned specific temporal phases.

Late period socio-political structure

Easter Island lacks a large corpus of ethnographic data and reliable early contact descriptions. Information collected during the early part of this century (Routledge 1919; Metraux 1940) and more recent ethnographic work by McCall (1979) permit a partial reconstruction of the socio-political structure for the latest period of the prehistoric cultural system (post AD 1722). Most of the information presented below derives from McCall (1979), who summarizes the local kinship structure.

The oral traditions presented by Metraux (1940, 121) state that shortly before the death of the founding king, Hotu Matu'a, the island was divided by the king among five of his six sons. The later period island divisions, however, present a much more complex distribution of descent lines and territorial divisions. McCall (1979) has identified five levels of segmentation

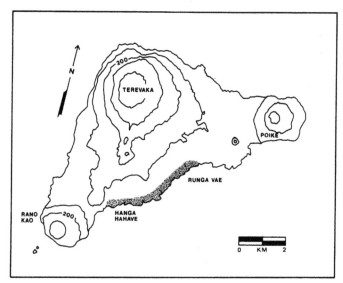

Fig. 8.1. Easter Island; the study area is shaded.

below the island-wide level. The island population is divided into two moieties, with the Tu'u Aro moiety occupying the northern half of the island, and the Hotu Iti moiety situated in the southern section. At the next level of segmentation were eleven *mata* or descent groups which were distributed around the island's circumference. Each *mata* occupied a defined territory which gave access to terrestrial as well as marine resources. Comprising a *mata* were multiple lineages, themselves composed of extended families or domestic groups. These in turn were composed of single nuclear family units.

McCall (1979, 124–5) interprets these *mata* descent groups as corporate units. Each group had a territory defined by boundary markers (*pipihoreko*). Ownership of the land was also validated by the use of toponyms and guarded by spirits (*akuaku*) which could inflict supernatural sanctions against those who committed infractions. Membership within the corporate group was defined primarily on the basis of patrilineal descent, although secondary membership in other groups may have been possible by demonstrating descent through a female line.

During the later part of the cultural sequence, a dual status system appears to have been established. According to Goldman (1970, 109–10) one status system was organized along traditional descent lines, with social position based on proximity to the founding ancestor. The second system was comprised of a set of warrior chiefs or *matatoa*. These individuals were the secular leaders of descent groups and appear to have controlled positions of authority. Holders of traditional status positions are said to have been limited to participation in purely religious functions.

This relationship between the hereditary chiefs and the position of warrior chief is hypothesized to have arisen out of conditions of increasing social instability which resulted from resource shortages brought on by environmental deterioration

(McCall 1979, 132; see also McCoy 1976). Thus, during the later period, the island population appears to have been composed of multiple descent groups in direct competition over such resources as fuel, water, and food.

The corporate significance of ritual centers

In this study of the socio-political structure of Easter Island, the corporate group will serve as the unit of analysis. Corporate groups in agrarian societies are landholding units of related individuals who share common concerns over territory, membership composition, and continuity of the local group. As a result, the spatial arrangement of ceremonial structures may reflect these concerns and permit the identification of local units. In this analysis a study of coastal religious structures attempts to identify the number of corporate groups present on the southern portion of the island.

In order to provide the link between ceremonial architecture and social organization, it must be demonstrated that corporate group identity is frequently expressed through collective activities above the individual level, such as shrine or temple construction. As a result of the short-term nature of visits by early explorers, and the late time period of more systematically collected data, much of the ethnographic data from Polynesia is limited and often anecdotal in nature, in my view hindering an examination of the relationships of interest. Therefore I have selected an ethnographic example from the African data. Collected by economic and social anthropologists, these data are detailed and comprehensive, and permit an examination of corporate group function.

In the following discussion of the Ibo of southeastern Nigeria, three issues are addressed. First, it is demonstrated that Ibo settlements are composed of a number of corporate bodies which meet the criteria for corporation presented below. Second, the shrines associated with the corporate unit and subunits are described in order to provide an appreciation of the number and variety of shrines which can exist within a social group. Third, the functions of the shrines and the reasons for their construction will be discussed.

Recent studies by Brown (1974) and Tiffany (1976) provide precise definitions of the attributes which are necessary for a group to be considered fully corporate. The primary attributes of a corporation are: (1) presumptive perpetuity, or the continuation of the corporate unit over time; (2) the concept of a unique identity; (3) rules for recruiting and excluding members; and (4) empirical evidence of the membership itself.

A corporate group also shares a set of common concerns and procedures, an organization for the conduct of affairs, and an autonomy of action. A corporate group may be further described and distinguished from other like groups on the basis of its *principles*. These principles are grounded in the rules of recruitment and include age, sex, ethnicity, locality, descent, common property interests, ritual and belief, occupation, rank, and voluntary association (Brown 1974).

They serve to define the membership boundaries of a group, the categories of common concern, and the prerequisites for its continuity (Smith 1974, 182).

The Ibo of southeastern Nigeria

The Ibo of southeastern Nigeria are subsistence farmers who raise their primary crop, yams, through hoe cultivation. In areas of lower population density (100–400 persons/square mile), Ibo farming settlements consist of aggregates of 4000–5000 persons, organized into village groups. The village group is the highest autonomous socio-political unit. It is composed of two or more villages or compound clusters located around a central meeting place or plaza (Jones 1949, 310). The village group is usually named after a mythical ancestor. Each component village is named after the founder and is composed of individual compounds of nuclear or extended families that may be grouped into hamlets. These hamlets may be composed of families who can trace descent from a great-grandfather (Udo 1965, 58).

The social structure of an Ibo community is based on agnatic descent. Each village group is recognized as a patriclan, although the uniting genealogy is probably fictitious (Jones 1949, 311). Each village may be composed of several major and/or minor lineages, the members of which tend to live in relatively close spatial proximity (Ardener 1959, 118).

Each village group is also a territorially organized entity, with each village the custodian of its particular segment. The property of a village consists of the land within the immediate vicinity of the compounds upon which yams, cocoyams, maize, vegetables, oil palms, and other trees are grown. Radiating out from the village group are the unoccupied farmlands which are subdivided among the resident population.

Land was the primary resource concern of the village and was closely managed for the benefit of the entire group (Meek 1937, 101). An individual's use of property for subsistence farming depended upon whether or not he could demonstrate agnatic affiliation to the maximal lineage or village (Jones 1961, 124). If group affiliation was not questioned, then land tenure was governed by three basic principles: (1) all land ultimately belongs to the community; (2) each person shall have security of tenure for the land he requires; and (3) no member shall be without land (Jones 1949, 313).

Community control over land was substantial, implemented through collaboration of family elders supported by warrior age grades (Meek 1937, 129). If property was needed for a communal facility such as a meeting house, it was taken without compensation. Unassigned parcels of land reverted to the community, which decided upon the disposition of the property, and, in some cases, the types and proportions of the crops to be planted (Jones 1949, 313).

Ownership of land passed to direct male descendants. If, however, the land was left unoccupied, it reverted to the village. In situations where land was insufficient to supply the subsistence needs of several sons, the most senior son received the property. The remaining sons were left to acquire land by alternate means which may have included land rental or land pledging.

These data demonstrate that Ibo communities function as corporate organizations. Each village has: (1) a unique identity in relation to other villages; (2) membership in the corporation depends on principles of descent; and (3) the organization is actively engaged in self-perpetuation through the management of land.

The construction of temples among the Ibo is intimately linked with ancestor worship and the lineage structure of the village group. In his study of a Nri community, Onwuejeogwu (1981) documents the relationship between lineage structure and temple construction. The organization of an Ibo village group is based on segmentary patrilineages. The minimal lineage is the smallest politically meaningful unit, with the founding ancestor usually removed by four or five generations from the present eldest member. These units are progressively grouped into minor, major, and maximal lineages. Organizational units above the minimal level are corporate entities (Onwuejeogwu 1981, 103–5). Temples within a community are found at the apex of lineage segments, that is, in the compound of the lineage head. Each temple is dedicated to the founding ancestor of the lineage or lineage segment. New temple construction occurs during the process of segmentation. The social position of the temple and its functions are determined by lineage status. Thus, every structurally significant ancestor in Nri society has a temple dedicated to him (1981, 38).

A temple is not a sacred area, but part of the domestic area of the custodian (the eldest son and head of the lineage), and is usually located in the center of the compound. Inside the temple is an altar to the ancestor as well as ritual paraphernalia and status items. At the temple, the lineage head greets visitors, conducts rituals, and engages in political and legal business.

Another important form of ritual construction is connected with supernatural beings called *Alusi*. The *Alusi* are forces which were created by the supreme spirit, *Chukwu*. These supernatural beings are associated with negative and positive roles which have a direct effect upon the well-being of the population. Important *Alusi* are the object of cults, some of which have temples constructed for them. A relationship is established with the force through ritual, with a temple being built upon the opening of the relationship. If an *Alusi* becomes too violent, the relationship is terminated, the site abandoned, and a new temple is established at another location (Onwuejeogwu 1981, 38). Not all *Alusi* have temples erected on their behalf. Smaller order shrines are more frequent. Each village recognizes five to ten *Alusi*, with the village group possessing up to six communal shrines. The role of the *Alusi* is best represented by the activities associated with the *Alusi* Ala, the earth deity.

Each of the component villages of a village group has a shrine dedicated to the earth deity. One of the village shrines, usually the most senior, is the location of a village group public sacrifice at one time during the year. Although the timing of the event may vary from community to community, the event occurs at important stages in the agricultural cycle such as before clearing land, before the planting of yams, or at the time of the yam harvest. During these events, sacrifices and offerings are made in order to ensure agricultural success. Additional public sacrifices may also be made on occasion, if called for as a result of divination (Meek 1937, 25–6).

Temporary shrines are also built when the need is perceived. When it is felt that an improper relationship exists between the village group and a particular deity, the elders of the community commission the ritual construction of a shrine. The community supplies yams for nearly one hundred male and female workers for a project that could take up to a year or more. Construction materials are also supplied by the community for the shrine, which is erected in a sacred grove near the center of the village group (Meek 1937, 49–52).

The location, type, and function of community shrines are often affected by population density and land tenure system of an area. In areas of high population density (750 persons/square mile) the land tenure system shifts towards a greater emphasis on individual ownership. As a result, the residential pattern is significantly different from that of the low population areas. In low population areas, the distinction between compound land and unoccupied farmland is maintained. Within compound land, territorial boundaries of compound clusters are well recognized and maintained. When the population of a village group becomes high, a new village is established away from the parent group and eventually becomes an autonomous political unit (Jones 1961, 122). At a certain point, this fissioning is not possible due to land shortages. Instead, the village population establishes compounds on the farmland, a process which eventually results in a group's territory being occupied by a continuous distribution of compounds. Agricultural practices gradually shift from bush fallow to yearly cultivation around the immediate compound area.

Under these conditions, the system of communal land tenure gradually shifts to one of individual ownership. Under the previous condition of sufficient farming land new plots of land tended to be given to the older men of the village, thus making the younger men economically dependent, yet providing a future security through inheritance. Under conditions of land pressure, greater security was found in personally owned land, and an aggressive individual could acquire more land than he needed for subsistence farming. In order to prevent encroachment by others, individually owned land was settled. This practice had the effect of preventing the formation of residential areas of closely related individuals.

This pattern had a significant effect upon the religious system and its architectural expression. Among the northeastern Ibo, where this dispersed pattern exists, corporate solidarity is low, and there are no cults associated with the lineages, and no ancestral shrines. Instead, there is a cult to a man's dead father which entails making offerings to the father's ghost (Jones 1961, 132). Thus, the regular pattern of temple construction found in areas exhibiting high corporate solidarity and lineage territories has changed to reflect the pattern of lineage dispersal under conditions of increasing land pressure.

The preceding ethnographic case shows that in lineage based corporate agrarian society, a strong relationship exists between the placement of ancestral shrines and structurally important kinship positions. This relationship appears to exist with lower population densities and the close residential proximity of related individuals. Under these conditions, the identification of ancestral shrines or temples could be used to reconstruct the lineage structure of a community. This apparent orderly pattern is complicated, however, by the presence of shrines dedicated to additional deities. Any reconstruction using religious architecture must be sensitive to the multiple functions of shrines and must try to distinguish, if possible, between those structures which identify social segments and those which do not.

Two additional considerations must also be recognized. The first of these is the degree of shrine preservation. Many smaller shrines may be constructed of thatch or other perishable materials which would leave little or no trace. In other situations a shrine may be a tree, or plot of land accompanied by a few ceramics or other portable items which would also leave few traces in the archaeological record. The implication is that almost any archaeological reconstruction will utilize only a partial set of the entire complement of religious shrines. Fortunately, on Easter Island many shrines are substantial constructions requiring a supra-family organization for their erection, thus permitting the identification of major social groups. Many smaller shrines erected by individuals or small groups of persons are not archaeologically visible, although they are presumed to have existed.

A second consideration is the discreteness of shrine location. Whether a shrine is part of a residential complex or spatially separate from the living area can affect identification. If a temple or shrine is located within a compound it may be difficult to distinguish from other structures. The manner of construction and proportions may be close to that of other domestic structures. Discrete shrine locations, on the other hand, facilitate the identification of ritual centers. On Easter Island, the majority of structures are separate from habitation areas and are located within 100–200 m of the shoreline. This ease of identification allows for a more reliable reconstruction.

Architectural typology of platform *ahu* and burial structures
Previous studies of Easter Island platform *ahu* (Metraux 1940; Smith 1961; Ayres 1973; McCoy 1976; Mulloy and

Table 8.1 *Ahu architectural attributes*

1. Central platform length: 3 m–14 m
2. Central platform length: 17 m–28 m
3. Central platform length: > 28 m
4. Platform rear wall: crude masonry
5. Platform rear wall: fine masonry
6. No wings
7. Wings
8. Statue
9. Red scoria top knot
10. Ramp
11. Crematorium
12. Plaza pavement
13. Crafted front retaining wall
14. Red scoria cornice

Figueroa 1978) have shown that the *ahu* are composed of different combinations of a limited set of architectural features including central platform, lateral wings, ramp, statues, crematorium, top knots, platform retaining wall cornices, and various seawall masonry styles. Of these features, the crematoria contain data most directly related to the activities connected with these structures. Deposits within crematoria are composed primarily of human bone mixed with beach pebbles, irregular stones, obsidian, and charcoal. Excavated crematoria at Ahu Vinapu (Mulloy 1961) and Ahu Akivi (Mulloy and Figueroa 1978) reveal that a variety of artifacts are found in crematoria matrices. At Ahu Vinapu bone fishhooks were numerous. At Ahu Akivi, stone disks, small statues, and stone and bone fishhooks were present. The occasional bones of chickens and rat have also been found. These data suggest that cremation of the dead and the presentation of votive offerings were two activities conducted

Table 8.2 *Percent occurrence of* ahu *attributes by cluster*

Cluster 1 (N = 8)
6(100): no wing   3(33.3): > 28 m
4(88.9): crude masonry   13(22.2): crafted front wall
8(88.9): statue   10(22.2): ramp
11(66.7): crematorium   5(11.1): fine masonry
2(55.6): 17 m–28 m   1(11.1): 3 m–14 m

Cluster 2 (N = 6)
2(100): 17 m–28 m   10(50.0): ramp
7(100): wings   11(50.0): crematorium
4(100): crude masonry   13(16.7): crafted front wall
8(100): statue

Cluster 3 (N = 6)
7(100): wings   14(83.0): red scoria cornice
8(100): statue   11(50.0): crematorium
5(100): fine masonry   9(33.0): top knot
10(100): ramp   12(33.0): plaza pavement
13(100): crafted front wall   3(16.7): > 28 m
2(83): 17 m–28 m

Cluster 4 (N = 10)
7(100): wings   10(30): ramp
1(100): 3 m–14 m   5(20): fine masonry
8(90): statue   9(10): top knot
4(80): crude masonry   12(10): plaza pavement
11(80): crematorium

Cluster 5 (N = 3)
2(100): 17m–28 m   4(100): crude masonry
6(100): no wing   9(100): top knot
8(100): statue   11(100): crematorium
13(100): crafted front wall   14(66.7): red scoria cornice
10(100): ramp   12(33.3): plaza pavement

at *ahu*. In addition, the presence of statues presumed to represent deified ancestors supports the working hypothesis that *ahu* are ritual centers dedicated to deceased kinsmen.

In order to determine if there are certain regular types of platform *ahu* composed of specific combinations of attributes, architectural data from the complete structures within the study area were analyzed. Fourteen architectural attributes from 33 complete structures (table 8.1) were analyzed using the multivariate grouping technique of cluster analysis (Wishart 1978). Ward's Method was selected as the algorithm to be used in the grouping procedures. This resulted in the definition of five homogenous types or groups of platform *ahu* (table 8.2).

Type 1 platform *ahu* possess the fullest complement of architectural features. They are defined by the presence of fine or crude seawall masonry, a paved ramp, statues with red scoria top knots, crafted platform front retaining walls with cornices, a crematorium, and a central platform length ranging from 14 to 28 m. Type 2 structures have central platforms of equivalent length and possess a crude masonry seawall, statues without top knots, wings, and a crematorium.

Type 3 structures are identical in all aspects to Type 2 *ahu* except that they do not have lateral wings paved with beach cobbles, and in most cases they do not have a frontal ramp. These structures are essentially rectangular platforms which range in length from 17 to 28 m. Type 4 *ahu* are small versions of Type 2 structures. The central platform ranges up to 14 m in length and possesses a crude masonry seawall, wings, a statue, a frontal ramp and crematorium. In contrast to Type 2 structures, the crematoria are very small and the wings tend to be level with the surrounding ground surface rather than elevated by the addition of fill.

Type 5 structures are miniature versions of Type 1 *ahu*. They range up to 14 m in central platform length and have a fine masonry seawall, statues with top knots, wings, and a crematorium. Unlike Type 1 structures, these *ahu* are located well inland from the coastline at distances of 1 km or more.

Easter Island interment structures are irregular basalt block structures which contain internal tombs averaging 3 m in length. Three major morphological types have been identified within the study area and consist of structures which are either semipyramidal, rectangular, or amorphous in form. Excavations at several of these structures (Seelenfreund 1982) reveal that each tomb contains multiple secondary burials of individuals from all age categories which were interred at different periods throughout the use of the structure.

The coastal settlement pattern

The obsidian hydration dating of platform *ahu* and burial structures permits a temporal examination of the distribution of each type of *ahu* and burial structure. For this stage in the analysis the prehistoric and protohistoric periods for Easter Island have been divided into thirteen one-hundred year analytical phases beginning at AD 700, with the first indications of residential settlement, and ending in AD 1864 with the arrival of the missionaries.

Phases 1–7 (AD 700–1400)

No *ahu* construction has been identified within the study area before AD 1300. During Phase 7 (AD 1301–1400) the first *ahu* appeared at Vaihu (Site 6-255), at Ure Uranga te Mahina (Site 7-575), and at Akahanga (Site 7-584) (fig. 8.2a). The platforms at these sites are buried or only partial structures and cannot be reliably typed, but are thought to represent Type 2 *ahu*. Two additional *ahu* were constructed during this period both of which are of the Type 2 category.

Phase 8 (AD 1401–1500)

Phase 8 witnessed the construction of a large number of platform *ahu* (fig. 8.2b). To the west at Hanga Hahave, a Type 2 and a Type 4 structure appear in association. Within the immediate area of Vaihu two Type 4 structures and two Type 2 structures were built. Ahu Vaihu was transformed from a Type 2 structure to a Type 1 *ahu*. To the east of Vaihu are seven Type 2 structures all of which are isolated platforms except for Ahu Akahanga (Site 7-584) which has a Type 3 platform and an unidentifiable structure in association. East of Akahanga five new *ahu* appeared, consisting of a mix of Types 2, 3, and 4.

Phase 9 (AD 1501–1600)

Ahu construction was less frequent during Phase 9 over most of the area except for the immediate zone around Hanga Hahave (fig. 8.2c). Site 5-78 was transformed from a Type 2 to a Type 1 *ahu*. Within the immediate area of this site three Type 2 structures were built along with a Type 3 structure further to the west. To the east of Hanga Hahave at Hanga Poukura a Type 1 structure was located. The seemingly sudden appearance of this structure in this phase is peculiar since all other Type 1 structures were preceded by Type 2 *ahu*. It is therefore probable that Ahu Hanga Poukura (Site 6-1, -2) contains a buried platform of the Type 2 variety. Ahu Vaihu (Site 6-255) remained a Type 1 *ahu*. In the area between Vaihu and Akahanga were constructed three Type 4 *ahu* and a single Type 2 structure. Ahu Ure Uranga te Mahina and Ahu Akahanga both took on the features of a Type 1, and within the immediate area several Type 3 structures were erected during this phase.

It is also proposed on the basis of obsidian dates from the Akahanga elite houses (*hare paenga*)(fig. 8.2a), that the elite complexes were constructed at this time and coincided with the erection of Type 1 *ahu* along the southern coast. An elite residential complex has not been found within the Vaihu area but it is highly probable that one once existed there, but has subsequently been destroyed through the scavenging of foundation stones.

Phase 10 (AD 1601–1700)

Platform *ahu* construction was limited during Phase 10 (fig. 8.2e). Additional Type 1 platforms were added to existing Type 1 sites at Ahu Hanga Poukura (Site 6-1, -2) and at Ahu Ure Uranga te Mahina. The rebuilding of structures can also be identified at *ahu* sites 7-32 and 12-460. Towards the end of

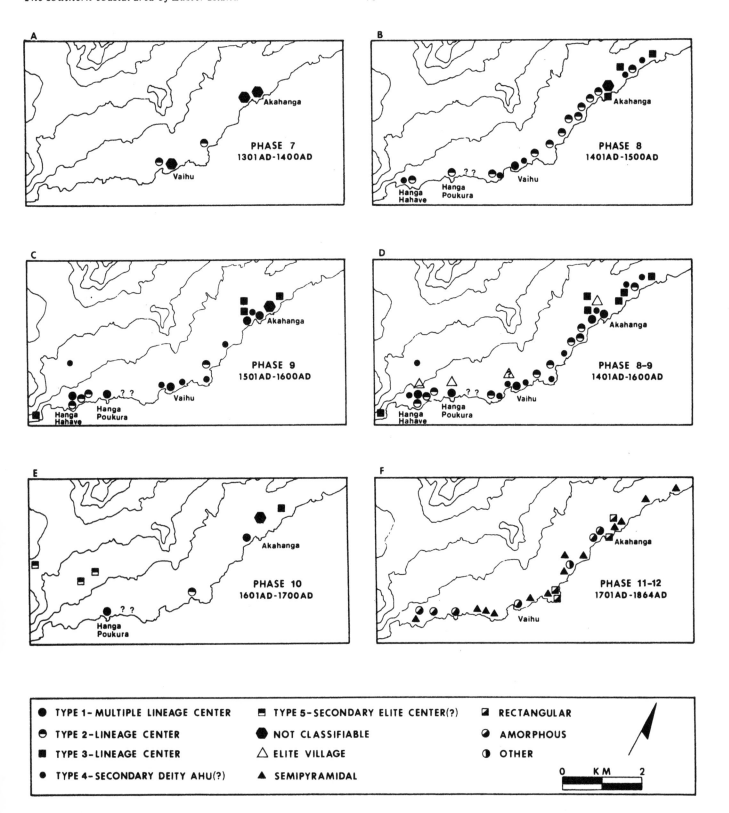

Fig. 8.2. Distribution of *ahu* and interment structures in the study area by phases.

this phase and in the first quarter of Phase 11, the Type 5 structures were built inland of Hanga Hahave.

Phases 11 and 12 (AD 1701–1864)

Phases 11 and 12 have been merged in the study of above ground burial locations since chronological control over these structures is limited. Obsidian hydration dates from excavated tombs at several sites indicate that the construction of semipyramidal structures had begun by AD 1692 at Site 7-220 and by AD 1736 at Site 8-374. Although this sample at present is very small, it is proposed that this building tradition began in the late 1600s (Stevenson 1984).

Figure 8.2f presents the distribution of burial structures. It is clear from this map that semipyramidal structures exhibit a tendency to form discrete clusters which are separated by areas without this structure type. The portions of the coastline where these structures rest are by and large removed from the locations of Type 1 platform *ahu* of Phase 10 and earlier. These intervening spaces contain amorphous rubble mounds which are superimposed over the Type 1 *ahu*. Rectangular *ahu* tend to co-occur amongst the semipyramidal structures.

The geographical distribution of platforms in the phase maps presented above, and their architectural attributes, provide data for the development of hypotheses concerning the size of the socio-political units served by each of the *ahu* and burial structures. Type 1 *ahu* appear to represent multiple lineage centers for several reasons. In contrast with the numerous Type 2, 3, and 4 *ahu*, only five Type 1 structures are present within the study area. Each of these structures is associated with an elite village complex. In addition, Type 1 *ahu* consistently exhibit evidence of greater labor investment as indicated by the presence of crafted central platform walls, lintels, top knots, larger and more numerous statues, and large crematoria. All of these attributes suggest a greater investment in initial construction, and probably a larger sized community served by the structure.

Located between Type 1 *ahu* are the most frequently occurring Type 2 and Type 3 *ahu*. These structures are hypothesized to represent *ahu* serving single lineages. These structures lack the refinements of Type 1 *ahu* as well as the association with elite residences. The small Type 4 *ahu* may represent structures which were constructed by organizational units below the lineage level such as occupational craftsmen or patrons of secondary deities. Crematoria at these structures are very small and suggest that mortuary rites were of less importance at these localities. The size of the socio-political unit served by such structures is presumed to have been quite small.

Type 5 *ahu* are problematical in their interpretation. These miniature versions of Type 1 *ahu* are few in number and date to the latest period of platform *ahu* construction. They may represent secondary elite centers. However, no elite residences or other indicators of rank are found in association with these structures; thus the role of Type 5 *ahu* as secondary elite centers remains tentative.

Conclusions

These hypotheses concerning the function and size of the groups served by each *ahu* permit an interpretation of the Easter Island settlement pattern on a temporal basis. The initial settlement of the southern coast began relatively late in the cultural sequence, around AD 1300. By the 1300s the first *ahu* were constructed. A proliferation of lineage *ahu* during Phase 8 may reflect a period of increased population growth and lineage fissioning, or the influx of peoples from other parts of the island. During this phase local lineages appeared to have retained their autonomy, as they exhibit little integration except around the area of Vaihu. At Vaihu the first multiple lineage center appeared during this phase, reflecting the increased integration of the lineages in this area. In Phase 9, multiple lineage centers appeared at Hanga Hahave (Site 5-78), Hanga Poukura (Sites 6-1, -2), Ure Uranga te Mahina (Site 7-575), and Akahanga (Site 7-584). The other major trend during this phase was the increased frequency of the small *ahu* possibly related to secondary deities or occupational groups.

Of particular interest during Phase 9 was the emergence of two multiple lineage centers and a single elite residential area at Akahanga. This arrangement of features leads to the hypothesis that two major sets of lineages, each with its own religious center, were institutionally integrated, with this integration reflected by the presence of a single elite residential complex. This association of multiple lineage centers did not suddenly arise in Phase 9, but appears to extend back to Phase 7. In Phase 7 lineage specific *ahu* were present at both locales and persisted through Phase 8. Thus the five multiple lineage centers reflect the presence of four politically autonomous groups which had developed by Phase 9, and continued unchanged until Phase 11.

In Phases 11 and 12 the coastal platform *ahu* fell into disuse and were replaced by newly constructed above ground interment structures. The semipyramidal structures form five discrete clusters along the coastline, removed from the multiple lineage centers of the previous phase. The unified multiple lineage center at Akahanga appears to have separated into two spatially discrete groups each with its burial locality removed from the elite center. Despite the shift in the form of mortuary practice from cremation to secondary burial and the location of tombs away from platform *ahu*, the basic organizational structure of the population remained intact. The four multiple lineage centers of Phase 10 gave way to five clusters of lineage specific tombs. The separation of the Akahanga population into two distinct groups reflected a decrease in the integration of this local unit. The hypothesis that this local group fissioned into two populations is not unrealistic since previous to Phase 11 a structural 'fault' in the organizational form of the population had always been manifested by the presence of adjacent multiple lineage centers. Only in Phase 11 did the component parts of the population manifest autonomous action relative to one another. Previous to this time the two populations had presumably been politically united.

Data from three platform *ahu* in the western section of the study area (Sites 5-209, 5-217, 5-297) suggest that platform *ahu* construction overlapped the construction of the above ground interment structures. These three secondary elite centers (Type 5) are spatially clustered inland of the Hanga Hahave area. This pattern suggests a resistance of the lineage groups in this area to the general changing trends in mortuary practice and/or religious perspective. Yet, at the same time the three small but elaborately constructed platform *ahu* suggest internal factionalization amongst the local population, a trend also noted for the Akahanga area. The continued use of platform *ahu* by the population inland of Hanga Hahave would also account for the limited construction of semipyramidal *ahu* along the coast.

The transformation during Phase 10 and Phase 11 from corporate territories marked by ancestral shrines (*ahu*) to clusters of burial tombs is similar in many respects to the ritual pattern described for the southern and northern Ibo. In areas of low to moderate Ibo population density, corporate solidarity is high and is expressed through a regular pattern of temple construction. In areas of high population density,

and individual ownership of land, there are no cults to the deceased ancestors, and no pattern of temple construction.

The population growth curve for the southern coastal area, inland of Akahanga, has been documented by Stevenson (1984). This reconstruction (fig. 8.3) shows a rapid increase in population beginning in Phase 5 and continuing up to Phase 9. The population from Phase 9 to Phase 12 is relatively stable, with some minor fluctuations in the latter two phases. There are some preliminary data to support the proposition that the island was undergoing deforestation and increased soil erosion. Radiocarbon dates from cores in the crater lakes suggest that this process had begun by 990 ± 70 bp (Flenley and King 1984). Thus by Phase 10, the cumulative effects of population growth and environmental deterioration may have resulted in a shortage of productive agricultural land (McCoy 1976). As a result, the maintenance of corporate territories appears to have given way to a more competitive strategy based on the acquisition of land through warfare. Within this context, the regular activities and supplications conducted on behalf of the ancestors connected with the land became less important, and were superseded by the cult of Orongo, and worship of the creator god Makemake (see Metraux 1940). Thus, although the transformation is not as marked as that noted between the northern and southern Ibo, there is evidence to suggest that corporate solidarity was substantially weakened on Easter Island by a decrease in arable land.

In summary, the settlement trajectory for the southern coast of Easter Island between AD 1300 and 1864 indicates a late but rapid settlement of the area followed by several hundred years of stable residence. Four autonomous political units can be identified prior to AD 1700, each composed of an elite and commoner population. Whether these groups were integrated at a higher level has not been detected archaeologically within the study area. After AD 1700, five socio-political units appear to be present. It is hypothesized that the corporate solidarity of these communities had been weakened in response to a decline in the availability of productive agricultural land. The inability of the ancestors to maintain the productivity of corporate territories eventually led to a decline in the construction of ancestral shrines, and the emergence of cults supporting a more competitive approach to resource acquisition.[1]

Note

[1] The settlement pattern data used in this study were documented in surveys conducted by Claudio Cristino and Patricia Vargas of the Centro de Estudios Isla de Pascua, Universidad de Chile. The generosity of these persons with their survey data made this study possible. This research was conducted with funding from the National Science Foundation (Grant BNS 8019713), the Hill Foundation, and the Explorers Club Exploration Fund.

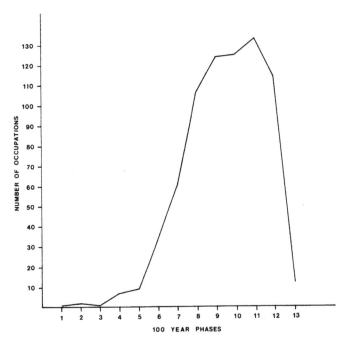

Fig. 8.3. Population growth curves for the Akahanga area.

Chapter 9

Turtles, priests, and the afterworld: a study in the iconographic interpretation of Polynesian petroglyphs

Barry Rolett

Recent archaeological studies attest to a burgeoning interest in the reconstruction of prehistoric thought patterns (Hodder 1982a, b; Leone 1982), based on the assumption that 'recovery of mind' is an attainable goal. This assumption is related to the general view that 'archaeology is a cultural science, and that all social strategies and adaptation must be understood as part of cultural, symbolically meaningful contexts' (Hodder 1982b, viii). It has been argued that the proper focus of archaeological studies centered on cognition should be particularistic rather than general:

> There can never be any direct predictive relationships between material culture and social behavior because in each particular context general symbolic principles, and general tendencies for the integration of belief and action are rearranged in particular ways as part of the strategies and intents of individuals and groups. The 'whole' is particular, dependent on contexts. (Hodder 1982a, 217)

This essay — an exploration into the archaeological study of cognition — focusses on a narrow topic of inquiry, turtle petroglyphs specifically in the Marquesas Islands of Eastern Polynesia, but situated within the broader context of Polynesian cultures. My interest in the significance of turtle motifs stems from the discovery of a remarkable petroglyph site (figs. 9.1, 9.2) on Nukuhiva Island, in the northern Marquesas. The Hatiheu Valley boulder site exhibits one of the finest arrays of petroglyphs hitherto known from the Marquesas. The eight turtles included among the representations that nearly cover the decorated face of the boulder are notable not only as the first turtle motifs recorded from the Marquesas, but also because of their evident deliberate arrangement in clusters and their execution in a patterned portrayal showing adherence to easily recognizable stylistic models.[1] Turtle petroglyphs are already well known from the Societies and other islands in Eastern Polynesia, so that discovery of similar motifs in the Marquesas seemed to open a promising avenue for comparative research. The decision to focus only on turtle motifs was made not because of any *a priori* assumption that other petroglyph types are less significant, but rather because turtle motifs are unambiguously identifiable representations, and because ethnographic evidence for the significance of turtles in Polynesian culture provided a convenient point of departure for research into the symbolic value of the motifs.

In focussing on turtle motifs, an attempt is made to demonstrate the usefulness of analyzing petroglyphs within a broad framework of ethnographic and archaeological data. Such an approach allows investigation into the possible meaning of iconographic subjects through reconstruction of their original context. But while this method is attractive in cases where there are no textual records to explain the context of an iconographic message, it has an important drawback which

Fig. 9.1. Petroglyph boulder in the Hatiheu Valley, Nukuhiva. Behind the boulder is a terraced ceremonial ground, the Kamuihei *tohua*.

has been noted by one of its chief advocates, André Leroi-Gourhan: the total value of the interpretation depends upon the value of the reconstruction (1975, 49). The nature of the archaeological record in most parts of the world is such that iconographic interpretation of prehistoric art through ethnographic inference has been more thoroughly explored in theory than in practice. In the Pacific, however, there is the advantage of a striking continuity between prehistoric and ethnographically documented cultures.

Despite the wealth of documentation for contact period Pacific Island cultures, few attempts have been made to analyze and interpret iconographic materials from this region by the proposition of hypotheses based on ethnological records. Moreover, the few investigators who have made use of ethnological records generally limited themselves to information given by native informants who were asked to explain the meaning of a specific motif (Ellis 1917, 346; Cox and Stasack 1970, 67—8). Such restricted use of the ethnographic record has limited potential because references to specific petroglyphs are exceedingly rare.

Most archaeological studies of Pacific Island petroglyphs have been carried out with the limited objective of compiling a descriptive inventory of motifs (e.g., Lavachery 1939; Linton 1925; Emory 1933; Cox and Stasack 1970; Frimigacci and Monnin 1980). Petroglyph inventories have been of considerable interest to researchers who have compared rock art motifs with ones known from mobiliary art and tattooing in an effort to define iconographic relationships between different islands and art forms (e.g., Handy 1938). However, the contribution of petrograph studies to such research has been relatively minor and the chief value of this comparative work has been to point out strong relationships between motifs found in mobiliary art and tattooing (von den Steinen 1928; Begouen 1928).

Recent work by Frimigacci and Monnin (1980) in New Caledonia exemplifies the contribution which can be made by inventory-oriented petroglyph studies. By analyzing the spatial distribution of motifs, Frimigacci and Monnin were able to identify associations that are characteristic of different geographic regions of this large island. These characteristic

Fig. 9.2. Detail of the petroglyphs on the Hatiheu petroglyph boulder shown in Figure 9.1.

associations effectively distinguish certain regions, and it has been suggested that they may reflect cultural sub-groupings (Frimigacci and Monnin 1980, 52). Spatial analysis of rock art motifs, a method pioneered by André Leroi-Gourhan in the study of Paleolithic cave art, is attractive both because it produces a *catalogue raisonné* of motifs and because it maintains a fundamental distinction between representation and meaning.

Form and space

In order to classify the petroglyphs at the Hatiheu Valley boulder site on Nukuhiva (fig. 9.1) I adopted the system proposed by Leroi-Gourhan (1982) in his study of Paleolithic cave art. This morphological framework comprises four successive levels, or 'figurative states', without implying directional changes from one state to another. Thus, I avoid one of the main problems with early research on Polynesian decorative art, namely that relationships between motifs were interpreted in an evolutionary manner even though there was no empirical evidence for succession. Leroi-Gourhan's figurative states vary from the pure geometric, consisting of non-representational signs, to the analytical figurative, which tends toward naturalistic representation.

Pure geometric figures are signs which, unlike elements of the other figurative states, cannot be identified without information from oral or written sources. Pure geometric figures from the Hatiheu site include crosses, quadrilaterals, circles, and arcs. The value of identifying these signs as a separate category is that the study of repeated associations

between signs and other motifs may reveal statistically significant relationships, as has been the case in Paleolithic cave art. Unfortunately, such a study is not possible at the present time because most Pacific Island petroglyph sites are only incompletely recorded and little attention has been given to spatial associations of motifs.

Geometric figurative elements are also signs, but unlike pure geometric elements, the subjects which they represent are relatively identifiable. These elements are generally geometricized forms of animal or human figures which are represented elsewhere in more naturalistic state. Stick-man (*etua*) motifs with upraised arms and legs astraddle, known from Hatiheu and other Marquesan sites (Suggs 1961, 144), as well as from Marquesan decorated bamboos (Begouen 1928), are a good example of geometric figurative elements. *Etua* motifs are clearly related to the full length anthropomorphic *tiki* figures which are highly developed in Marquesan statuary and mobiliary art.

The *synthetic figurative* is an intermediary stage between the geometric figurative, tending towards non-figurative representations, and the *analytical figurative*, in which animals are portrayed with near accuracy of natural morphology. Synthetic figurative elements express essentials of form without the detail of the analytical figurative. The animal figures from the Hatiheu boulder are synthetic figurative motifs. They include three types of turtles, two fish, an unidentified supernatural animal, and a jungle fowl (fig. 9.1). The large fish carved in bas relief, dominating the other animals, is readily identifiable as a dolphin fish or *mahimahi*

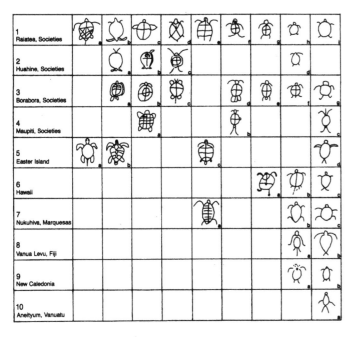

Fig. 9.3. Distribution of turtle petroglyph motifs in Oceania.

(*Corphyraena*). The turtle types are distinguished by the shape of the carapace, the size of the flippers, and the presence or absence of a line across the carapace. Those with the dorsal lines have a pointed carapace and larger front than back flippers (fig. 9.3, 7a). The three of this type are grouped with four others that also have pointed shells but differ by the absence of the dorsal line and a less pronounced difference between the front and back flippers (fig. 9.3. 7b). The third type, represented by three examples, one of which is situated well away from the group of other turtles, has an oval shaped carapace and front and back flippers of nearly equal size (fig. 9.3, 7c).

When the Hatiheu turtle motifs are compared with ones known from other Pacific Island sites, a number of stylistic trends become apparent. The Hatiheu motifs are abbreviated forms that express the essential features of natural morphology using a minimal number of lines. In contrast, two motifs from Easter Island (fig. 9.3, 5a, b) approach visual accuracy, while the other turtle figures shown in fig. 9.3 are geometricized and abbreviated forms in various degrees of development. Society Islands' turtle motifs exhibit the greatest diversity, varying from motifs displaying certain naturalistic elements (fig. 9.3, 1a–c, 2a, b, 4a) to others which are abbreviated (fig. 9.3, 1h, i, 2d, 3g, 4c), and geometricized (fig. 9.3, 1c–g, 2c, 3a–f).

Figure 9.3 presents the range of variation in all reported Pacific Island turtle petroglyph motifs. These are known mainly from Eastern Polynesia, with rare examples from Fiji, New Caledonia, and Vanuatu. In the absence of counts which would quantify the relative frequencies of the different motifs,

we are forced to rely upon non-systematic observations for an idea of their geographical distribution. Turtle motifs have been recorded on four of the Society Islands (Raiatea, Huahine, Borabora, and Maupiti), and Emory (1933) has noted that they are the most frequently encountered motif there. In contrast, in most of the other islands, turtles are comparatively rare. In places where they are rare, the motifs are usually isolated, while in the Societies and on Nukuhiva they are often found grouped in clusters similar to those characteristic of the Hatiheu Valley boulder.

Figure 9.3 highlights several stylistic trends. First, there are notable similarities between the abbreviated turtle motifs from the Societies, Marquesas, Hawai'i, and New Caledonia. Those from Fiji and Vanuatu are somewhat at variance from the other abbreviated forms. Moreover, there is a strong tradition in the Societies and Easter Island which involves geometrically patterned motifs. The patterned figures display close adherence to established aesthetic traditions, for some of their characteristic geometricized forms have been recorded from multiple sites on the same island. A good example is item 3d in figure 9.3, a prominently represented motif at Emory's *ofai honu* (Emory 1933), as well as at another nearby site recorded by myself in 1981. It is also interesting that items 3b, 3d, 3e, and 4b from figure 9.3 depict the front flippers departing from the head, a characteristic trait of Fijian motifs.

The turtle motifs are most obviously classified, however, by the degree of visual accuracy which they exhibit. There are two modes of departure from the most morphologically accurate motifs (fig. 9.3, 5a–b): (1) geometricization of the forms into patterned figures; and (2) abbreviation of the forms into simple figures with a minimum number of lines. Depiction of sexual dimorphism may account for some of the variability among motifs; those with long tails are probably males. Sexual differentiation on the basis of this criterion is particularly marked among motifs from Fiji, Hawai'i, and Borabora.

In the Marquesas, where the turtles like other figures in rock art are depicted in abbreviated form, more naturalistic turtle motifs are known from mobiliary art (von den Steinen 1923, fig. 215) and a highly geometricized form was widely employed in tattooing (Handy 1922).

The Marquesan cultural context

The Hatiheu Valley boulder is located in the interior of the valley on a slope near the upper portion of a series of paved stone terraces comprising a ceremonial ground, or *tohua*. A megalithic raised platform, notable both for its elaborate stonework and for an ancient banyan (*Ficus* sp.) growing on one corner, lies at the lower end of the terraces (figs. 9.4, 9.5). Judged on the basis of the size of the platform, its proximity to the *tohua*, the quality of the dry masonry construction, and the presence of the banyan (traditionally associated with sacred places), this stone structure is interpreted as a *me'ae*, the focal point of Marquesan religious ceremonies.[2]

Fig. 9.4. The Teipoka *me'ae*, Hatiheu Valley, Nukuhiva. The *me'ae* is situated at the end of a terraced ceremonial ground, on the edge of which is the illustrated petroglyph boulder.

Although it is difficult to distinguish between Marquesan *me'ae* and residential house platforms on the basis of masonry construction alone, *me'ae* are generally larger and more elaborately built than house platforms (Linton 1925, 34).

There is some evidence of a functional distinction between two types of *me'ae*, those that were reserved primarily for ceremonies related to the disposal of the dead, and those that were the scene of a wider range of ceremonies, but generally of lesser importance than the mortuary rites. Mortuary *me'ae* are nearly all located in secluded parts of upper valleys (Linton 1925, 33; Gracia 1843, 57–8), while public *me'ae* are usually found in the vicinity of residential areas, especially near the intersections of commonly travelled paths (Gracia 1843, 59). Missionary records list thirteen *me'ae* in Hatiheu. This site is most likely Me'ae Te Ipoka, dedicated to Tevanauaua, god who accords victory (CM Ms I, 14).

Von den Steinen (1928) visited Me'ae Te Ipoka in the late nineteenth century and identified the site as the traditional residence of the inspirational priest or *taua* of Hatiheu. Marquesan *taua* were distinguished from the rest of the

population by their perceived ability to communicate directly with the deities (*atua*), most of whom Marquesans considered to be the spirits of deceased *taua* and chiefs (*hakaiki*). The Marquesan term for deity, *atua*, was also applied to certain *taua* who achieved divine status during the course of their lives, but the number of *taua* who attained this level of importance was probably no more than one or two per island (Vincendon-Dumoulin 1843, 226). All other *taua* were elevated to deified status after death through a series of ceremonies highlighted by numerous human sacrifices. *Atua* were believed to exercise supernatural power over the elements, being able to provide rich harvests or make the land sterile, and to inflict sickness or death at will. Less powerful than the *atua* but closely linked with them, *taua* possessed the ability to determine the cause of calamities affecting the population and to foresee danger (Vincendon-Dumoulin 1843, 227). The spiritual link between *taua* and *atua* manifested itself in self-induced trances, during which the *taua* was possessed by the *atua* which he either trapped by catching it in his hands, or which entered directly into his body (Gracia 1843, 46). The *taua* spoke oracles during the trances, which always occurred

Fig. 9.5. The lower retaining wall of Teipoka *me'ae*. Marquesan *me'ae* are noted for their massiveness and the excellence of their construction. The wall height is 3.8 meters.

on the *me'ae*, transmitting information communicated to him by the *atua* in an unnatural, squeaky voice produced in the manner of a ventriloquist. Oracles spoken by the *taua* often called for human victims or offerings of food to be brought upon the *me'ae* in order to satisfy the wishes of the *atua*. Such commands were supported by the power of the *hakaiki*, who were considered to be direct descendants of certain *atua* and who in some cases were themselves also *taua* (Gracia 1843, 47).

Descriptions of *me'ae* by early nineteenth-century visitors to the Marquesas project vivid images of the sites and religious ceremonies performed at them. Stone and wooden anthropomorphic representations, some of which were more than two meters tall, seem to have been a nearly universal feature of mortuary *me'ae* on Nukuhiva (Stewart 1831, 290; Tautain 1897, 669); these also appeared, less commonly, on public *me'ae* (Linton 1925, 32). These images, known as *tiki*, were sculpted in a highly conventionalized style but appear to have represented various different *atua*, especially deified *hakaiki* and *taua* (Tautain 1897, 673, 677).

House structures with pointed roofs likened by early visitors to obelisks were also a characteristic feature of mortuary *me'ae* (Porter 1822, 110). These structures, known as *ha'e tua* (literally, pointed house), were presided over by the *taua* and were dedicated to the tribal tutelar gods who were often believed to inhabit them (Handy 1923, 49). The *ha'e tua* and tress in the vicinity of the *me'ae* were draped with streamers of white bark cloth, identifying the area as a *tapu* precinct (Porter 1822, 116). Porter's account of a visit to a *me'ae* includes the following description:

The obelisks [*ha'e tua*] are about thirty-five feet in height, and about the base of them were hung the heads of hogs and tortoises, as I was informed, as offerings to their gods. On the right of this grove, distant only a few paces, were four splendid war canoes, furnished with their outriggers, and decorated with ornaments of human hair, coral shells, etc., with an abundance of white streamers. Their heads were placed toward the mountain, and in the stern of each was a figure of a man with a paddle steering, in full dress, ornamented

with plumes, earrings made to represent those formed
of whales' teeth, and every other ornament of the
fashion of the country. One of the canoes was more
splendid than the others, and was situated nearer the
grove. I inquired who the dignified personage might be
who was seated in her stern, and was informed that this
was the priest who had been killed, not long since, by
the Happahs. The stench here was intolerable from the
number of offerings which had been made, but, attracted
by curiosity, I went to examine the canoes more minutely,
and found the bodies of two of the Typees, whom we
had killed, in a bloated state, at the bottom of that of
the priest, and many other human carcasses, with the
flesh still on them, lying about the canoe. (Porter 1822,
110–11)

Porter's valuable description identifies the significance
of the *me'ae* as related to the recent death of a priest, or *taua*.
It is of particular interest to note that the 'tortoise' heads
were hung about the base of the *ha'e tua* and the *me'ae*. In
all likelihood, these were heads of the green turtle (*Chelonia
mydas*). Although the hawksbill turtle (*Eretmochelys
imbricata*) was valued as the source of tortoise shell used in
the manufacture of ornaments, the green turtle appears to
have been regarded with special religious significance. One
indication of the high esteem accorded the green turtle is that
after Christian influence in the Marquesas prevailed against
the ceremonial use of human victims, the green turtle or *honu*
was substituted in their place (Jardin 1862, 74). Further
evidence of the religious and ceremonial value of turtles is
given in a myth recorded by Handy (1930, 35). In the myth,
two men engage in building a raised stone platform (*paepae*)
to commemorate the death of a close relative. Upon nearing
completion of the *paepae*, the men set out on a special fishing
expedition to capture turtles for use in connection with
ceremonies associated with final completion of the structure.
When the *paepae* was finished and the ceremony involving the
turtles had been enacted, the spirit of the honored relative,
still lingering until that time about the earth, made its final
passage to the afterworld.

The reference to turtles in connection with a memorial
ceremony seems related to the Marquesan practice of holding
celebrations to commemorate the death of an individual.
Feasting was an important part of such occasions, as was the
ritual offering of food to the *atua* believed to be responsible
for helping the spirit of the deceased (Handy 1923, 217).
According to Gracia (1843, 117), memorial ceremonies were
held one lunar month after death and again after ten lunar
months. Offerings were viewed as essential in ensuring a
successful passage of the spirit to its final resting place in the
afterworld. This is well illustrated by the response given to
Porter in answer to his questions about why the dead enemy
warriors had been placed in the canoe of a *taua* killed in
recent hostilities with the neighboring valley. Porter was
informed through his interpreter that the *taua* was on his
way to the afterworld and that a 'crew' of ten enemy warriors

was needed in order to paddle his canoe there (1822, 111).
Gracia (1843, 45) also noted that seven to ten human sacrifices
generally were necessary in order to elevate the spirit of a
taua to the status of *atua*. The description of the *taua*'s passage
to the afterworld in terms of a canoe voyage is an appropriate
metaphor because deification of the *taua* after death essentially
involved a transition from earth to the afterworld, the
antipodes of which were considered to be the dwelling place
of the *atua*. Thus the turtle offerings made in connection
with the memorial ceremony mentioned in the myth, like
the human victims placed in the canoe of the *taua*, may be
viewed as serving the purpose of effecting a successful
transition, in the sense of actual physical displacement, from
earth to the afterworld.

In addition to their value in connection with memorial
ceremonies, turtles were also important in other religious
rites. Catholic missionary records indicate that occasions on
which human victims or food offerings were left on the
me'ae included ceremonies designed to obtain victory in war
(CM Ms. II, 42), to bring rain (CM Ms. II, 38), and to obtain
help from the gods in avenging an enemy who for some reason
was beyond the reach of the intended aggressor (CM Ms. II, 44).
Certain species of the Marquesan plant and animal worlds
were regarded as particularly suitable offerings to the gods
and these were made *tapu*. Delmas' 1927 listing of *tapu*
plants and animals for each valley on Nukuhiva demonstrates
a high degree of inter-valley variability, reinforcing the
conclusion that the imposition of a *tapu*, whether temporary
or permanent, was within the power of an individual *taua*
(Handy 1923, 259; Gracia 1843, 52).

The *tapu* on the turtle appears to have been one of the
strongest and most culturally ingrained. In the eighteenth-
century missionary record of William Crook (n.d., 55), and in
Jardin's natural history of the Marquesas (1862, 74), the
turtle is said to have been reserved for consumption by high
status individuals. Another source states that turtles were
'dedicated to the gods' (CM Ms. I, 14). However, these general
statements are insufficient to reveal the full extent to which
Marquesan behavior toward a particular species was affected
by its *tapu* status. Such information can be derived only from
examination of specific cases in which actual behavior in
connection with a *tapu* species was recorded. Although specific
cases involving the turtle are absent in the ethnohistoric
literature, valuable inferences may be drawn from examination
of an event recorded by Gracia (1843, 53–4) involving a red
pig, among the most *tapu* of all animals. Gracia, who had
purchased the pig, was surprised at the rough manner in which
his Marquesan helper proceeded to drive it to the house. Yet
despite the youth's unrestrained abuse in delivering the pig,
he objected fearfully to Gracia's suggestion that he kill it.
After the pig had met its fate, the boy nonetheless consented
to cook part of it for the missionaries, although he would not
eat any of the meat himself, or even any of the other food
cooked in the same pot. Instead, the Marquesan youth took
his own separate portion of uncooked meat and kindled a

new fire to prepare his own meal, being careful to use different utensils than those that had been used to prepare the missionaries' food.

Several inferences emerge from Gracia's episode, regarding the cultural significance of Marquesan food *tapu.* First, the fact that a food was *tapu* did not necessarily prohibit all but high status individuals such as *taua, hakaiki,* or missionaries from eating of it. Rather, low status individuals, such as the youth in Gracia's account, were permitted to eat meat from a *tapu* animal provided that they partook of portions cooked and served separately from those portions prepared for the high status individuals. In this context, it is possible that the food remains of feasts held on the *me'ae* were suspended from the walls of the *ha'e tua* and hung from branches of the trees in the religious precinct because that food was *tapu* to all but the participants in the ceremony. Moreover, there is evidence that participants in such ceremonies were subject to the influence of the *tapu* only during the period of the ceremony (see Porter 1822, 115 for temporary *tapus* associated with particular ceremonies). Finally, although low status individuals apparently were restricted from killing a *tapu* animal, other behavior toward the living animals was less strictly controlled, as evidenced by the youth's rough treatment of the pig as he drove it to the mission.

Direct ethnohistoric evidence to test the validity of these inferences as they pertain to Marquesan behavior regarding turtles is available only with reference to fishing. Apparently, special ceremonies were held in connection with planning fishing expeditions to catch turtles for use in ceremonies, and the fishermen were *tapu* both during the ceremony and the ensuing fishing expedition. Porter witnessed a *me'ae* ceremony which he was informed was related to the success of the turtle hunt:

> I have seen Gattanewa with all his sons, and many others sitting for hours together clapping their hands and singing before a number of little wooden gods laid out in small houses erected for the occasion, and ornamented with strips of cloth. They were such houses as a child would have made, of about two feet long and eighteen inches high, and no less than ten or twelve of them in a cluster, like a small village. By the side of these were several canoes, furnished with their paddles, seines, harpoons, and other fishing apparatus, and round the whole a line was drawn to show that the place was tabooed. Within this line was Gattanewa and others, like overgrown babies, singing and clapping their hands, sometimes laughing and talking, and appearing to give their ceremony no attention . . . I enquired the cause of this ceremony of Gattanewa; he told me he was going to catch tortoise for the gods, and that he should have to pray to them several days and nights for success, during which time he would be tabooed, and dare not enter a house frequented by women. (Porter 1822, 115)

Edward Robarts, an early nineteenth-century beachcomber, also referred to the *tapu* on men fishing for turtles, noting

that he and a *hakaiki* he accompanied were not allowed 'during the time of searching for turtle to go among females' (Dening 1974, 251).

Pan-Polynesian comparison

The demonstrable derivation of all Polynesian cultures from a common ancestral tradition makes the comparative approach a fruitful method of research in this area (see Green, this volume). Inter-archipelago comparison of the cultural significance of turtles in Polynesia demonstrates that the observed religious significance of turtles in the Marquesas reflects concepts originally rooted in Ancestral Polynesian culture. Comparative data can also serve as a basis for drawing inferences concerning aspects of Marquesan culture for which adequate documentation is lacking.

Turtles played a central role in certain ceremonies held at religious sites in the Tuamotu Islands of Eastern Polynesia. According to the Catholic missionary Montiton (1874, 378–9), who witnessed these ceremonies during the mid-nineteenth century, turtles were beheaded and disemboweled at the temple site (*marae*), then cooked in special ovens and eaten by the ceremonial priests and their assistants. After this first serving, the turtle meat was divided and distributed to other men of the community but apparently not to women or children. In the Central Polynesian island of Tongareva, the beachcomber Lamont participated in a *marae* ceremony that involved turtle feasting (Lamont 1867, 182–3). The turtle was beheaded and disemboweled on the *marae* and taken to the community meeting place where it was served to Lamont and three chiefs. Surrounded by a group of onlookers who complimented his generosity when he shared pieces of the meat with them, Lamont threw some of the meat to the wives of the chiefs, who, to his great surprise, recoiled in terror, shouting '*huie atua!*' (prohibited). Lamont noted that after the ceremony he was treated with increased respect in the community and accorded the highest ranking title, that of *ariki* (see Buck 1932, 91–2 for an analysis of Lamont's account). The practice of similar ceremonies involving turtle feasting in the Cooks and Society Islands is suggested by an observation in the missionary narrative of John Williams:

> The turtle was considered by the Rarotongans and Tahitians as most sacred. A part of every one caught was offered to the gods, and the rest cooked with sacred fire, and partaken of by the king and principal chiefs only. (Williams 1838, 429)

The widespread Polynesian distribution of turtle ceremonies is further evidenced by ethnographic notes from Anuta collected by Kirch and Rosendahl (1973, 26) identifying a specialized *marae* (located in the immediate vicinity of the principal pre-Christian-era *marae*) as one where turtles and porpoises were cooked and eaten in religious ceremonies. A Rarotongan chief portrayed in the frontispiece of Williams' narrative had turtle motifs tattooed on his knees, although the rest of his tattoos were geometric motifs. Williams (1838, 463) identified the chief as Tepo and stated that the tattoos were executed 'in consequence of the death of his ninth child'. Records of the cultural significance of turtles in other island groups are less specific and generally refer only to the *tapu* surrounding them that restricted their consumption by persons other than high status individuals. In addition to those noted for the Marquesas, tabus regarding the consumption of turtles are known from the Society Islands (Henry 1928, 381), the Tuamotus (Montiton 1874, 369), Mangareva (Buck 1938, 91), the Cook Islands (Williams 1838, 429; Lamont 1867, 182–3), Hawai'i (Stewart 1826, 365), Easter Island (Barthel 1978, 142), Samoa (Buck 1930, 522), the Tokelau Islands (MacGregor 1937, 100), Futuna (Burrows 1936, 103), and 'Uvea (Burrows 1937, 144). In Melanesia, restrictions on fishing for turtles and on eating them have been reported from the Lau Islands, Fiji (Thompson 1940, 137, 154) and the Loyalties (Ray 1917, 290; Guiart 1963, 285, 289).

Comparative research also reveals that archaeological associations between turtle petroglyphs and religiously significant sites exist in the Society Islands and in Easter Island, in addition to the Marquesas. In the Societies, associations between turtle petroglyphs and stone structures are of two types: (1) cases where turtle motifs are found engraved on stones used in the exterior wall construction of *marae* and raised platforms (*paepae*) known to have been elite residences; and (2) cases where turtle motifs are engraved on boulders situated near raised stone structures of religious significance. The first case is by far the most common.

Turtle motifs associated with *marae* in the Society Islands are engraved on quarried limestone slabs forming the facing wall of the *ahu*, the long narrow structure which was the focal point of *marae* ceremonies. Although Emory (1933) found turtle petroglyphs at only five of the 114 *marae* he recorded in the Leeward Islands, three of those *marae* (Manunu, Anini, and Tainuu) are among the largest in the archipelago. *Marae* Tainuu, at Tevaitoa, Raiatea, is the largest of all, being 162 feet long and 20 feet wide. Turtle motifs are engraved on two of the facing stones of *Marae* Tainuu (fig. 9.3, 1b, d, 1h–i) and on the basalt cornerstone of a nearby *paepae* (fig. 9.3, 1a) which Emory recorded as the residence of the chief of Tevaitoa (Emory 1933, 154). *Marae* Manunu and Anini on Huahine are of a distinct type; both sites have a smaller platform built on top of the *ahu*, a feature unknown from other *marae* (Emory 1933, 34). Two of the *marae* (Manunu and Rauhuru) with turtle petroglyphs are at Maeva, where the *marae* of all the principal families of Huahine Nui were clustered together in a group of twenty-five structures. There are two boulder sites, on Borabora and Maupiti, with impressive groups of turtle petroglyphs but apparently neither of these sites is associated with raised stone structures (Emory 1933, 173, 175). Drawings of these petroglyph groups and detailed information about the Leeward Islands *marae* are given in Emory (1933).

On Easter Island a turtle motif (fig. 9.3, 1d) is engraved on a slab of an important religious structure, the *ahu* Ihu Arero (Lavachery 1939, 35). Other motifs, including representations of 'birdmen', octopus, and possibly whales,

are associated with the turtle, but apparently this site is the only religious structure on Easter Island that is directly associated with animal motif petroglyphs (Lavachery 1939, 110).

Interpretation

Little is known regarding the motivations for executing petroglyphs in Polynesia, even in island groups such as the Societies, Marquesas, and Hawai'i, where petroglyph sites are relatively common. This gap in the ethnographic and archaeological record of Polynesia is especially striking in consideration of our clearer understanding of the motivations for other art forms such as tattooing, and the carving of stone monuments. Two problems in interpreting petroglyphs are: (1) iconographic significance can vary in both time and space; and (2) the motivation for executing a particular work, whether it be religious, social, or aesthetic, must be demonstrated if an attempt is made to distinguish between these often closely related sources of inspiration (Leroi-Gourhan 1975, 50). The first problem, variability of iconographic significance in time and space, raises the question of the extent to which ethnographic data from the European contact period accounts are relevant to the interpretation of petroglyphs which (except in rare cases involving European subject matter or direct association with datable cultural deposits) cannot yet be directly dated. One effective means of establishing the time depth of certain concepts characteristic of Polynesian cultures is to demonstrate, through inter-island group comparison, that the underlying themes can be traced back to the common ancestral cultural tradition. Concepts assignable to this ancestral tradition – such as the religious significance of turtles – can be used with confidence in proposing ethnologically based interpretations of petroglyphs. It is likely, however, that even as there is variability among Polynesian concepts concerning the cultural significance of turtles (presumably resulting from divergence and differentiation in isolated island groups), the iconographic significance of turtle petroglyphs probably also developed differently in each island group. More complete documentation of petroglyph sites in the Marquesas and other archipelagoes will provide an increasingly firmer basis for defining the nature of this variability in terms of archaeological context.

The second problem, that of distinguishing between religious, social, and aesthetic sources of inspiration, is particularly complex because such sources of inspiration were so closely linked in Polynesian cultures. Even the first-hand observers whose accounts form the basis of reconstructions of the traditional cultures were unclear about such distinctions. For example, Gracia (1843, 55) states that Marquesan men met regularly at public *me'ae* on occasions which involved both religious ceremonies and feasting, and that even the feasting seems to have been regarded as a kind of religious act, because it included putting food to the mouths of the *tiki* and attaching uneaten remains of the feast to the walls of the thatched house built on the *me'ae*. There were no clearly defined boundaries between the realms of religious, social, and aesthetic concerns. Rather, Marquesan culture was characterized by the intertwining of these aspects of culture, and it is by keeping this consideration in the forefront that an attempt at interpretation of the Hatiheu turtle petroglyphs can best be made.

The significance of turtles in religious ceremonies involving treatment of the dead, as suggested by the myth recorded by Handy and by Porter's description of a mortuary *me'ae*, indicates a connection between turtles and the passage to the afterworld. Marquesans believed both in an underworld (*Hawaiki*) and in the heavens (*aki*). Dordillon (1931, 156) lists three stratified levels of *Hawaiki*: (1) *Hawaiki ta uka* (uppermost); (2) *Hawaiki vaveka* (middle); and (3) *Hawaiki ta ao* (lowermost). The spirits of commoners were believed to have little chance of attaining the lowest, most desirable level of *Hawaiki*. If the death of a commoner was not honored by the proper mortuary rites it was believed that the spirit could not leave earth but would remain to haunt the living (Delmas 1927, 52–3). Entry to the afterworld could also be made through the heavens, and it is interesting to note that the heavens were believed to be linked with the underworld, so that the highest level of *aki* corresponded to the lowest level of *Hawaiki* (Delmas 1927).

The turtle may have been associated with *Hawaiki* because of its ability to dive to great ocean depths. More significant, however, is the turtle's ability to pass from the depths of the ocean to the land, where it lays its eggs. In this metaphorical sense, turtles are able to cross the boundary between two separate worlds. The Marquesan *taua* was similarly held in awe because of his ability to communicate between the world of mortals and that of the deities. I suggest that the religious significance of turtles in the Marquesas, and in Polynesian cultures generally, is related to a symbolic association between turtles and the transcendence of boundaries between worlds. That Polynesians did, in fact, view turtles in terms of this ability to cross these boundaries is illustrated by certain Tuamotuan chants associated with turtle ceremonies. One such chant, recited as the turtle was ritually killed, runs as follows:

Ka ma te po, ka ma te ao.
Koia Tu, koia Ragi;
Mata-iki, Mata-ho.
Tagi i te po, tagi i te ao,
Hura tana pu ha i katau e,
Kia mate!

The nether world, the upper
world is freed of restrictions.
There is Tu, there is Ragi;
Mata-iki, Mata-ho.
Sounding in the nether world,
sounding in the upper world.

Their trumpet is heard on the right,
Heralding the death of the victim.

(Emory 1947, 75)

The contrasts of above and below, and of inland and seaward, are common themes in other chants recited during turtle ceremonies (Emory 1947, 75, 78–80). Turtles, we surmise, then, were symbolically associated with *taua* because, like their human counterparts, they could transcend boundaries between worlds. Likewise, as a symbol of the transcendence between worlds, turtles were viewed as particularly appropriate for use in connection with mortuary and memorial ceremonies, the purpose of which was to assist the successful passage of a spirit from earth through the stratified layers of the afterworld to its final destination.

This interpretation of Marquesan turtle petroglyphs found in Hatiheu Valley represents an effort to incorporate the analysis of iconographic materials into the study of Polynesian prehistory. The approach employed involves investigation into the possible meaning of petroglyphs through reconstruction of their original context and the proposition of hypotheses based upon ethnological records. This method of studying iconographic themes within a cultural context could also be applied in research on other petroglyph motifs. Indeed, the range of its potential application extends to the analysis of all iconographic themes and materials for which there are relevant ethnological records. 'Recovery of mind', or the reconstruction of prehistoric thought patterns, should now be viewed not only as an attainable goal but as a promising avenue for future research.[3]

Notes

[1] Suggs (1961, 145, 147) mentions having found turtle petroglyphs on Nukuhiva, at Ha'atuatua and in Hatiheu, but the specific motifs were not recorded.

[2] Different terms, *me'ae* and *ahu*, were used with the same significance in various parts of the Marquesas. Following the precedent set by Linton (1925, 31), and in order to simplify matters, the term *me'ae* is used as a general designation for all such sites in this paper.

[3] My opportunity to visit the Marquesas Islands was made possible by a fellowship from the Thomas J. Watson Foundation. Work on the paper began at Yale University under the supervision of Richard Pearson and I thank him for his encouragement, as well as for having invited me to present the results of my research at the XIth International Congress of Anthropological and Ethnological Sciences. I am also grateful for valuable comments and criticism that I have received from Patrick Kirch, Douglas Oliver, Tom Dye, Patrick McCoy, Paul Cleghorn, and Robert Suggs. Finally, I am indebted to Monseigneur Alain Le Cleach and Severin 'Matu' Katupa of Nukuhiva for having shared their knowledge of the Hatiheu Valley petroglyph boulder with me, and to David Kiphuth of the Yale Peabody Museum for having made the drawing of it from my photographs.

88

REFERENCES

Aberle, D. F 1983. The proto-speech community as a focus for historical reconstruction. Paper presented at the 11th International Congress of Anthropological and Ethnological Sciences, Vancouver, British Columbia.

Adams, R. N. 1975. *Energy and Structure: A Theory of Social Power*. Austin, University of Texas Press.

Adams, R. W. 1984. '*In the Land of Strangers*': *A Century of European Contact with Tana 1774–1874*. Pacific Research Monograph 9. Canberra, Australian National University.

Adams, W. Y. 1978. On migration and diffusion as rival paradigms. In P. G. Duke, J. Ebert, G. Langemann and A. P. Buchner (eds.), *Diffusion and Migration: Their Roles in Cultural Development*. CHACMOOL, The Archaeological Association of the University of Calgary.

Adams, W. Y. 1979. On the argument from ceramics to history: a challenge based on evidence from Medieval Nubia. *Current Anthropology* 20:727–44.

Adams, W. Y., D. P. Van Gerven and R. S. Levy 1978. The retreat from migrationism. *Annual Review of Anthropology* 7:483–532.

Alkire, W. H. 1965. *Lamotrek Atoll and Inter-Island Socioeconomic Ties*. Illinois Studies in Anthropology No. 5. Urbana, University of Illinois Press.

Alkire, W. H. 1977. *An Introduction to the Peoples and Cultures of Micronesia*, 2nd edn. Menlo Park, Calif., Cummings.

Allen, J. 1977. Sea traffic, trade, and expanding horizons. In J. Allen, J. Golson, and R. Jones (eds.), *Sunda and Sahul: Prehistoric Studies in Southeast Asia, Melanesia, and Australia*. London, Academic Press, 387–417.

Allen, J. 1982. Pre-contact trade in Papua New Guinea. In R. J. May and H. Nelson (eds.), *Melanesia: Beyond Diversity*. Canberra, Australian National University, 193–205.

Allen, M. S. 1981. An analysis of the Mauna Kea Adze Quarry archaeobotanical assemblage. Unpublished M.A. thesis, University of Hawai'i, Honolulu.

Allen, M. S. 1984. A review of archaeobotany and palaeoethnobotany in Hawai'i. *Hawai'ian Archaeology* 1:19–30.

Ambrose, W. R. and R. C. Green 1972. Fifth millennium BC transport of obsidian from New Britain to the Solomon Islands. *Nature* 237:31.

Anell, B. 1955. Contribution to the history of fishing in the southern seas. *Studia Ethnographica Upsaliensia* 9. Uppsala, Almqvist and Wiksells Boktryckeri.

Ardener, E. 1959. Lineage and locality among the Mba-Ise Ibo. *Africa* 29:113–33.

Aubert de la Rue, E. 1938. Sur la nature et l'origine probable des pierres portées en pendentifs à l'île Tanna. *L'Anthropologie* 48:249–260.

Axelrod, R. 1984. *The Evolution of Cooperation*. New York, Basic Books.

Axelrod, R., and W. D. Hamilton 1981. The evolution of cooperation. *Science* 211:1390–6.

Ayres, W. S. 1970. Archaeological survey and excavations, Kamana-Nui Valley, Moanalua Ahupua'a South Halawa Valley, Halawa Ahupua'a. *Departmental Report Series* 70–8. Honolulu, Department of Anthropology, B.P. Bishop Museum.

Ayres, W. S. 1973. The cultural context of Easter Island religious structures. Ph.D. dissertation. Tulane University.

Babcock, T. F. 1977. A re-analysis of pottery from fortified sites on Taveuni, Fiji. *Archaeology and Physical Anthropology in Oceania* 7:112–34.

Bailey, G. N. 1983. Concepts of time in Quaternary prehistory. *Annual Review of Anthropology* 12:165–92.

Barnett, H. G. 1949. *Palauan Society*. Eugene, University of Oregon Press.

Barnett, H. G. 1960. *Being a Palauan*. New York, Holt, Rinehart and Winston.

Barrau, J. 1965. L'Humide et le sec. *Journal of the Polynesian Society* 74:329–45.

Barrera, W., Jr, 1971. Anaehoomalu: a Hawaiian oasis. *Pacific Anthropological Records* 15. Honolulu, Department of Anthropology, B.P. Bishop Museum.

Barrera, W., Jr, and P. V. Kirch 1973. Basaltic glass artefacts from Hawaii: their dating and prehistoric uses. *Journal of the Polynesian Society* 82:176–87.

Barthel, T. 1978. *The Eighth Land: The Polynesian Discovery and Settlement of Easter Island*. Honolulu, University of Hawai'i Press.

Bastin, R. 1981. Economic enterprise in a Tannese village. In M. Allen (ed.), *Vanuatu: Politics, Economics and Ritual in Island Melanesia*. Sydney, Academic Press, 337–55.

Bayliss-Smith, T. 1978. Maximum populations and standard populations: the carrying capacity question. In D. Green, C. Haselgroves, and M. Spriggs (eds.), *Social Organization and Settlement*, Part I. BAR International Series 47. Oxford, 129–51.

Bayliss-Smith, T. 1980. Population pressure, resources, and welfare: towards a more realistic measure of carrying capacity. In H. C. Brookfield (ed.), *Population-Environment Relations in Tropical Islands: The Case of Eastern Fiji*. Man in the Biosphere, Technical Notes 13. Paris, UNESCO, 61–93.

Begouen, H. 1928. Deux bambous pyrograves. *Bulletin de la Société d'Histoire Naturelle de Toulouse* 57:223–32.

Bellwood, P. 1978. *Man's Conquest of the Pacific*. Auckland, Collins.

Bellwood, P. 1979. Settlement Patterns. In J. D. Jennings (ed.), *The Prehistory of Polynesia*. Cambridge, Harvard University Press.

Bellwood, P. 1979. *Man's Conquest of the Pacific*. New York, Oxford University Press.

Berndt, R. M., and C. H. Berndt 1977. *The World of the First Australians*, rev. edn. Sydney, Ure Smith.

Best, S. 1977. Archaeological investigations on Lakeba, Lau Group, Fiji. *New Zealand Archaeological Association Newsletter* 20: 28–38.

Biggs, B. 1979. Proto-Polynesian word list II. *Working Papers in Anthropology, Archaeology, Linguistics and Maori Studies* 52. Auckland, Department of Anthropology, University of Auckland.

Birks, L. 1973. *Archaeological Excavations at Sigatoka Dune, Fiji*. Bulletin of the Fiji Museum 1.

Birks, L., and H. Birks 1967. A brief report on excavations at Sigatoka, Fiji. *New Zealand Archaeological Association Newsletter* 10: 16–25.

Birks, L., and H. Birks 1978. Archaeological excavations at Site VL 16/81, Yanuca Island, Fiji. *Oceanic Prehistory Records* 6, University of Auckland.

Blake, N. M., B. P. Hawkins, R. L. Kirk, K. Bhatia, P. Brown, R. M. Garruto and D. C. Gajdusek 1983. A population genetic study of the Banks and Torres Islands (Vanuatu) and of the Santa Cruz Islands and Polynesian Outliers (Solomon Islands). *American Journal of Physical Anthropology* 62:343–61.

Blumenstock, D. I., and S. Price 1967. Climates of the States: Hawaii. Environmental Science Data Service, *Climatology of the United States* 60–51. Washington, D.C., Government Printing Office.

Blust, R. A. 1972a. Proto-Oceanic addenda with cognates in non-Oceanic Austronesian languages. *Working Papers in Linguistics* 4:1–43. Honolulu, University of Hawai'i.

Blust, R. A. 1972b. Additions to 'Proto-Austronesian addenda' and 'Proto-Oceanic addenda with cognates in non-Oceanic Austronesian languages'. *Working Papers in Linguistics* 4 (8): 1–17. Honolulu, University of Hawai'i.

Bonnemaison, J. 1979. Les voyages et L'enracinement: Formes de fixation et de mobilité dans les sociétés traditionelles des Nouvelles-Hébrides. *L'Espace Géographique* 4:303–18.

Bonnemaison, J. 1981. Review [of Spriggs 1981]. *Journal de la Société des Océanistes* 70–1:126–9.

Bonnemaison, J. 1983. *The Tree and the Canoe*. Paper given at 15th Pacific Science Congress, Dunedin, New Zealand, 1–11 February 1983.

Brown, D. E. 1974. Corporations and social classification. *Current Anthropology* 15:29–52.

Brown, J. M. 1925. *The Riddle of the Pacific*. London.

Brunton, R. 1979. Kava and the daily dissolution of society on Tanna, New Hebrides. *Mankind* 12(2):93–103.

Brunton, R. 1981. The origins of the John Frum Movement: a sociological explanation. In M. Allen (ed.), *Vanuatu: Politics, Economics and Ritual in Island Melanesia*. Sydney, Academic Press, 357–77.

Buck, P. 1930. *Material Culture of Samoa*. Bernice P. Bishop Museum Bulletin 72. Honolulu.

Buck, P. 1932. *Ethnology of Tongareva*. Bernice P. Bishop Museum Bulletin 92. Honolulu.

Buck, P. 1938. *Ethnology of Mangareva*. Bernice P. Bishop Museum Bulletin 157. Honolulu.

Burrows, E. G. 1936. *Ethnology of Futuna*. Bernice P. Bishop Museum Bulletin 138. Honolulu.

Burrows, E. G. 1937. *Ethnology of Uvea (Wallis Island)*. Bernice P. Bishop Museum Bulletin 145. Honolulu.

Burrows, E. G. 1939. Breed and border in Polynesia. *American Anthropologist* 41:1–21.

Butler, B. M. 1984. A preliminary report on the 1983 archaeological survey of Aimeliik State, Republic of Palau. Ms. on file, Center for Archaeological Investigations, Southern Illinois University at Carbondale.

Capell, A. 1960. *Anthropology and linguistics of Futuna-Aniwa, New Hebrides*. Oceania Linguistic Monograph 5.

Carney, J. N., and A. McFarlane 1979. *Geology of Tanna, Aneityum, Futuna and Aniwa*. Port Vila, British service.

Carneiro, R. L. 1970. A theory of the origin of the state. *Science* 169: 733–8.

Chapman, P. S., and P. V. Kirch 1979. Archaeological excavations at seven sites, Southeast Maui, Hawaiian Islands. *Departmental Report Series* 79–1. Honolulu, Department of Anthropology, B. P. Bishop Museum.

Ching, F. K. W. 1971. The Archaeology of South Kohala and North Kona: Surface Survey Kailua-Kawaihae Road Corridor. *Hawaii State Archaeological Journal* 71-1. Honolulu, Department of Land and Natural Resources, State of Hawai'i.

Christensen, C. C., and P. V. Kirch 1981. Non-marine molluscs from archaeological sites on Tikopia, Solomon Islands. *Pacific Science* 35:75–88:

Clark, E. 1953. *Lady with a Spear*. New York, Harper.

Clark, J. T. 1983. Radiocarbon chronology. In J. T. Clark and P. V. Kirch (eds.), *Archaeological Investigations of the Mudlane-Waimea-Kawaihae Road Corridor, Island of Hawaii*. *Departmental Report Series* 83-1; 317–23. Honolulu, Department of Anthropology, B. P. Bishop Museum.

Clark, J. T., and P. V. Kirch (eds.) 1983. *Archaeological Investigations of the Mudlane-Waimea-Kawaihae Road Corridor, Island of Hawaii*. *Departmental Report Series* 83-1. Honolulu, Department of Anthropology, B. P. Bishop Museum.

Clark, J. T., and J. Terrell 1978. Archaeology in Oceania. In B. J. Siegel, A. R. Beals and S. A. Tyler (eds.), *Annual Review of Anthropology* 7:293–319. Palo Alto, Calif., Annual Reviews.

Clark, R. 1978. The New Hebridean Outliers. In S. A. Wurm and L. Carrington (eds.), *Second International Conference on Austronesian Linguistics: Proceedings*. Pacific Linguistics C61: 911–28.

Clark, R. 1982. Proto-Polynesian birds. In J. Siikala (ed.), *Oceanic Studies: Essays in Honour of Aarne A. Koskinen.* Transactions of the Finnish Anthropological Society 11. Helsinki.

Cleghorn, P. L. 1980. The Hilina Pali Petroglyph Cave, Hawaii Island: a report on preliminary archaeological investigations. *Departmental Report Series* 80–1. Honolulu, Department of Anthropology, B. P. Bishop Museum.

Cleghorn, P. L. 1982. The Mauna Kea Adze Quarry: Technological analyses and experimental tests. Ph.D. dissertation. Honolulu, University of Hawai'i.

CM Ms. (n.d.) Typescript of notes from the Catholic Mission (Taiohae, Nukuhiva) copies by E. S. C. Handy, and filed in the Bernice P. Bishop Museum Library, Honolulu.

Codrington, R. H. 1891. *The Melanesians: Studies in their Anthropology and Folklore.* Oxford, Clarendon Press.

Colley, H., and R. P. Ash 1971. *The Geology of Erromango.* Port Vila, British Service.

Cook, J. [J. C. Beaglehole (ed.)] 1969. *The Journals of Captain James Cook, Volume II: The Voyage of the Resolution and Adventure 1772–1775.* Cambridge, University Press.

Copeland, J. 1860. Letter, 26 March 1860. *Reformed Presbyterian Magazine*, October 1860:344–8.

Cordy, R. H. 1981. *A Study of Prehistoric Social Change: The Development of Complex Societies in the Hawaiian Islands.* New York, Academic Press.

Cordy, R. H. 1983a. Settlement patterns of complex societies in the Pacific. Paper presented at the 15th Pacific Science Congress, Dunedin, New Zealand.

Cordy, R. H. 1983b. Social stratification in Micronesia. Paper presented at the Society for American Archaeology meetings.

Cordy, R. H. in press. Settlement patterns in complex societies in the Pacific. *New Zealand Journal of Archaeology* 7.

Cordy, R. H., and H. D. Tuggle 1976. Bellows, Oahu, Hawaiian Islands: new work and new interpretation. *Archaeology and Physical Anthropology in Oceania* 54:207–35.

Corning, P. A. 1983. *The Synergism Hypothesis: A Theory of Progressive Evolution.* New York, McGraw-Hill.

Cox, J. H., and E. Stasack 1970. *Hawaiian Petroglyphs.* Bernice P. Bishop Museum Special Publication 60. Honolulu.

Cristino, C., and P. Vargas 1980. Prospeccion arqueologica de Isla de Pascua. In C. Cristino (ed.), *Estudios Sobre la Isla de Pascua.* Santiago, Universidad de Chile, 193–226.

Cristino, C., P. Vargas and R. Izaurieta 1981. *Atlas Arqueologico de Isla de Pascua.* Santiago, Universidad de Chile.

Crook, W. P. MSS. Account of the Marquesas Islands. Sydney, The Mitchell Library.

Danielsson, B. 1967. Kia ora Keneti. In G. Highland (ed.), *Polynesian Culture History.* Honolulu, B. P. Bishop Museum.

Davenport, W. H. 1962. Red feather money. *Scientific American* 206:94–103.

Davenport, W. H. 1964. Notes on Santa Cruz voyaging. *Journal of the Polynesian Society* 73:134–42.

Davidson, J. M. 1974. Samoan structural remains and settlement patterns. In R. C. Green and J. M. Davidson (eds.), *Archaeology in Western Samoa, Vol. II.* Bulletin of the Auckland Institute and Museum 7. Auckland.

Davidson, J. M. 1977. Western Polynesia and Fiji: Prehistoric contact, diffusion and differentiation in adjacent archipelagos. *World Archaeology* 9:82–94.

Davidson, J. W. 1975. *Peter Dillon of Vanikoro: Chevalier of the South Seas.* Melbourne, Oxford University Press.

Davis, D. D. 1983. Investigating the diffusion of stylistic innovations. *Advances in Archaeological Method and Theory* 6:53–89.

Dean, J. S., R. C. Euler, G. J. Gumerman, R. H. Hevly and T. N. V. Karlstrom 1985. Human behavior, demography, and paleoenvironment on the Colorado Plateaus. *American Antiquity* (in press).

Delmas, Père S. 1927. *La Religion ou le Paganisme des Marquisiens.* Paris, Beauchesne.

Dening, G. (ed.) 1974. *The Marquesan Journal of Edward Robarts, 1787–1824.* Canberra, Australian National University Press.

Diener, P. 1982. The evolution of dysfunction. *Culture* 2(2):43–51.

Dillon, P. 1829. *Narrative and Successful Result of a Voyage in the South Seas ... to Ascertain the Actual Fate of La Perouse's Expedition ...* 2 vols. London, Hurst, Chace, and Co.

Dordillon, R. 1931. *Grammaire et Dictionnaire de la Langue des Iles Marquises.* Travaux et Mémoires de l'Institut d'Ethnologie 17. Paris.

Dumont D'Urville, J. S. C. 1833. *Voyage de la Corvette l'Astrolabe ... Pendant les Années 1826 ... 1829 ... Histoire du Voyage,* vol. 5. Paris, J. Tastu.

Dunnell, R. C. 1978. Style and function: a fundamental dichotomy. *American Antiquity* 43:192–202.

Dunnell, R. C. 1980. Evolutionary theory and archaeology. *Advances in Archaeological Method and Theory* 3:35–99.

Dunnell, R. C. 1982a. Science, social science and common sense: the agonizing dilemma of modern archaeology. *Journal of Anthropological Research* 38:1–25.

Dunnell, R. C. 1982b. Americanist archaeological literature: 1981. *American Journal of Archaeology* 86:509–29.

Dyen, I. ms. The linguistic evidence for early Austronesian social organization. Paper prepared at Yale University, New Haven, 1981.

Dyen, I., and D. F. Aberle 1974. *Lexical Reconstruction: The Case of the Proto-Athapaskan Kinship System.* Cambridge, University Press.

Earle, T. 1978. Economic and social organization of a complex chiefdom: The Halele'a District, Kauai, Hawaii. *Anthropological Papers of the Museum of Anthropology, University of Michigan* 63.

Ekholm, K. 1978. External exchange and the transformation of Central African global systems. In J. Friedman and M. J. Rowlands (eds.), *The Evolution of Social Systems.* London, Duckworth, 115–36.

Ellis, W. 1917. *Narrative of a Tour Through Hawaii.* Honolulu, The Hawaiian Gazette.

Emory, K. P. 1933. *Stone Remains in the Society Islands.* Bernice P. Bishop Museum Bulletin 116. Honolulu.

Emory, K. P. 1947. *Tuamotuan Religious Structures and Ceremonies.* Bernice P. Bishop Museum Bulletin 191. Honolulu.

Emory, K. P. 1979. The Societies. In J. D. Jennings (ed.), *The Prehistory of Polynesia.* Cambridge, Harvard University Press.

Emory, K. P. and Y. H. Sinoto 1969. Age of the sites in the South Point Area, Ka'u, Hawaii. *Pacific Anthropological Records* 8. Honolulu, Department of Anthropology, B. P. Bishop Museum.

Feinberg, R. 1981. *Anuta: Social Structure of a Polynesian Island.* The Institute for Polynesian Studies.

Firth, R. 1936. *We, The Tikopia.* London, George Allen and Unwin.

Firth, R. 1939. *Primitive Polynesian Economy.* London, George Routledge and Sons.

Firth, R. 1954. Anuta and Tikopia: symbiotic elements in social organization. *Journal of the Polynesian Society* 63:87–131.

Firth, R. 1959. Ritual adzes in Tikopia. In J. D. Freeman and W. R. Geddes (eds.), *Anthropology in the South Seas.* New Plymouth, Thomas Avery and Sons, 149–59.

Firth, R. 1961. *History and Traditions of Tikopia.* Wellington, The Polynesian Society.

Flannery, K. V. 1972. The cultural evolution of civilizations. *Annual Review of Ecology and Systematics* 3:399–426.

Flenley, J. R., and S. M. King 1984. Late Quaternary pollen records from Easter Island. *Nature* 307:47–50.

Force, R. W. 1960. *Leadership and Culture Change in Palau.* Fieldiana Publications in Anthropology 50. Chicago, Chicago Natural History Museum.

Force, R. W. and M. Force 1972. *Just One House: A Description and Analysis of Kinship in the Palau Islands.* Bernice P. Bishop Museum Bulletin 235. Honolulu.

Fornander, A. 1969. *An Account of the Polynesian Race . . . ,* Vol. II. Reprint of the 1879 edition. Rutland, Vermont, Charles E. Tuttle Co. Publishers.

Fosberg, R. (ed.). 1963. *Man's Place in the Island Ecosystem.* Honolulu, B. P. Bishop Museum.

Fried, M. 1967. *The Evolution of Political Society.* New York, Random House.

Friedman, J. 1981. Notes on structure and history in Oceania. *Folk* 23:275–95.

Friedman, J. 1982. Catastrophe and continuity in social evolution. In C. Renfrew, M. J. Rowlands and B. A. Segraves (eds.), *Theory and Explanation in Archaeology.* New York, Academic Press, 175–96.

Frimigacci, D. 1970. Fouilles archéologiques a Vatcha (près de Vao), Ile des Pins: compte rendu préliminaire. *Etudes Mélanésiennes,* N.S., 21–5:23–42.

Frimigacci, D., and J. Monnin 1980. Un inventaire de petroglyphes de Nouvelle Calédonie (Grande Terre et Iles). *Journal de la Société des Océanistes* 36:17–60.

Frost, E. L. 1974. *Archaeological Excavations of Fortified Sites on Taveuni, Fiji.* Asian and Pacific Archaeology Series 6. Honolulu, University of Hawai'i.

Frost, E. L. 1979. Fiji. In J. D. Jennings (ed.), *The Prehistory of Polynesia.* Cambridge, Harvard University Press.

Geddie, J. 1855. Letter, 3 October 1854. *Missionary Register of the Presbyterian Church of Nova Scotia,* August 1855:124–6.

Geraghty, P. A. 1983. *The History of the Fijian Languages.* Oceanic Linguistics Special Publication No. 19. Honolulu, University of Hawai'i.

Gifford, E. W. 1949. Excavations in Viti Levu. *Journal of the Polynesian Society* 58:83–90.

Gifford, E. W. 1951. *Archaeological Excavations in Fiji.* Anthropological Records 13:3. Berkeley and Los Angeles, University of California Press.

Godelier, M. 1977. *Perspectives in Marxist Anthropology.* Cambridge, University Press.

Godelier, M. 1978. Infrastructures, society, and history. *Current Anthropology* 19(4):763–71.

Goldman, I. 1970. *Ancient Polynesian Society.* Chicago, University Press.

Golovnin, V. M. n.d. [G. R. V. Barratt (ed.)] *The Russian Sloop-of-War Diana at Tana Island July 1809.* Unpublished translation by courtesy of G. R. V. Barratt.

Goodenough, W. 1957. Oceania and the problem of controls in the study of cultural and human evolution. *Journal of the Polynesian Society* 66:146–55.

Goodenough, W. H. 1983. Phylogenetically related cultural traditions. Paper presented at the XIth International Congress of Anthropological and Ethnological Sciences. Vancouver, British Columbia.

Gould, S. J., D. M. Raup, H. J. Sepkoski, T. J. M. Schopf and D. S. Simberloff 1977. The shape of evolution: a comparison of real and random clades. *Paleobiology* 3:23–40.

Grace, G. W. 1969. A Proto-Oceanic finder list. *Working Papers in Linguistics* 1:39–84. Honolulu, University of Hawai'i.

Gracia, L. 1843. *Lettres sur les Iles Marquises ou Mémoires pour Servir a l'Etude Religieuse, Morale, Politique, et Statistique des Iles Marquises et de l'Océanie Orientale.* Paris, Gaume Frères.

Green, R. C. 1963a. A suggested revision of the Fiji sequence. *Journal of the Polynesian Society* 72:235–53.

Green, R. C. 1963b. Two collections of pottery from Sigatoka, Fiji. *Journal of the Polynesian Society* 72:261–4.

Green, R. C. 1967. The immediate origin of the Polynesians. In G. A. Highland, R. W. Force, A. Howard, M. Kelly and Y. H. Sinoto (eds.), *Polynesian Culture History, Essays in Honor of Kenneth P. Emory.* Honolulu, B. P. Bishop Museum.

Green, R. C. 1967. Settlement patterns: four case studies from Polynesia. *Asian and Pacific Archaeology Series* 1:101–32. Honolulu, Social Sciences Research Institute.

Green, R. C. 1970a. Settlement pattern archaeology in Polynesia. In R. C. Green and M. Kelly (eds.), *Studies in Oceanic Culture History, Vol. I, Pacific Anthropological Records* 11. Honolulu, Bernice P. Bishop Museum.

Green, R. C. 1970b. Radiocarbon dating in the Makaha Valley. In R. C. Green (ed.), *Makaha Valley Historical Project Interim Report No. 2. Pacific Anthropological Records* 10, 97–104. Honolulu, B. P. Bishop Museum.

Green, R. C. 1971. Anuta's position in the subgrouping of Polynesia's languages. *Journal of the Polynesian Society* 80:355–70.

Green, R. C. 1974. A review of portable artifacts from Western Samoa. In R. C. Green and J. M. Davidson (eds.), *Archaeology in Western Samoa, Vol. II, Bulletin of the Auckland Institute and Museum* 7. Auckland.

Green, R. C. 1979a. Lapita. In J. D. Jennings (ed.), *The Prehistory of Polynesia.* Cambridge, Harvard University Press.

Green, R. C. 1979b. Peruvian or Polynesian: the stone-lined earth oven of Easter Island. *New Zealand Archaeological Association Newsletter* 22:92–6.

Green, R. C. 1980. Makaha before 1880 A.D.: Makaha Valley Historical Project summary report No. 5. *Pacific Anthropological Records* 31. Honolulu, B. P. Bishop Museum.

Green, R. C. 1981. Location of the Polynesian homeland: a continuing problem. In J. Hollyman and A. Pawley (eds.), *Studies in Pacific Languages and Cultures in Honour of Bruce Biggs.* Auckland, Linguistic Society of New Zealand.

Green, R. C. 1982. Models for the Lapita cultural complex: an evaluation of some current proposals. *New Zealand Journal of Archaeology* 4:7–20.

Green, R. C. in press, a. Settlement pattern studies in Oceania: introduction to a symposium. *New Zealand Journal of Archaeology* 6.

Green, R. C. in press, b. Lapita fishing: the evidence of site SE-RF-2 from the Main Reef Islands, Santa Cruz Group, Solomons. In A. J. Anderson (ed.), *Traditional Fishing in the Pacific, Pacific Anthropological Records.* Honolulu, B. P. Bishop Museum.

Green, R. C., and J. S. Mitchell 1983. New Caledonian culture history: a review of the archaeological sequence. *New Zealand Journal of Archaeology* 5:19–67.

Green, R. C., K. Green, R. A. Rappaport, A. Rappaport and J. M. Davidson 1967. Archaeology on the island of Mo'orea, French Polynesia. *Anthropological Papers of the American Museum of Natural History* 51:111–230.

Griffin, P. B. and G. W. Lovelace (eds.) 1977. Survey and salvage – Honoapi'ilani Highway. *ARCH Occasional Papers* 77-1. Lawai, Hawai'i, Archaeological Research Center Hawai'i, Inc.

Groube, L. M. 1971. Tonga, Lapita pottery, and Polynesian origins. *Journal of the Polynesian Society* 80:278–316.

Groube, L. M. n.d. [1972]. Aneityum, Erromango Fieldnotes. Manuscript in Archives, Department of Prehistory, R.S.Pac.S, Australian National University.

Groube, L. M. 1975. Archaeological research on Aneityum. *South Pacific Bulletin* 25(3):27–30.

Guiart, J. 1956. *Un Siècle et Demi de Contacts Culturels à Tanna,*

Nouvelles-Hebrides. Publications de la Société des Océanistes 5, Musée de l'Homme, Paris.

Guiart, J. 1963. *Structure de la Chefferie en Melanesie du Sud.* Travaux et Mémoires de l'Institut d'Ethnologie, LXVI. Paris.

Gumerman, G. J., D. Snyder and W. B. Masse 1981. *An Archaeological Reconnaissance in the Palau Archipelago, Western Caroline Islands, Micronesia.* Center for Archaeological Investigations Research Paper 23. Southern Illinois University at Carbondale.

Haas, J. 1982. *The Evolution of the Prehistoric State.* New York, Columbia University Press.

Hale, H. 1846. Ethnography and Philology. *United States Exploring Expedition, Volume VI.* Philadelphia, Sherman.

Hammatt, H. H. and S. D. Clark 1980. Archaeological testing and salvage excavations of a 155 acre (Ginter) parcel in Na Ahupua'a Pahoehoe, La'aloa and Kapala'alaea, Kona, Hawaii Island. *ARCH* 14–152. Lawai, Hawai'i, Archaeological Research Center Hawai'i, Inc.

Handy, E. S. C. 1923. *The Native Culture in the Marquesas.* Bernice P. Bishop Museum Bulletin 9. Honolulu.

Handy, E. S. C. 1930. *Marquesan Legends.* Bernice P. Bishop Museum Bulletin 69, Honolulu.

Handy, W. C. 1922. *Tattooing in the Marquesas.* Bernice P. Bishop Museum Bulletin 1. Honolulu.

Handy, W. C. 1938. *L'art des Iles Marquises.* Paris, Les Editions d'Art et d'Histoire.

Harding, T. G. 1967. *Voyagers of the Vitiaz Strait.* Seattle, University of Washington Press.

Harner, M. J. 1970. Population pressure and the social evolution of agriculturalists. *Southwestern Journal of Anthropology* 26: 67–86.

Hassan, F. A. 1981. *Demographic Archaeology.* New York, Academic Press.

Hayden, B. 1975. The carrying capacity dilemma. *American Antiquity* 40, memoir 30:205–21.

Hayden, B. 1983. Social characteristics of early Austronesian colonizers. *Indo-Pacific Prehistory Association Bulletin* 4:123–34.

Henry, T. 1928. *Ancient Tahiti.* Bernice P. Bishop Museum Bulletin 48. Honolulu.

Hocart, A. M. 1915. Ethnographic sketch of Fiji. *Man* 15:73–7.

Hodder, I. 1978. Social organisation and human interaction: the development of some tentative hypotheses in terms of material culture. In I. Hodder (ed.), *The Spatial Organisation of Culture.* Pittsburg, University of Pittsburg Press.

Hodder, I. 1982a. *Symbols in Action.* Cambridge, University Press.

Hodder, I. (ed.) 1982b. *Symbolic and Structural Archaeology.* Cambridge, University Press.

Hommon, R. J. 1975. Use and control of Hawaiian inter-island channels. Polynesian Hawaii A.D. 1400–1794. Unpublished manuscript. Honolulu, Office of the Governor of Hawai'i.

Hommon, R. J. 1976. The formation of primitive states in pre-contact Hawaii. Ph.D. dissertation. Tucson, University of Arizona.

Hommon, R. J. 1980. National Register of Historic Places multiple resource nomination form for the historic resources of Kaho'olawe. (Prepared for the U.S. Navy.)

Hommon, R. J. 1983. Kaho'olawe archaeological excavations 1981. Honolulu, Science Management, Inc.

Hope, G. S., and M. J. T. Spriggs 1982. A preliminary pollen sequence from Aneityum Island, Southern Vanuatu. *Indo-Pacific Prehistory Association Bulletin* 3:88–94.

Howells, W. W. 1973. *The Pacific Islanders.* Charles Scribner's Sons, New York.

Hughes, P. J., and G. Hope 1979. Prehistoric man-induced degradation of the Lakeba landscape: evidence from two inland swamps. In H. C. Brookfield (ed.), *Lakeba: Environmental change, population dynamics and resource use.* Paris, UNESCO.

Hughes, P. J., and R. J. Lampert 1977. Occupational disturbance and types of archaeological deposit. *Journal of Archaeological Science* 4:135–40.

Hunt, T. L. 1980. Toward Fiji's past: archaeological research on southwestern Viti Levu. Unpublished Master's thesis, University of Auckland.

Hunt T. L. 1981a. New evidence for early horticulture in Fiji. *Journal of the Polynesian Society* 90:259–66.

Hunt, T. L. 1981b. Review of Parry, John T., Ring-ditch fortifications in the Rewa Delta, Fiji: air photo interpretation and analysis. *Journal of the Polynesian Society* 90:139–41.

Inglis, J. 1882. *A Dictionary of the Aneityumese Language.* London, Williams and Norgate.

Inglis, J. 1890. *Bible Illustrations from the New Hebrides.* London, Nelson and Sons.

Irwin, G. 1978. The development of Mailu as a specialized trading and manufacturing center in Papuan prehistory. *Mankind* 11:403–15.

Jardin, E. 1862. *Essai sur l'Histoire Naturelle de l'Archipel des Marquises.* Paris, J. B. Bailliere.

Jennings, J. 1979. *The Prehistory of Polynesia.* Cambridge, Harvard University Press.

Jennings, J. D., R. Holmer, and G. Jackmond 1982. Samoan village pattern: four examples. *Journal of the Polynesian Society* 91: 81–102.

Jermann, J. V., and R. C. Dunnell 1979. Some limitations of isopleth mapping in archaeology. *Anthropological Research Papers, Arizona State University* 15:31–60.

Johannes, R. E. 1981. *Words of the Lagoon: Fishing and Marine Lore in the Palau District of Micronesia.* Berkeley, University of California Press.

Johnson, G. A. 1978. Information sources and the development of decision-making organizations. In C. Redman, M. J. Berman, E. Curtin, W. Langhorne, Jr, N. Versaggi, and J. Wanser (eds.), *Social Archaeology: Beyond Subsistence and Dating.* New York, Academic Press.

Jones, G. I. 1949. Ibo land tenure. *Africa* 19:309–23.

Jones, G. I. 1961. Ecology and social structure among the north eastern Ibo. *Africa* 31:117–33.

Kaeppler, A. 1978. Exchange patterns in goods and spouses: Fiji, Tonga, and Samoa. *Mankind* 11:246–52.

Kamakau, S. M. 1961. *Ruling Chiefs of Hawaii.* Honolulu, The Kamehameha Schools Press.

Kaplan, S. A. 1976. Ethnological and biogeographical significance of pottery sherds from Nissan Island, Papua New Guinea. *Fieldiana: Anthropology* 66(3). Chicago, Field Museum of Natural History.

Keate, G. 1788. *An Account of the Pelew Islands.* London, G. Nichol.

Keesing, R. M. 1982. *Kwaio Religion.* New York, Columbia University Press.

Kelly, M. and J. T. Clark 1980. Kawainui Marsh, Oahu: Historical and archaeological studies. *Departmental Report Series* 80–3. Honolulu, Department of Anthropology, B. P. Bishop Museum.

Kikuchi, W. K. 1973. Hawaiian aquacultural systems. Ph.D. dissertation. Tucson, University of Arizona.

Kirch, P. V. 1971. Archaeological excavations at Palauea, southeast Maui, Hawaiian Islands. *Archaeology and Physical Anthropology in Oceania* 6:62–86.

Kirch, P. V. 1975a. Radiocarbon and hydration-rind dating of prehistoric sites in Halawa Valley. In P. V. Kirch and M. Kelly (eds.), Prehistory and ecology in a windward Hawaiian valley: Halawa Valley, Molokai. *Pacific Anthropological Records* 24. Honolulu, Department of Anthropology, B. P. Bishop Museum.

Kirch, P. V. 1975b. Excavations at sites A1-3 and A1-4: early settlement and ecology in Halawa Valley. In P. V. Kirch and M. Kelly (eds.), Prehistory and Ecology in a windward Hawaiian valley: Halawa Valley, Molokai. *Pacific Anthropological Records* 24. Honolulu, Bernice P. Bishop Museum.

Kirch, P. V. 1979a. Late prehistoric and early historic settlement-subsistence systems in the Anahulu Valley, Oahu. *Departmental Report Series* 79-2. Honolulu, Department of Anthropology, B. P. Bishop Museum.

Kirch, P. V. 1979b. Marine exploitation in prehistoric Hawaii: archaeological excavations at Kalahuipua'a, Hawaii Island. *Pacific Anthropological Records* 29. Honolulu, Department of Anthropology, B. P. Bishop Museum.

Kirch, P. V. 1979c. Archaeology and the evolution of Polynesian culture. *Archaeology* 32(5):44–52.

Kirch, P. V. 1980a. The archaeological study of adaptation: theoretical and methodological issues. In M. Schiffer (ed.), *Advances in Archaeological Method and Theory* 3:101–56. New York, Academic Press.

Kirch, P. V. 1980b. Polynesian prehistory: cultural adaptation in island ecosystems. *American Scientist* 64:39–48.

Kirch, P. V. 1982a. Advances in Polynesian prehistory: three decades in review. *Advances in World Archaeology* 1:51–97. New York, Academic Press.

Kirch, P. V. 1982b. The impact of the prehistoric Polynesians on the Hawaiian ecosystem. *Pacific Science* 36:1–14.

Kirch, P. V. 1982c. A revision of the Anuta sequence. *Journal of the Polynesian Society* 91:245–54.

Kirch, P. V. 1983a. Introduction. In J. T. Clark and P. V. Kirch (eds.), Archaeological Investigations of the Mudlane-Waimea-Kawaihae Road Corridor, Island of Hawaii. *Departmental Report Series* 80–1. Honolulu, Department of Anthropology, B. P. Bishop Museum.

Kirch, P. V. 1983b. An archaeological exploration of Vanikoro, Santa Cruz Islands, Eastern Melanesia. *New Zealand Journal of Archaeology* 5:69–113.

Kirch, P. V. 1983c. Man's role in modifying tropical and subtropical Polynesian ecosystems. *Archaeology in Oceania* 18:26–31.

Kirch, P. V. 1984. *The Evolution of the Polynesian Chiefdoms.* Cambridge, University Press.

Kirch, P. V. 1985a. *Feathered Gods and Fishhooks: An Introduction to Hawaiian Archaeology and Prehistory.* Honolulu, University of Hawaii Press.

Kirch, P. V. 1985b. On the genetic and cultural relationships of certain Polynesian Outlier populations. *American Journal of Physical Anthropology.*

Kirch, P. V., and C. C. Christensen 1980. Nonmarine molluscs and paleoecology at Barber's Point, Oahu. Manuscript, Department of Anthropology, B. P. Bishop Musuem, Honolulu.

Kirch, P. V. and T. S. Dye 1979. Ethno-archaeology and the development of Polynesian fishing strategies. *Journal of the Polynesian Society* 88:53–76.

Kirch, P. V. and M. Kelly (eds.) 1975. Prehistory and ecology in a windward Hawaiian valley: Halawa Valley, Molokai. *Pacific Anthropological Records* 24. Honolulu, Department of Anthropology, B. P. Bishop Museum.

Kirch, P. V. and P. Rosendahl 1973. Archaeological investigation of Anuta. *Pacific Anthropological Records* 21:25–108.

Kirch, P. V. and D. E. Yen 1982. *Tikopia: The Prehistory and Ecology of a Polynesian Outlier.* B. P. Bishop Museum Bulletin 238.

Klein, J., J. C. Lerman, P. E. Damon and E. K. Ralph 1982. Calibration of radiocarbon dates: tables based on the consensus data of the workshop on calibrating the radiocarbon time scale. *Radiocarbon* 24:103–50.

Krämer, A. 1919. In G. Thilenius (ed.), *Ergebnisse der Sudsee-Expedition 1908–1910.* II. Ethnographie; B. Mikronesien. Band 3, Teilband 2. Hamburg, Friederichsen, (Anon. translation available through Human Relations Area Files.)

Kubary, J. S. 1895. *Ethnographische Beitrage zur Kenntnis des Karolinen Archipels.* Leiden, P. W. M. (Anon. translation available through Human Relations Area Files.)

Ladd, E. J. 1973. Kaneaki temple site – an excavation report. In E. J.

Ladd (ed.), Makaha Valley Historical Project Interim Report No. 4, *Pacific Anthropological Records* 19. Honolulu, Department of Anthropology, B. P. Bishop Museum.

Lambert, R. 1971. Botanical identification of impressions on archaeological potsherds from Sigatoka. Final Report No. 3. *Records of the Fiji Museum* 1(5):124–48.

Lamont, E. H. 1867. *Wild Life Among the Pacific Islanders.* London, Hurst and Blackett.

Lavachery, H. 1939. *Les Pétroglyphes de l'Ile de Pacques.* Anvers, De Sikkel.

Leach, J. W. and E. Leach (eds.) 1983. *The Kula: New Perspectives on Massim Exchange.* Cambridge, University Press.

Lee, R. B. 1979. *The !Kung San: Men, Women and Work in a Foraging Society.* Cambridge, University Press.

Lee, R. B., and I. DeVore (eds.) 1968. *Man the Hunter.* Chicago, Aldine.

Leenhouts, P. W. 1955. *The Genus Canarium in the Pacific.* B. P. Bishop Museum Bulletin 216.

Leone, M. 1982. Some opinions about recovering mind. *American Antiquity* 47:742–60.

Leroi-Gourhan, A. 1975. Iconographie et interprétation. In *Symposium International sur les religions de la préhistoire.* Capo di Ponte, Centro Comuno di Studi Preistorici.

Leroi-Gourhan, A. 1982. *The Dawn of European Art.* Cambridge, University Press.

Levison, M., R. G. Ward and J. W. Webb 1973. *The Settlement of Polynesia. A Computer Simulation.* Minneapolis, University of Minnesota Press.

Lincoln, P. C. (ed.) 1979. Proto-Oceanic cognate sets. Unpublished computer printout. Honolulu, Department of Linguistics, University of Hawai'i.

Lindstrom, L. 1981a. Achieving Wisdom: Knowledge and Politics on Tanna (Vanuatu). Ph.D. Thesis, University of California, Berkeley. Ann Arbor, University Microfilms.

Lindstrom, L. 1981b. Bigman or chief? Knowledge and political process on Tanna. *Kroeber Anthropological Society Papers* 57–8: 122–46.

Lindstrom, L. 1984. Doctor, lawyer, wise man, priest: big men and knowledge in Melanesia. *Man* N.S. 19:291–309.

Linton, R. 1925. *Archaeology of the Marquesas Islands.* Bernice P. Bishop Museum Bulletin 29. Honolulu.

Lucking, L. J. 1981. An archaeological investigation of the prehistoric Palauan terraces. Ms. on file, Historic Preservation Office, U.S. Trust Territory of the Pacific Islands, Saipan.

Lynch, J. 1978. Proto-South Hebridean and Proto-Oceanic. In S. Wurm and L. Carrington (eds.), Second International Conference on Austronesian Linguistics: Proceedings, *Pacific Linguistics* C61:717–79. Canberra.

McArthur, N. 1974. Population and prehistory: the late Phase on Aneityum. Unpublished Ph.D. Thesis. Canberra, Australian National University.

McArthur, N. 1978. 'And, Behold, the Plague was Begun among the People'. In N. Gunson (ed.), *The Changing Pacific: Essays in Honour of H. E. Maude.* Oxford, University Press, 273–84.

McCall, G. 1979. Kinship and environment on Easter Island: some observations and speculations. *Mankind* 12:119–37.

McCluer, J. 1790–2. Voyage to the Pelew Islands in the H. C. Snow Panther. Ms. on file, Palau Museum, typescript 1974. Original in British Museum, London.

McCoy, P. C. 1976. *Easter Island Settlement Patterns in the Late Prehistoric and Protohistoric Periods.* Easter Island Committee Bulletin 5. New York, International Fund for Monuments.

McCoy, P. C. 1977. The Mauna Kea Adze Quarry Project: a summary of the 1975 field investigation. *Journal of the Polynesian Society* 86:223–44.

MacGregor, G. 1937. *Ethnology of Tokelau Islands.* Bernice P. Bishop Museum Bulletin 146. Honolulu.

McKnight, R. K. 1960. Competition in Palau. Unpublished Ph.D. thesis, Ohio State University.

McLean, R. F. 1980. The land–sea interface of small tropical islands: morphodynamics and man. In H. C. Brookfield (ed.), *Population-Environment Relations in Tropical Islands: The Case of Eastern Fiji*. Paris, UNESCO.

Maddock, K. 1972. *The Australian Aborigines: A Portrait of Their Society*. Baltimore, Penguin.

Malinowski, B. 1922. *Argonauts of the Western Pacific*. London, George Routledge and Sons.

Malo, D. 1951. *Hawaiian Antiquities*. Bishop Museum Special Publication 2, Special Edition, translated from the Hawai'ian by Dr Nathaniel B. Emerson. Honolulu, B. P. Bishop Museum Press.

Masse, W. B., D. Snyder and G. J. Gumerman 1983. A millennium of fishing and shell fishing in the Palau Islands, Micronesia. Paper presented at the 15th Pacific Science Congress, Dunedin, New Zealand.

Masse, W. B., D. Snyder and G. J. Gumerman 1984. Prehistoric and historic settlement in the Palau Islands, Micronesia. *New Zealand Journal of Archaeology* (in press).

Mauss, M. 1923. Essai sur le don. *L'Année Sociologique*.

Mayr, E. 1959. Typological versus population thinking. In *Evolution and Anthropology: A Centennial Appraisal*. The Anthropological Society of Washington.

Mayr, E. 1982. *The Growth of Biological Thought*. Belknap Press of Harvard University, Cambridge.

Mead, M. 1957. Introduction to Polynesia as a laboratory for the development of models in the study of cultural evolution. *Journal of the Polynesian Society* 66:145.

Mead, S. M., L. Birks, H. Birks and E. Shaw 1975. *The Lapita pottery of Fiji and its associations*. The Polynesian Society Memoir 38, Wellington.

Medway, Lord, and A. G. Marshall 1975. Terrestrial vertebrates of the New Hebrides: Origin and distribution. *Philosophical Transactions of the Royal Society of London*, series B 272–423–66.

Meek, C. K. 1937. *Law and Authority in a Nigerian Tribe*. New York, Barnes and Noble.

Metraux, A. 1940. *Ethnology of Easter Island*. Bernice P. Bishop Museum Bulletin 160. Honolulu.

Michels, J. W., C. M. Stevenson, I. S. T. Tsong, and G. Smith 1984. The obsidian hydration rates for Easter Island. In W. Ayres (ed.), *Recent Easter Island Archaeology*. University of Oregon Occasional Papers in Anthropology, Eugene.

Modjeska, N. 1977. *Production among the Duna*. Unpublished Ph.D. thesis. Canberra, Australian National University.

Montiton, A. 1874. Les Paumotus. *Les Missions Catholiques* 6 (Jan.–Dec. 1874).

Moore, J. A. 1983. The trouble with know-it-alls: information as a social and ecological resource. In J. A. Moore and A. S. Keene (eds.), *Archaeological Hammers and Theories*. New York, Academic Press, 173–91.

Morgenstein, M., and T. J. Riley 1974. Hydration-rind dating of basaltic glass: a new method for archaeological chronologies. *Asian Perspectives* 17:145–59.

Morgenstein, M. and P. Rosendahl 1976. Basaltic glass hydration dating in Hawaiian archaeology. In R. E. Taylor (ed.), *Advances in Obsidian Glass Studies*. New Jersey, Noyes Press, 141–64.

Mulloy, W. 1961. The ceremonial center of Vinapu. In T. Heyerdahl and E. Ferdon (eds.), *The Archaeology of Easter Island*. Monographs of the School of American Research and the Museum of New Mexico No. 24. Santa Fe, 181–220.

Mulloy, W. and G. Figueroa 1978. The A Kivi-Vai Teka complex and its relationship to Easter Island architectural prehistory. *Asian*

and Pacific Archaeology Series 8. Honolulu, University of Hawai'i.

Murakami, G. M. 1983. Identification of charcoal from Kaho'olawe archaeological sites. Appendix B in *Kaho'olawe excavations 1981*, by R. J. Hommon. Honolulu, Science Management, Inc.

Nakamura, W. T. 1933. A study of the variation in annual rainfall of Oahu Island (Hawaiian Islands) based on the Law of Probabilities. *Monthly Weather Review* 61:354–60.

Newman, T. S. n.d. [1970]. *Hawaiian Fishing and Farming on the Island of Hawaii, A.D. 1778*. Honolulu, Division of State Parks, Department of Land and Natural Resources, State of Hawai'i.

Nicklin, K. 1971. Stability and innovation in pottery manufacture. *World Archaeology* 3:13–48.

Olson, L. 1983. Hawaiian volcanic glass applied 'dating' and 'sourcing': archaeological context. In J. T. Clark and P. V. Kirch (eds.), Archaeological Investigations of the Mudlane-Waimea-Kawaihae Road Corridor, Island of Hawaii, *Departmental Report Series* 83-1. Honolulu, Department of Anthropology, B. P. Bishop Museum.

Onwuejeogwu, M. A. 1981. *An Ibo Civilization*. London, Ethnographica Ltd.

O'Reilly, P. 1954. Abri sous roche à gravures, Nailou district de Cakaudrove, Vanua Levu, îles Fidji. *Journal de la Société des Océanistes* 10:178–9.

Osborne, D. 1966. *The Archaeology of the Palau Islands: An Intensive Survey*. Bernice P. Bishop Museum Bulletin 230. Honolulu.

Osborne, D. 1979. *Archaeological Test Excavations, Palau Islands, 1968–1969. Micronesica* Supplement No. 1.

Otterbein, K. 1970. *The Evolution of War*. New Haven, Human Relations Area Files Press.

Parry, J. 1977. *Ring-Ditch Fortifications in the Rewa Delta, Fiji: Air Photo Interpretation and Analysis*. Bulletin of the Fiji Museum 3.

Pawley, A. K. 1981. Melanesian diversity and Polynesian homogeneity: a unified explanation for language. In J. Hollyman and A. Pawley (eds.), *Studies in Pacific Languages and Cultures in Honour of Bruce Biggs*. Auckland, Linguistic Society of New Zealand.

Pawley, A. K. 1982a. The etymology of Samoan *taupou*. In R. Carle *et al.* (eds.), *Gava: Studies in Austronesian Languages and Cultures Dedicated to Hans Kahler*. Berlin, Dietrich Reimer Verlag.

Pawley, A. K. 1982b. Rubbish-man, commoner, big man, chief? Linguistic evidence for hereditary chieftainship in Proto-Oceanic society. In J. Siikala (ed.), *Oceanic Studies: Essays in Honour of Aarne A. Koskinen*, Transactions of the Finnish Anthropological Society 11. Helsinki.

Pawley, A. K. in press. Proto-Oceanic terms for 'person': a problem in semantic reconstruction. In V. Ascon and R. Leed (eds.), *Festschrift for Gordon Fairbanks*. Honolulu, University of Hawai'i Press.

Pawley, A. K. ms. Linguistic evidence for reconstructing PPN society. Lecture notes, Department of Linguistics, University of Hawai'i (1975).

Pawley, A. K., and R. C. Green 1971. Lexical evidence for the Proto-Polynesian homeland. *Te Reo* 14:1–36.

Pawley, A. K., and R. C. Green 1973. Dating the dispersal of the Oceanic languages. *Oceanic Linguistics* 12:1–67.

Pawley, A. K., and R. C. Green in press. The Proto-Oceanic language community: distribution, diversification, dispersal dates. *Journal of Pacific History*.

Pearson, R. J., P. V. Kirch and M. Pietrusewsky 1971. An early prehistoric site at Bellows Beach, Waimanalo, Oahu, Hawaiian Islands. *Archaeology and Physical Anthropology in Oceania* 6: 204–34.

Pielou, E. C. 1979. Interpretation of paleoecological similarity matrices. *Paleobiology* 5:435–43.

Pielou, E. C. 1983. Spatial and temporal change in biogeography: gradual or abrupt? In R. W. Sims, J. H. Price, and P. E. S. Walley (eds.), *Evolution, Time and Space: The Emergence of the Biosphere*. Academic Press, London.

Porter, D. 1822. *Journal of a Cruise Made to the Pacific Ocean by Captain David Porter, in the United States Frigate Essex, in the Years 1812, 1813, and 1814*. New York.

Portlock, N. 1968. *A Voyage Round the World . . . Performed in 1785, 1786, 1787 and 1788 . . .* [Facsimile of 1789 edition]. New York, Da Capo Press.

Prescott, J. R., G. B. Robertson, and R. C. Green 1982. Thermoluminescence dating of Pacific Island pottery: successes and failures. *Archaeology in Oceania* 17:142–7.

Prickett, N. J. 1979. Prehistoric occupation in the Moikau Valley, Palliser Bay. In B. F. and H. H. Leach (eds.), *Prehistoric Man in Palliser Bay*, National Museum Bulletin 21. Wellington.

Prickett, N. J. 1982. An archaeologist's guide to the Maori dwelling. *New Zealand Journal of Archaeology* 4:111–47.

Quantin, P. 1979. *Archipel des Nouvelles-Hébrides: Sols et Quelques Données du Milieu Naturel: Erromango, Tanna, Aniwa, Anatom, Foutouna*. Paris, ORSTOM.

Radcliffe-Brown, A. R. 1952. *Structure and Function in Primitive Society*. London, Cohen and West.

Rappaport, R. 1968. *Pigs for the Ancestors*. New Haven, Yale University Press.

Rappaport, R. A. 1978. Maladaption in social systems. In J. Friedman and M. J. Rowlands (eds.), *The Evolution of Social Systems*. Pittsburgh, University Press.

Rathje, W. L. 1972. Praise the gods and pass the metates: a hypothesis of the development of lowland rainforest civilizations in Mesoamerica. In M. P. Leone (ed.), *Contemporary Archaeology*. Carbondale, Southern Illinois University Press, 365–92.

Ray, S. 1917. The language and people of Lifu, Loyalty Islands. *Journal of the Royal Anthropological Institute of Great Britain and Ireland* 47:239–322.

Renfrew, C. 1982. Polity and power: interaction, intensification and exploitation. In *An Island Polity: The Archaeology of Exploitation in Melos*. Cambridge, University Press, 264–90.

Renfrew, C. 1984. *Approaches to Social Archaeology*. Cambridge, Harvard University Press.

Richerson, P. J. 1977. Ecology and human ecology: a comparison of theories in the biological and social sciences. *American Ethnologist* 4(1):1–26.

Riesenfeld, A. 1950. *The Megalithic Culture of Melanesia*. Leiden, E. J. Brill.

Ripperton, J. C., and E. Y. Hosaka 1942. Vegetation zones of Hawaii. *Agricultural Experiment Station Bulletin* 89. Honolulu, University of Hawai'i.

Rivers, W. H. R. 1914. *The History of Melanesian Society*. Cambridge, University Press.

Rosendahl, P. H. 1972a. Aboriginal agriculture and residence patterns in upland Lapakahi, Island of Hawaii. Ph.D. dissertation. Honolulu, Department of Anthropology, University of Hawai'i.

Rosendahl, P. H. 1972b. Archaeological salvage of the Hapuna-Anaehoomalu Section of the Kailua-Kawaihae Road (Queen Kaahumanu Highway), Island of Hawaii. *Departmental Report Series* 72-5. Honolulu, Department of Anthropology, B. P. Bishop Museum.

Rosendahl, P. H. 1973. Archaeological salvage of the Ke'ahole to Anaehoomalu Section of the Kailua-Kawaihae Road (Queen Kaahumanu Highway), Island of Hawaii. *Departmental Report Series* 73-3. Honolulu, Department of Anthropology, B. P. Bishop Museum.

Rosendahl, P. H. 1976. Archaeological investigations in upland Kaneohe. *Departmental Report Series* 76-1. Honolulu Department of Anthropology, B. P. Bishop Museum.

Routledge, C. S. 1919. *The Mystery of Easter Island*. London, Sifton Praed.

Rowland, M. J., and S. Best 1980. Survey and excavation on the Kedekede hillfort, Lakeba Island, Lau group, Fiji. *Archaeology and Physical Anthropology in Oceania* 15:29–50.

Ruse, M. 1982. *Darwinism Defended*. Addison-Wesley, London.

Ruyle, E. 1973. Genetic and cultural pools: some suggestions for a unified theory of biocultural evolution. *Human Ecology* 1(3): 201–16.

Rye, O. S. 1981. *Pottery Technology: Principles and Reconstruction*. Manuals on Archaeology 4. Taraxacum, Washington.

Sahlins, M. D. 1957. Differentiation by adaptation in Polynesian societies. *Journal of the Polynesian Society* 66:291–300.

Sahlins, M. D. 1958. *Social stratification in Polynesia*. University of Washington Press, Seattle.

Sahlins, M. D. 1963. Poor man, rich man, big-man, chief: political types in Melanesia and Polynesia. *Comparative Studies in Society and History* 5:285–303.

Sahlins, M. D. 1972. *Stone Age Economics*. Chicago, Aldine-Atherton.

Sahlins, M. D. 1973. Class and kinship in 19th-century Hawaii. Paper delivered at the University of Hawai'i, 9 May 1973.

Sahlins, M. D. 1974. Historical anthropology of the Hawaiian Kingdom. Research proposal submitted to the National Science Foundation. Honolulu, B. P. Bishop Museum.

Sahlins, M. D. 1983. Other times, other customs: the anthropology of history. *American Anthropologist* 85:517–44.

Sanders, W. T. and B. J. Price 1968. *Mesoamerica: The Evolution of a Civilization*. New York, Random House.

Schilt, A. R. 1980. Archaeological investigations in specified areas of the Hanalei Wildlife Refuge, Hanalei Valley, Kauai. Typescript report. Honolulu, Library, B. P. Bishop Museum.

Schilt, A. R. 1984. Subsistence and conflict in Kona, Hawaii. An archaeological study of the Kuakini Highway Realignment Corridor. *Departmental Report Series* 84-1. Honolulu, Department of Anthropology, B. P. Bishop Museum.

Schmid, M. 1975. La flore et la végétation de la partie méridionale de l'archipel des Nouvelles-Hébrides. *Philosophical Transactions of the Royal Society of London*, series B, 272:329–42.

Schmitt, R. C. 1968. *Demographic Statistics of Hawaii: 1778–1965*. Honolulu, University of Hawai'i Press.

Schmitt, R. C. 1970. Famine mortality in Hawaii. *Journal of Pacific History* 4:109–15.

Schmitt, R. C. 1971. New estimates of the pre-censal population of Hawaii. *Journal of the Polynesian Society* 80:237–42.

Seelenfreund, A. 1982. Easter Island burial practices. Ms. on file, Department of Anthropology, University of Otago, New Zealand.

Semper, K. 1982. *The Palauan Islands in the Pacific Ocean*, translated by Mark L. Berg. Micronesian Area Research Center, University of Guam (orig. 1873).

Service, E. R. 1967. *Primitive Social Organization: An Evolutionary Perspective*. New York, Random House.

Service, E. R. 1975. *Origins of the State and Civilization: The Process of Cultural Evolution*. New York, Norton.

Shaw, E. 1967. A reanalysis of pottery from Navatu and Vuda, Fiji. Unpublished Master's thesis, University of Auckland.

Shutler, M. E. and R. Shutler 1966. A preliminary report of archaeological excavations in the southern New Hebrides. *Asian Perspectives* 9:157–66.

Shutler, R. 1970. A radiocarbon chronology for the New Hebrides. *Proceedings 8th International Congress of Anthropological and Ethnological Sciences* Vol. 3:135–7. Tokyo and Kyoto, Science Council of Japan.

Shutler, R. and M. E. Shutler 1975. *Oceanic Prehistory*. Menlo Park, Cummings.

Sinoto, Y. H. 1979. The Marquesas. In J. D. Jennings (ed.), *The Prehistory of Polynesia*. Cambridge, Harvard University Press.

Sinoto, Y. H. and M. Kelly 1975. Archaeological and historical surveys of Pakini-Nui and Pakini-Iki coastal sites; Waiahukini, Kailikii, and Hawea, Ka'u, Hawaii. *Departmental Report Series* 75-1. Honolulu, Department of Anthropology, B. P. Bishop Museum.

Smith, C. S. 1961. A temporal sequence derived from certain ahu. In T. Heyerdahl and E. Ferdon (eds.), *The Archaeology of Easter Island*. Monographs of the School of American Research and the Museum of New Mexico 24. Santa Fe, 181–220.

Smith, D. R. 1983. *Palauan Social Structure*. New Brunswick, N. J., Rutgers University Press.

Smith, M. G. 1974. *Corporations and Society*. London, Duckworth.

Sober, E. 1980. Evolution, population thinking and essentialism. *Philosophy of Science* 47:350–83.

Spate, O. H. K. 1978. The Pacific as an artefact. In N. Gunson (ed.), *The Changing Pacific: Essays in Honour of H. E. Maude*. Melbourne, Oxford University Press, 32–45.

Spriggs, M. J. T. 1981a. Prehistoric human-induced landscape enhancement in the Pacific: examples and implications. Revised version of a paper presented at the conference on Prehistoric Intensive Agriculture in the Tropics, 17–20 August 1981. Australian National University.

Spriggs, M. J. T. 1981b. Vegetable kingdoms: taro irrigation and Pacific prehistory. Unpublished Ph.D. thesis. Canberra, Australian National University.

Spriggs, M. J. T. 1984. The Lapita Cultural Complex: origins, distribution, contemporaries and successors. *Journal of Pacific History* 19(3 and 4):46–65.

Spriggs, M. J. T. 1984. 'A School in Every District': missionary manipulation of traditional social and spatial structure on Aneityum Island, Southern Vanuatu. *Journal of Pacific History* 19:202–23.

Spriggs, M. J. T. 1985. Why irrigation matters in Pacific prehistory. *Journal of Pacific History* 20:23–41.

Steinen, K. von den. 1928. *Die Marquesander und ihre Kunst*. Berlin, Ernst Vohsen.

Stevenson, C. M. 1984. Corporate descent group structure in Easter Island prehistory. Ph.D. dissertation. Pennsylvania State University.

Stewart, C. S. 1826. *Narrative of a Residence in the Sandwich Islands, During the Years 1823, 1824, and 1825 . . .* London, H. Fisher and P. Jackson.

Stewart, C. S. 1831. *A Visit to the South Seas in the U.S. Ship Vincennes . . .* New York, John P. Haven.

Suggs, R. C. 1961. The archaeology of Nuku Hiva, Marquesas Islands, French Polynesia. *Anthropological Papers of the American Museum of Natural History* 49:1–205.

Tautain, M. le Dr 1897. Notes sur les constructions et monuments des Marqueises. *Anthropologie* 8:667–78.

Terray, E. 1972. *Marxism and 'Primitive' Societies*. New York, Monthly Review Press.

Terrell, J. E. in press. *Passage to Prehistory: Science and Prehistory in the Pacific Islands*. Cambridge, University Press.

Thompson, L. 1938. The culture history of the Lau Islands, Fiji. *American Anthropologist* 40:181–97.

Thompson, L. 1940. *Southern Lau, Fiji: An Ethnography*. Bernice P. Bishop Museum Bulletin 162. Honolulu.

Tiffany, S. 1976. The cognatic descent groups of contemporary Samoa. *Man* 10:430–47.

Trotter, M. M. 1979. Niue Island archaeological survey. *Canterbury Museum Bulletin* 7. Christchurch.

Tryon, D. T. 1976. *New Hebrides Languages: An Internal Classification*. *Pacific Linguistics, Series C* 50.

Tuggle, H. D., and P. B. Griffin 1973. Lapakahi Hawaii: archaeological studies. *Asian and Pacific Archaeology Series* 5. Honolulu, Social Science Research Institute, University of Hawai'i.

Tuggle, H. D., and M. M. Tomonari-Tuggle 1980. Prehistoric agriculture in Kohala, Hawaii. *Journal of Field Archaeology* 7:297–312.

Udo, R. K. 1965. Disintegration of nucleated settlement in eastern Nigeria. *Geographical Review* 60:53–67.

Vancouver, G. 1967. *A Voyage of Discovery to the North Pacific Ocean and Round the World* [Reprint of the 1798 edition]. New York, Da Capo Press.

Vayda, A. P. and B. J. McCay 1975. New directions in ecology and ecological anthropology. In B. J. Siegel, A. R. Beals and S. A. Tyler (eds.), *Annual Review of Anthropology* 4:293–306. Palo Alto, Calif., Annual Reviews.

Vincendon-Dumoulin, D. A. 1843. *Iles Marquises ou Nouka-Hiva: Histoire, Géographie, Moeurs et Considérations Générales*. Paris, Arthus Bertrand.

Wallerstein, I. 1974. *The Modern World-System*. New York, Academic Press.

Ward, G. K. 1976. The archaeology of settlements associated with the chert industry of Ulawa. In R. C. Green and M. M. Cresswell (eds.), *Southeast Solomon Islands Cultural History*. Wellington, Royal Society of New Zealand, 161–80.

Ward, R. J., J. W. Webb and M. Levison 1973. The settlement of the Polynesian outliers: a computer simulation. *Journal of the Polynesian Society* 82:330–42.

Ward, R. H. 1967. Genetic studies on Fijians. Unpublished Master's thesis. University of Auckland.

Webb, M. C. 1975. The flag follows trade: an essay on the necessary interaction of military and commercial factors in state formation. In C. C. Lamberg-Karlovsky and J. A. Sabloff (eds.), *Ancient Civilization and Trade*. Albuquerque, University of New Mexico Press, 155–210.

Webster, D. 1975. Warfare and the evolution of the state: a reconsideration. *American Antiquity* 40:464–70.

Weisler, M., and P. V. Kirch 1985. The structure of settlement space at Kawela, Molokai, Hawai'ian Islands. *New Zealand Journal of Archaeology* 7:129–58.

White, J. P. and J. Allen. 1980. Melanesian prehistory: some recent advances. *Science* 207:728–34.

Williams, J. 1838. *A Narrative of Missionary Enterprises in the South Sea Islands*. London, John Snow.

Wilson, E. O. 1975. *Sociobiology: The New Synthesis*. Cambridge, Harvard University Press.

Wishart, D. 1978. Clustan 1C user's manual. Computer Centre, University College, London.

Wittfogel, K. A. 1957. *Oriental Despotism*. New Haven, Yale University Press.

Wolf, E. 1982. *Europe and the People Without History*. Berkeley, University of California Press.

Wright, H. T. 1977. Recent research on the origin of the state. In B. J. Siegel (ed.), *Annual Review of Anthropology* 6:379–98. Palo Alto, Calif., Annual Reviews.

Wright, H. T. and Johnson, G. A. 1975. Population, exchange, and early state formation in southwestern Iran. *American Anthropologist* 77:267–89.

Yen, D. E., P. V. Kirch, P. H. Rosendahl and T. J. Riley 1972. Prehistoric agriculture in the upper valley of Makaha, Oahu. In E. J. Ladd and D. E. Yen (eds.), Makaha Valley Historical Project Interim Report No. 3, *Pacific Anthropological Records* 18:59–94. Honolulu, Department of Anthropology, B. P. Bishop Museum.

INDEX

For EU product safety concerns, contact us at Calle de José Abascal, 56–1°,
28003 Madrid, Spain or eugpsr@cambridge.org.

www.ingramcontent.com/pod-product-compliance
Ingram Content Group UK Ltd.
Pitfield, Milton Keynes, MK11 3LW, UK
UKHW030905150625
459647UK00025B/2878